Titu Cusi: A 16th-Century Account of the Conquest

Introduction, Spanish Modernization, English Translation and Notes
by Nicole Delia Legnani, with prologue by Frank Salomon

*Instrucción del Inga don Diego de Castro Titu Cusi Yupangui
para el muy ilustre Señor el Licenciado Lope García de Castro*

Instruction of the Inqa Don Diego de Castro Titu Kusi Yupanki
for His Most Illustrious Lord Licentiate Lope García de Castro
(1570)

Published by Harvard University
David Rockefeller Center for Latin American Studies

Distributed by Harvard University Press
Cambridge, Massachusetts
London, England
2005

Library of Congress Cataloging-in-Publication Data

Yupangui, Diego de Castro, titu cusi, 16th cent.
[Relación de la conquista del Perú. English & Spanish]
Titu Cusi, a 16th-century account of the conquest : Instrucción del
Inga Don Diego de Castro Titu Cusi Yupangui para el muy ilustre Señor el
Licenciado Lope García de Castro = Instruction of the Inqa don Diego
de Castro Titu Kusi Yupanki for His Most Illustrious Lord Licentiate Lope
García de Castro (1570) / introduction, Spanish modernization, English
translation, and notes by Nicole Delia Legnani.
    p. cm.
"Derives from a senior thesis defended by Nicole Delia Legnani in
January 2003 in the Department of Romance Languages and Literatures
at Harvard University"—Foreword.
Includes bibliographical references.
ISBN-13: 978-0-674-01973-7 (Harvard University Press : pbk. : alk.
paper)
ISBN-10: 0-674-01973-3 (Harvard University Press : pbk. : alk. paper)
1. Peru—History—Conquest, 1522–1548. 2. Peru—Histor—1548–1820.
I. Legnani, Nicole Delia, 1980–   . II. David Rockefeller Center
for Latin American Studies. III. Title. IV. Title: Instrucción del Inga don
Diego de Castro Titu Cusi Yupangui para el muy ilustre Señor el Licenciado
Lope García de Castro. V. Title: Instruction of the Inqa don Diego de
Castro Titu Kusi Yupanki for His Most Illustrious Lord Licentiate Lope
García de Castro.
F3442.Y8513 2005a
985'.0—dc22

                                                    2005019194

Contents

Preface

By Frank Salomon

The book in your hands is a rare legacy from the Inka world. It was dated in the year 1570: late in a four-decade era of "fight-and-talk" relations between an Inka rump state fortified in the Peruvian jungle and the newly consolidated Viceroyalty of Peru. At that time Titu Cusi Yupanqui, heir to the title Child of the Sun, was literally under the guns of Spain. Counteroffensively, he took up another European weapon: writing. Nicole Legnani invites us to study the strange verbal salvo he and his two Spanish collaborators fired at those who would erase Inka titles of inheritance and nobility. Although couched as a chronicle, and marked by European rhetoric of the era, his *Instrucción* was also intended to make a legal point: the Pizarran conquest of Peru in 1532–35 had been invalid, because the legitimate Inka sovereign had never given offense to Spain. This belated Peruvian extension of the Las Casian dissident current originating in Mexico carries between its lines a daring argument. Titu Cusi still thought it possible that the Inka dynasty could become a Christian royal house, peers alongside the greatest crowns of Europe. The slow death of this hope was to become a central theme of Andean culture.

Titu Cusi's testimony of stubborn Inka hope is a core primary source for Latin American history. Legnani's translation will interest students of New World history, Latin American Studies, Spanish, and anthropology. In the framework of hemispheric Native American Studies, it stands among the indispensable documents of the indigenous past.

The *Instrucción* is also a passionately dramatic book. It resounds with the Iberian language of its time, Spanish drama's "golden century." Titu Cusi had (to readers of English) an almost Elizabethan vision of "my father Mankhu Inka" as tragic monarch. By rendering in modern dialogue the many speeches Titu Cusi imputes to Inkas (male and female) and to their foes, Legnani brings to life the intended emotional appeal of the narrative. Titu Cusi and his Spanish collaborators were not wrong to think the story of Mankhu's breakdown and humiliation, of his fury and martyrdom, and of his son's ambitions for vindication would prove enduringly memorable.

Finally, we can thank Legnani for helping readers of English make contact with the rich matrix of scholarship Peruvian and other scholars have built around the memory of the besieged Inka redoubt. The questions she and Titu Cusi put before us are searching ones, close to the core of any serious attempt at an Andean-centered view of Latin American origins.

Frank Salomon is a Professor in the Department of Anthropology, University of Wisconsin–Madison.

Foreword

This book derives from a senior thesis in Latin American Studies defended in January 2003 by Nicole Delia Legnani in the Department of Romance Languages and Literatures, Harvard University. Recipient of a Hoopes Prize in the Humanities that year, Legnani's thesis was the first modernized Spanish version and the only complete English translation of Titu Cusi's *Instrucción*.

Titu Cusi's text is pivotal to a better understanding of the processes involved in the Conquest of the Incas. It provides an example of an indigenous, Andean reformulation of the strategies of survival and adaptation during the long reign of Spanish domination that began in 1532.

The first section, "A Necessary Contextualization," speaks to the non-specialist, didactically presenting the general circumstances under which Titu Cusi's text was composed as a peculiar "relación" in 1570. In the Introduction, and then through the notes of the modern Spanish and English translations, Legnani explains the specific features of her modernized version and translation.

This book will be most helpful in classes and discussions, in both English and Spanish, of Latin American colonial literature and Latin American studies. In fact, beyond the work's obvious philologic qualities and original insights, the spirit of the text lies in its educational value and potential. Nicole Legnani's outstanding contribution gives voice to an indigenous culture, one that has resisted complete assimilation during more than four hundred years of Western presence in the Andes. We hope this book facilitates the study of the Incas and the Andean area in the years to come.

José Antonio Mazzotti
Gardner Cowles Associate Professor of Romance Languages and Literatures
Harvard University
Cambridge, Massachusetts, July 2005

A Necessary Contextualization

When Francisco Pizarro and other Spanish conquistadors stationed in Panama undertook their first exploration of the littoral of the Southern Sea (now known as the Pacific Ocean) in 1524, the Tawantinsuyu under the Inqa Wayna Qhapaq stretched from Acosbamba in southern Colombia, through the coast and highlands of Ecuador, Peru and Bolivia, reaching its borders along the Maulle river in Chile and the departments of Mendoza and Tucumán in northwestern Argentina. Tawantinsuyu, which in Quechua means "the four lands joined together," was the name the Inqas gave to the world under their control, a world where the chaos of thousands of ethnicities, languages and societies found their place in the Inqa social order. Reciprocity and kinship—the redistribution of goods, human labor, lands and water to maximize the biodiversity found between desert coasts and snow-capped mountains—were characteristics of Andean societies before the advent of the Inqanate in the Andean world.

For more than a thousand years before the Inqas founded the center of the Tawantinsuyu in Cuzco, in the southern highlands of Peru, other societies and states such as the Moche, Nazca, Wari and Tiwanaku (to name just a few) had elaborate irrigation systems, *andenes*—agricultural balconies, to plant on what would otherwise be inaccessible steep slopes—and constructed roadways, and with these technological advances a complex system of beliefs which gave meaning to a natural world dominated by extremes. During the four hundred years that the Inqas dominated the Andean social landscape (1,100~1532 A.D.), they were able to organize massive populations, extensive territories and productions by building their state on the traditional cornerstones of kinship and reciprocity, and a moiety social structure. Yet these efforts were not met without conflict, and their methods were not free of coercion: local deities were taken hostage by the Inqa conquerors, brought to Cuzco and forced to accept their place in the hierarchy dominated by the state-sponsored religion; rebellious populations were forcibly removed and relocated.

Reconstructions of the Inqa past are largely based on the conflicting ideals of the Spanish conquistadors and their chroniclers. They presented the Tawantinsuyu as a pre-Hispanic utopia, a bountiful *pax incaica*, which had prepared its inhabitants for Christianity in a New World free of the evils that plagued medieval Europe or, alternatively, a tyranny that had massacred and enslaved entire populations for the benefit of the illegitimate rulers in Cuzco. Contemporary political thinkers in the Andean

world have likewise invoked stereotypes to satisfy modern political agen-
das when attempting to reconcile conflicting identities through the projection of one national history. In this way, the Tawantinsuyu has been characterized as a primitive communist society, a socialist empire or a totali-
tarian theocracy, the dictatorship of one ethnic group over many.
Increasingly, it has become the salient symbol for unity and cooperation
among the indigenous peoples of the Andean region.

The Spanish chroniclers were given the task of ordering Inqa narratives
into a format and in terms that a European audience could understand.
The term "empire," when used to describe the Inqas' rule over the Andean
world, is thus understood in this context as an attempt to establish a parallel between the Roman empire and the Inqa presence in the
Tawantinsuyu. In a similar fashion, *sheep* was synonymous for *llama*, *lion*
for *puma* and *God* for *Wiraqucha*. Structurally, the cyclical and repetitive
forms of Inqa narrative were "translated" to construct a linear narrative or
a genealogy on European terms. The need for genealogies was particularly
necessary during the first four decades of the Spanish arrival in the
Tawantinsuyu.

The Inqas did not possess an alphabet or glyphs as forms of writing;
rather, information was encoded in a system of knotted strings known as
khipu, which could be used for accounting or story-telling. The *khiphuka-*
mayuq were "those who gave order to the *khipu*," knowledgeable in the
composition and the "reading" of these colorful knotted strings. Each
Inqa was the founder of his own lineage (*panaqa*) and each *panaqa* was
responsible to the memory of their Inqa. Upon the death of an Inqa, the
khipukamayuq were ordered to compose a history of his exploits that
would be recited and performed in rituals before the mummy of the Inqa;
it was believed that the Inqa "spoke" to his descendants through these
performances.

The Spanish who were able to witness these recitations compared them
to the *romanceros* and *villancicos* of the Spanish oral tradition, emphasiz-
ing in their accounts the importance of music and dance in these performances. The comparison made with these popular forms of Spanish orality,
however, failed to appreciate the role of the *khipukamayuq* in legitimating
political actors in what was a cultural production for the benefit of the ruling elite in Cuzco. Over the past decade, research in linguistics and the discovery of a transliterated fragment of one of these Inqa epics have shown
that these narratives were in fact composed and recited in "the secret language of the Inqas," an Aymara with a heavy Puquina substrate, which
would not have been understood by the native inhabitants of the Cuzco

region. The experience of one of these epic performances could, instead, be compared to the Latin mass in medieval Europe wherein only an elite could understand the words being recited by the officiates from the Holy Book, but the religious signification was understood by the majority of worshipers through the sinesthetic experience of ritual motions, the repetition of prayers, music and incense. The *khipus* made for honoring the memory of the Inqa should thus be distinguished from the cultural production in Quechua, which was the *lingua franca* of the Inqanate, whose orality may not differ from the epics sung in Aymara-Puquina so much in their formal structure but, at the very least, in their modes of production and reception.

Competition among the *panaqas* led to conflicting histories of the exploits of the Inqas; at the same time, the compilations of narratives by Cieza de León or Juan de Betanzos have allowed researchers to identify mythic cycles, among these the founding of Cuzco by the Ayar brothers and the war with the Chankas, an ethnic group from the Ayacucho region. The rhythm and direction of the Inqa conquests are always portrayed in an outward clockwise spiral from the center of the Tawantinsuyu, Cuzco; likewise, "new" conquests were conceived as living extensions of old conquests in these narratives. For example, Wayna Qhapaq, the last Inqa to rule in the Tawantinsuyu without contact with the Spanish conquistadors, and responsible for extending the Inqanate's limits to Acosbamba in Southern Colombia and the Maulle River in Southern Chile, is also portrayed as having conquered the Chankas. This may be because the Inqa was conceived as reliving and extending the exploits of his predecessors and thus engaged the collective memory of the Inqas in Cuzco by performing "prior" conquests in rituals. In Southern Peru, indigenous communities perform one event of the conquest on a yearly basis, often the encounter between Ataw Wallpa and Francisco Pizarro in Cajamarca, and documentation of such performances exists from the late 16th and early 17th centuries. The importance of this "historic" event is not conceived in linear terms but is seen as vital to the life and memory of the community.

By the time Francisco Pizarro and Diego de Almagro made their third trip along the coast of the Tawantinsuyu in 1532, they had already founded (in 1527) San Miguel de Piura, the first Spanish settlement off the coast of Northern Peru, without the authorization of the Governor of Panama, who had only given them permission to explore the littoral of the Southern Sea. At the time, Wayna Qhapaq was still ruling the Inqanate whose borders he had extended and was troubled by the news of their arrival. Though their stay was brief, for the Governor had only given them permission to explore until March 1528, they left pestilence and disease in their wake. It has been suggested that Wayna Qhapaq himself later died of smallpox, one of the deadly diseases brought by the conquistadors. The explorers brought back to Panama llamas and alpacas, textiles and a cup made of gold to persuade the Governor that the conquest of Peru would be a profitable enterprise.

"Peru" was a neologism, born from an error in translation between the explorers and the natives during an encounter on their second trip, which has been poignantly narrated in the *Comentarios Reales* by the Inca Garcilaso de la Vega. Pizarro left for Spain to receive permission from King of Spain and Holy Roman Emperor Carlos V to conquer Peru. In the Capitulación de Toledo, the contract signed between the Crown and Pizarro, Francisco Pizarro was made the Governor of Nueva Castilla and Captain General of the territory from Tumbes, on the northern coast of Peru, to Chincha, on the southern coast of Peru. The contract also stipulated the presence of treasury officials and notaries of the Crown, as well as clergy to ensure the evangelization of the natives. Almagro, Pizarro's partner in the previous explorations, was only made mayor of Tumbes, and he was, understandably, upset when he learned of Pizarro's governorship. Quarrels over the territorial limits and powers established by the Capitulación de Toledo would eventually lead to wars between the two conquistadors and their followers.

When Pizarro and his men set out to conquer Nueva Castilla, the political situation of the Inqanate was one of turmoil. Waskar Inqa and Ataw Wallpa, both sons of Wayna Qhapaq and of mothers who belonged to competing *panaqas*, had been engaged in a bloody and merciless war of succession following the death of the Inqa. It has been estimated that at least one third of the population of the Tawantinsuyu had been ravaged by war and disease; Waskar Inqa's followers in Cuzco had been tortured and killed by Ataw Wallpa's armies, and Waskar Inqa himself was being held prisoner by the newly hailed Inqa. Inqa Ataw Wallpa was returning to Cuzco, after having quelled rebellions in the northern Tawantinsuyu and celebrated his victory over Waskar in Quito, and had stopped in Cajamarca to heal a battle wound when he learned of the Spanish presence on the northern Peruvian coast. The conquistadors, led by Pizarro and Almagro, had already ravaged villages. The encounter between Ataw Wallpa, Francisco Pizarro, Fray Vicente de Valverde and their indigenous interpreter in Cajamarca, on November 16, 1532, is also known as the "Dialogue of Cajamarca" and has become symbolic of the conquest and the traumatic clash between cultures. More than thirty thousand unarmed men, women and children had congregated in the main square of Cajamarca to see the new Inqa and his entourage receive little over a hundred sixty conquistadors who had prepared an ambush. There are conflicting accounts of the meeting between the conquistadors and the Inqa, but the recurring theme is the "sacrilege" committed by Ataw Wallpa when he was presented with the Bible as a source of divine authority that he was forced to accept, along with the Holy Roman Emperor Carlos V as his overlord. When Ataw Wallpa threw the Bible to the ground, the conquistadors opened fire and the Inqa was taken prisoner. This "dialogue" and subsequent massacre has become symbolic for the entire conquest of Peru.

Ataw Wallpa was held in captivity while his ransom was collected. (While in prison, he nonetheless ordered the execution of Waskar Inqa.) Ataw Wallpa was executed on July 26, 1533, less than one year after the first encounter. His execution was not viewed favorably by the Spanish crown, who worried that if the regicide being perpetrated in the New World were legitimated, it might become common in Spain as well. For this reason, the controversy in the chronicles as to whether Ataw Wallpa had indeed been the "legitimate" or "bastard" son of Wayna Qhapaq, and therefore rightful heir to the Inqanate, was also an exercise in exculpating or blaming Pizarro and his men for the crimes of Cajamarca.

Following the death of Ataw Wallpa, the conquistadors led by Francisco Pizarro began their long march to Cuzco. On the way there, Thupaq Wallpa was named successor to the Inqanate but was poisoned during the trip. In November 1533, the conquistadors arrived in Cuzco after meeting with Manku Inqa, another son of Wayna Qhapaq, on the outskirts of the center of the Tawantinsuyu. The Spaniards presented themselves as partisans of the *panaqa* of Waskar Inqa and were thus received favorably by the cusqueño population, and Manku Inqa was proclaimed the legitimate successor to Wayna Qhapaq. Less than two years later, relations between Manku Inqa and the Spaniards had deteriorated, and the friendship between Francisco Pizarro and Diego de Almagro had been further strained when the latter was named the Governor of Nueva Toledo by Carlos V. The boundaries between Nueva Castilla and Nueva Toledo were unclear, and control over Cuzco was the sticking point. Almagro agreed, however, to leave with the high priest of the Inqanate, Willaq Umu (Wila Uma in the *Instrucción*), for the conquest of Chile. Upon the return of Wila Uma, Manku Inqa took advantage of Francisco Pizarro's trip to Lima to rebel and place Cuzco and the conquistadors under siege in May 1536.

The long siege of Cuzco and the eventual victory of the Spanish took on epic dimensions, including the miraculous manifestation of the Virgin

Mary and the Apostle Santiago, who, on his white horse, waged war with the Inqas as he had with the moors during the reconquest of Spain. Notwithstanding the losses in Cuzco, Manku Inqa and his followers managed to escape and establish an Inqanate in Vilcabamba parallel to the emerging colonial state in Cuzco and Lima. From Vilcabamba, the neo-Inqa state controlled the highland corridors in Ayacucho, Junin and Huánuco between the two major centers of colonial Peru, Cuzco and Lima. Manku Inqa also followed closely the hostilities between the followers of Almagro and Pizarro and was himself attacked in Vilcabamba several times by Gonzalo Pizarro, the half brother of Francisco Pizarro, and Pawllu Inqa.

A year after the almagristas assassinated Francisco Pizarro in 1541, Manku Inqa sheltered almagristas in Vilcabamba. The following year Carlos V passed the Leyes Nuevas (New Laws), which placed the administration of the Spanish American kingdoms under the authority of officials named by the Crown and not by the conquistadors. These laws also stipulated that the lands—and, mainly, the natives—that had been placed under the "protection" (*encomendados*) of the conquistadors (making them *encomenderos*) were not hereditary titles. These laws coincided with the arrival of the first viceroy in Lima, who was authorized to negotiate a truce with Manku Inqa.

The warring factions among the conquistadors were now divided between those who were loyal to Emperor Carlos V and his officials (*realistas*) and those who wanted to rule Peru for themselves. The latter faction included Gonzalo Pizarro who, in 1548, was punished, imprisoned and executed for treason. The *Instrucción* repeatedly mistakes Gonzalo for the other Pizarro brothers, thus constructing a Pizarro character whose actions embody the collective misdeeds of the Pizarros and the conquistadors in Peru. Manku Inqa was betrayed by the *almagristas* he had protected in Vilcabamba, who assassinated him in 1545, ostensibly to reconcile themselves with the *pizarristas*, who were engaged in a war against the *realistas* now that they had found a common grievance against the Leyes Nuevas. Following the death of Manku Inqa, the Inqas of Vilcabamba continued to attack the Spanish, making it even more difficult for the representatives of the Crown to govern an increasingly hostile and chaotic territory, on all fronts.

Following the death of Manku Inqa, the Inqas of Vilcabamba adopted a two-pronged approach to oust the Spanish from the Tawantinsuyu. On the one hand, they negotiated the introduction of Sayri Thupaq and his Quya (spouse and sister) into colonial society on Spanish terms, i.e., as the "legitimate" heir to the Inqa throne. Sayri Thupaq ceased hostilities with the Crown and was thus recognized as a noble with hereditary titles, lands and a yearly salary. At the same time, the *crónicas* and *informaciones* were written by *cronistas*, Spanish officials or conquistadors who were commissioned by the colonial administration to make sense of the cultures and societies native to the territories which now formed part of a Spanish American kingdom and were subjects of the king of Spain. (The information was collected and compiled from many sources and did not rely solely on the authors' experiences.) The *crónicas* were official documents of the conquest, narrating the actions taken by the conquistadors, the native populations, Crown officials and clergy. They were used to make policies as to the evangelization of the natives and the distribution of land and labor between the Crown, the Church and the conquistadors. One of the characteristics of the *crónicas* is an acceptance or rejection of the arguments used by Fray Bartolomé de las Casas in the major theological debate of the time, whether or not the native peoples of the Americas had souls.

Fray Bartolomé de las Casas, the Bishop of Chiapas, considered the founder of *indigenismo*, argued that the conquistadors were more pagan than the natives whose natures and societies were predisposed toward Christianity. The destruction wrought in the Americas was counterproductive to the evangelical work of the Church, and thus treasonous, because the conquistadors impeded the natural extension of the reconquest of Spain in the new Spanish territories. His ideas were in part responsible for the promulgation of the Leyes Nuevas (as well as the Crown's prerogative to have more control over the administration and exploitation of the American kingdoms). Fray Bartolomé de las Casas maintained a network of clergy throughout the Americas, among whom was Fray Domingo de Santo Tomás, who argued in favor of an alliance between the kurakas of the Mantaro Valley in Peru and the Church, instead of the system of *encomiendas* (and later *corregimientos*) which favored the conquistadors. Fray Domingo de Santo Tomás is also known for his important linguistic contributions, namely the first grammar and lexicon of Quechua.

Although Sayri Thupaq was assimilated into colonial society on Spanish terms, the Inqas of Vilcabamba continued their attacks on the Spanish. To the dismay of the viceroy in Lima, Titu Kusi Yupanki sent a letter in 1559 "clarifying" the Inqa succession, claiming that Thupaq Amaru was Manku Inqa's legitimate heir. This meant that over the next ten years the Spanish viceroys and governors were involved in both fighting the Inqas and reinitiating the peace negotiations, while the lands, titles and salaries granted to Sayri Thupaq, Quya Kusi Warkay and their descendants allowed the Inqas of Vilcabamba to fund their military campaigns and support their followers. The lands, strategically located between Vilcabamba and Cuzco, gave the Inqas safe passage into the center of the Tawantinsuyu. Vilcabamba [Willka pampa] means "sacred and speaking ground" or a "land of oracles" in Aymara and Quechua. While the Inqas still controlled Vilcabamba, the Viceroyalty of Peru and the Tawantinsuyu coexisted and parallel orders of landscape, history and religion reigned in the Andean region.

Along the borders of Vilcabamba, the Inqas and Spanish officials negotiated, signed treaties, exchanged letters and made shows of force and power for more than ten years after Sayri Thupaq's ceremonial exit into colonial Peru. From 1564 to 1569, the Licentiate Lope García de Castro governed Peru; despite the peace treaty of Acobamba, the skirmishes between the Spanish and the Inqas intensified. During those years, a messianic movement called the Taki Unquy, centered in Ayacucho, caught the attention of the colonial authorities, who did not hesitate in assuming a link between its leadership and Vilcabamba.

When the *Instrucción* was composed by Inqa Titu Kusi Yupanki in 1570, he already had experience narrating his father's story for the purpose of receiving favors from the colonial authorities with the aid of his mestizo scribe, Martín de Pando. The *instrucción* or *relación* had a specific function within the legal framework of the Spanish conquest: often addressed to the king, it requested immediate gratification or relief for the services that the author or the petitioner had rendered to the Crown. As such, its veracity was legitimated by the eye-witness testimony of the person requesting the favor. The *Instrucción* differs greatly from the traditional format in that it is addressed to the former governor of Peru, Licentiate Lope García de Castro, with the hope that he would learn, recite and argue Manku Inqa's history and Titu Kusi Yupanki's case before the King of Spain. Furthermore, the *Instrucción* narrates Manku Inqa's grievances with the Spanish, which Titu Kusi Yupanki could not have witnessed. Yet the title of this narrative suggests that Titu Kusi Yupanki may have felt justified giving an eye-witness testimony of his father's life as a traditional recitation of the *khipukamayuq* composed to honor the memory of an Inqa and his *panaqa*. This subtext is made evident in the syntax and semantic fields of the *Instrucción*, which are reminiscent of Quechua and Aymara. Fray Marcos García and Fray Diego Ortiz were new additions to a project that had become increasingly urgent with the arrival of the new viceroy, Francisco de Toledo, in Lima in November 1569.

Francisco de Toledo's administration changed the sociopolitical order and the discourse of colonial Peru. Instead of viewing the Spanish presence in Peru as a Christian continuation of the Inqa Empire, he legitimated the conquest in Spain's traditional recognition of a people's right to revolt against a tyrannical monarch. Evidence for the tyranny of the Inqas was found in the Inqa's own wars of conquest. Since they were illegitimate rulers, there was no longer a need to negotiate or to offer terms for peace which recognized their nobility. Furthermore, native forms of social organization would only perpetrate their barbarity and idolatry and had to be eliminated. The direct consequences of this alteration in colonial policy meant greater vehemence in the extirpations of idolatry, the transformation of the Andean landscape with the *reducciones*, which aimed to structure the life of Andean men and women around the Spanish-style village and town, and the invasion of Vilcabamba in 1572. In 1572, there were no qualms as to whether Inqa Thupaq Amaru could be beheaded by a Spanish authority. By then, the Inqas of Vilcabamba were considered treasonous subjects of the King of Spain who had usurped his authority in what was now Spanish territory.

Introduction

Prior Editions of the Instrucción del Inga Don Diego de Castro Titu Cusi Yupangui para el muy Ilustre Señor el Licenciado Lope García de Castro

The *Instrucción* was first published in its entirety in 1916 by Horacio H. Urteaga and Carlos A. Romero as *Relación de la conquista del Perú y hechos del Inca Manco II*,[1] which included Romero's biography of Titu Kusi Yupanki as well as transcriptions of historical documents relevant to the Vilcabamba neo-Inqa[2] state in appendices. The edition was based on a copy made by Doctor Manuel González de la Rosa of the manuscript in the Biblioteca del Escorial, Spain. Marcos Jiménez de la Espada, however, had already published selected passages of the *Instrucción* in 1877, namely the chapter on Manku Inqa's death and the certification of authenticity given to the narrative toward the end of the text, in the Apéndice 18 to his edition of Cieza de León's *La Guerra de Quito*. Jiménez de la Espada gave the title *Relación de como los españoles entraron en el Perú y el subceso que tuvo Mango Inga en el tiempo que entre ellos vivió*[3] to this narrative.

Urteaga, in his prologue to the 1916 edition, explicitly sees the publication of the *Relación de la Conquista del Perú y hechos del Inca Manco II* as a political act. He refers to the text as a vindication for "the humiliations of 1879"[4] (1916 Edition: VIII), a reference to the Battle of the Pacific and the Chilean invasion of Lima, and much of his prologue centers around the failed relationship between Lima and the provinces to create "one ethnic unity and national consciousness"[5] (XVI). He is interested in promoting the "mestizo consciousness"[6] and not that of the "ignorant Indian"[7] (VIII). He chooses to date his prologue on "Independence Day 1916"[8] and writes that the *Relación* serves as a reminder "to Peru that in her past a written future can be discerned, because the race that founded the Empire of the Incas, lives: only that she is bound and immobilized by our selfishness: Untie her and set her free!"[9] (XVII). Romero's biography similarly reflects the liberal views of Limeños, struggling with their search for a national identity at the turn of the 20th century in post-bellum Peru by turning to the country's pre-Hispanic roots. He chastises the conquistadors as "more barbarian than the very Indians"[10] (XXI) and argues that had the conquistadors followed the example of the Inqas and continued governing the Empire according to its laws, Spain would still be the most powerful nation of the world (XXI). Romero, especially in the latter estimation of the conquest's failures, is replicating and extending one of the ideological strands explored by the *Instrucción*. The aim of the 1916 edition is clearly to raise the "Peruvian national consciousness" by widespread dissemination of the text that seems to embody for the editors the promise of a new "mestizo" morality.

Aside from the liberal and early indigenista discourses of its prologue and biography, the edition itself is noteworthy because of Romero's carefully documented footnotes and the care taken to present a faithful transcription of the manuscript in El Escorial. More documentation about the neo-Inqa Vilcabamba state has since been discovered (cf. Dunbar Temple: 614–29; Guillén Guillén 1994: 247–278; Nowack and Julien: 15–81; Nowack 2004: 139–179), and the glosses of foreign terms to Spanish often recur solely to Quechua, although the editors are quick to recognize words of Caribbean origin.

The 1973 edition by Francisco A. Carrillo, entitled *Relación de la conquista de Perú*,[11] is based solely on the 1916 edition, conserves its orthography and part of its footnotes (reducing these from 100 to 33) and does not reproduce the appendices. The punctuation was done by Marco Martos and Carlos Garayar (9).

Unlike the Urteaga and Romero prologues, Carrillo stresses "the Indian point of view [. . .] the history of one aspect of the conquest seen, felt or heard at first hand by none other than [Titu Kusi Yupanki]"[12] (7). The Spanish of the text is noted as "already in the full process of mestizaje"[13] and the long monologues in the text are given with "Indian soul, voice and sonority"[14] (8). The purpose of this 1973 edition was to make the text more accessible to a public beyond academic circles.

Miscegenation, or *mestizaje*, between the conquistadors and the natives has led Peruvian historians and literary critics to view "the mixing of races" as a harmonious reconciliation between two diametrically opposed forces during the conquest, the conqueror and the conquered, as a framework both to comprehend the social fabric produced in Latin America from the conquest and to insert literary production within a structurally stable analysis. Dunbar Temple, a Peruvian historian writing in the 1950s who was in great part responsible for refueling historians' interest in the Inqas of Vilcabamba, wrote on the *inevitability* of the neo-Inqanate's defeat in 1572 by Viceroy Toledo:

Though we should not lose sight, on all occasions, of the indisputable fact that the Incas of Vilcabamba defended, with admirable justic and heroicity that renders them honorable in the face of history, their rights to a land and an Empire which were theirs, it is necessary to be aware, at the same time, that Titu Cusi and his captains had already made themselves subject to the Crown [by the Capitulation of Acobamba], that **the authority of Spain was being imposed by the force of the Conquest**, that this had been recognized by the very same Indians, **and embedded biologically by the incipient, yet by no means less powerful, mestizaje.**[15] (618)

The inevitability of the Inqas' defeat in Vilcabamba is seen as the inescapable consequence of *mestizaje* as the inexorable force leading to the rapid hispanization of colonial Peru's ethnic demographics and thus cultural make-up. Similar ideas in literary criticism of Latin American "hybrid" texts[16] addressed what was seen as an overall tendency to assimilate indigenous sources into "Hispanic" culture as a process of "acculturation." The term "transculturation," coined by the Cuban anthropologist Fernando Ortiz in 1940 and later used by the Uruguayan critic Angel Rama, rejected the projection of a unilateral tendency of native sources to be absorbed by the dominant Hispanic culture, and rather allowed for a more egalitarian "mixing" whereby both Hispanic culture and native cultures were "transculturated." The term "transculturation," however, does not lose the implied emphasis of harmonious syncretism. Antonio Cornejo Polar later proposed the term "contradictory whole" to analyze the corpus of Peruvian literature, rejecting previous attempts to resolve social and cultural forces that historically and socially have not been reconciled, but rather co-exist in constant struggle and opposition (1983: 37–50). Carlos-García Bedoya did not include Titu Kusi Yupanki's *Instrucción* in the section of Andean chroniclers in his book, *La literatura peruana en el periodo de estabilización colonial (1580–1789)*, precisely because it precedes Viceroy Toledo's consolidation of colonial Perú; the imposition of Spanish colonial domination over Peruvian territory had not concluded (171–77; 171 note 399). Nevertheless, if we were to accept Dunbar Temple's view that Toledo's victory was inevitable because of the reconciling forces of miscegenation, the *Instrucción* would necessarily be read as an integral indicator of Toledo's *fated* victorious campaign over the Inqas of Vilcabamba. The scholarly activity of historians and literary critics, who have continuously edited and re-edited the text, illustrates the *Instrucción*'s saliency in understanding Perú's colonial past and present and mirrors our own conceptual frameworks for determining a text's character (i.e., literary, historical, anthropological, etc.) and the manner in which we proceed in our construction of heuristic categories through which we may read these texts.

The 1985 edition by Luis Millones, entitled *Ynstruçion del Ynga Don Diego de Castro Titu Cussi Yupangui para el muy ilustre señor el licenciado Lope Garçia de Castro, governador que fue destos reynos del Piru, tocante a los negoçios que con su majestad, en su nonbre, por su poder a de tratar; la cual es esta que se sigue (1570)* was the first full edition to be directly based on the manuscript in El Escorial. Julio García Miranda and Laura Gutiérrez transcribed the original faithfully, choosing not to omit repetitions or correct the grammar and spelling; by respecting the linguistic anomalies of the text, Millones provides an edition interesting not only to historical and literary researchers but to linguists as well; his questions and suggestions are duly noted in this edition, and my reading of possible Aymara words in the text would not have been possible had it not been for his edition.

His prologue was likewise the first to systematically address the multiple authorship of the text—"a translation written in precarious circumstances"[17] (Millones 1985: 11)—and he calls his readers' attention to the Spanish and Quechua narrative structures, words, syntax and semantic fields, mythical undercurrents "which being expressed as episodic seem to be structural in Andean society"[18] (Millones 1985: 13). The text is not valued for its relative historical veracity but for its own "criteria for truth"[19] which "tended more towards the reconstruction of customs rather than chronological or geographical certainty of the narrated facts"[20] (Millones 1985: 17). The complex relationships between the historical figures of Titu Kusi Yupanki, Martín de Pando, fray Marcos García, fray Diego Ortiz, their authorship of the text, the juncture between orality and the written word, were given a framework through which readers of the *Instrucción* could question the "mestizo"[21] label that had been stamped on the text as a category for its literary and historical analysis. This edition and its prologue set the stage for subsequent literary studies[22] of the *Instrucción* such as those by Jakfalvi-Leyva, Chang-Rodríguez, Lienhard, and Mazzotti. My own modernized version of the text is mainly based on the Millones edition and owes much to its prologue, although my version is cross-referenced with some differences found in the earlier and later editions.

In 1988, the *Instrucción* was again published under the title *En el encuentro de dos mundos: los Incas de Vilcabamba. Instrucción del inga Don Diego Tito Cussi Yupanqui (1570)* by María del Carmen Martín Rubio with a prologue by Francisco Valcárcel. Martín Rubio characterized the *Instrucción* as a "recollection directed to Felipe II of Spain"[23] and as a product of "cultural simbiosis" (1988 Edition: 121). The edition ostensibly modernizes the text to make it accessible to a wider public, but fails to change the 16th-century orthography in many instances (most notoriously the <x>, <ss> and <ç>) leaving the text mottled with [sic] and no more intelligible to readers unfamiliar with 16th-century Spanish. Furthermore, Martín Rubio does not gloss the majority of the indigenous words for her readers, and when she does she makes no attempt to follow modern Quechua orthography.[24] Her decision not to modernize proper nouns or toponymy renders reference to a modern map of Peruvian territory difficult. The result is an inconsistent edition that is neither modernization nor transcription.

Liliana Regalado de Hurtado's edition, published as *Instrucción al Licenciado Don Lope García de Castro (1570)* in 1992, is also plagued by inaccuracies, omissions and incoherent punctuation. The glossary of indigenous words provided at the end of the text commits basic errors (such as ascribing the Caribbean word "chicha" to Quechua) or mixes Spanish and Quechua orthographic rules, thereby producing hybrid spellings. Regalado de Hurtado's reading of the text emphasizes Spanish influences, asserting that Titu Kusi Yupanki was easily able to understand and make himself understood in Spanish because of his "acculturation" with the Spanish and the "mestizo" minority living in Vilcabamba at the time (XIII). Yet the will of Felipe Kispi Titu, Titu Kusi Yupanki's son and heir, written in the City of Kings (Lima) in 1578, had to be translated into Spanish (in Dunbar Temple: 629). That Felipe Kispi Titu required an interpreter to write his last will and testament after having lived in Lima for six years awaiting his exile to New Spain (which never came to fruition) is not indicative of the kind of "acculturation" or cultural "mestizaje" Regalado de Hurtado asserts he would have been exposed to in Vilcabamba before Toledo's conquest of the neo-Inqa state in 1572—at least with respect to the languages being spoken there: predominantly indigenous with a minimal Spanish presence, mainly embodied by Titu Kusi Yupanki's translator and secretary, Martín de Pando, and the two Spanish Augustine missionaries who arrived during the latter two years of Titu Kusi Yupanki's reign.

Though much of Regalado de Hurtado's historical analysis depends on Guillén Guillén 1984 (cf. XIV–V), she is quick to criticize his anachronistic division between "nationalists" or "patriots" (XVI) yet writes that, "critical or not of the [colonial] system, Martín de Pando was, as was frequent among those of his social group [mestizo], an opportunist"[25] (XXXIV). Regalado de Hurtado asserts along the same vein that Titu Kusi Yupanki's message to be alert and resist the Spaniards "is not proclaimed as his own, rather, in any case, inherited from his father Manco Inca, a message badly disguised in the imaginary speeches of his progenitor [. . .]"[26] (XVIII). Regalado de Hurtado's edition was aimed at expanding the knowledge of this text beyond academic circles, like the 1985 and 1988 editions, and was also a transcription of microfilm copies of the manuscript in El Escorial.[27]

There has been only one full translation of the *Instrucción* into another language—German—by Martin Lienhard, about which, unfortunately, I am unable to comment. Translated passages of the *Instrucción* to English appeared in Bingham's *Lost City of the Incas*, in the chapter "The Story of the Last 4 Incas" (43–78). This chapter also contains translations of the earlier correspondence between Titu Kusi Yupanki and Lope García de Castro, interspersed with sections of the Augustine Friar Calancha's *Moralizing Chronicle of the Order of Saint Augustine in Peru*, which refer to Friar Diego Ortiz's martyrdom. Selections of the *Instrucción* were later translated into English by Michael Jimenez and included in the collection *New Iberian World: A Documentary History of the Discovery and Settlement of Latin America to the Early 19th Century*, edited by John H. Parry and Robert C. Keith in 1984.

This bilingual edition includes the first modernization of the *Instrucción* as well its first full translation into English and uses a reduced version of the opening rubric for its title: *Instrucción del Inga Don Diego de Castro Titu Cusi Yupangui para el muy ilustre Señor el Licenciado Lope García de Castro* and *Instruction of the Inqa Don Diego de Castro Titu Kusi Yupanki for His Most Illustrious Lord Licentiate Lope García de Castro*. It is my hope that this edition will make the *Instrucción* more accessible to readers of modern Spanish and English alike and that the annotations will prove useful to those unfamiliar with the history of early colonial Peru and Andean linguistics. Published references and works are supplemented by primary sources from the Archivo Histórico Regional del Cuzco and the Archivo Arzobispal del Cuzco.

The Fate of Translators: A Note on This Edition

It may be the fate of translators to suffer a premature death for their betrayals. In the *Instrucción*, Antonico, the "Indian tongue"[28] interpreting for the Spaniards, betrays his masters when he warns Manku Inqa of Juan Pizarro's scheme to seize him once again for more ransom; he later betrays his new master, Manku Inqa, when he attempts an escape with other Spaniards back to Cuzco. When caught, he receives a fitting death, to die "by mouth"[29] as he betrayed with his "tongue": he is given as fodder for the ritual cannibalism practiced by the Moyo Moyo living on the eastern side of the Andean cordillera. Martín de Pando, Titu Kusi Yupanki's "scribe," and Fray Diego Ortiz, who collaborated in the composition of the *Instrucción*, suffered similar fates when they were blamed for Titu Kusi Yupanki's death.[30] It is my hope that by recognizing my own "betrayals" of and "loyalties" to the different voices[31] juxtaposed in the *Instrucción*, I may be saved from a similar fate.

The *Instrucción* presents several difficulties for a translator. It is, in itself, a loose translation of what could have been originally one or several Quechua-Aymara oral narratives, and its multiple authorship offers many layers of interpretation. Likewise, a modernization (as the very term suggests) implies a betrayal of the 17th-century manuscript copy of the text dated to 1570. I have, for example, unraveled the paragraphs containing dialogue to render these more "dramatic" passages into something resembling what a contemporary reader might recognize as a script, one more conducive to being read aloud or even performed, "[. . .] assimilating the passage[s] to our Western system even if, in the end, we 'legitimize' this text by having it approximate our own [theatrical] tradition" (Harrison 1989: 92). I have also placed page breaks at the beginning of every chapter or rubric heading in order to facilitate a bilingual parallel reading of the text.

Any Hispanic, theatrical influences should be addressed, however, in order to recognize possible sources for the *Instrucción*'s dialogic structure, which is uncanny for a text whose title makes a claim to its insertion within the legal genre of the Hispanic *relación*, addressed to the King, detailing personal feats in favor of the Sovereign in the hope of receiving retribution by the Crown. An important body of colonial plays written in Quechua deserves our attention for comparison to the dramatic passages in the *Instrucción*.

According to Lohmann Villena, the first play performed in the Viceroyalty of Peru was the staged representation of Corpus Christi in 1563 to celebrate the closure of the Tridentine Assembly. An *Auto de la gula*[32] was recited, and its title suggests that the *auto* may have been a farce (or a derivation of the medieval morality plays). *Autos* continued to be performed in Lima, especially to celebrate Corpus Christi, and there is indication that an *auto* was performed in Arequipa in 1564. Not all of these *autos* were sacramental in theme, and the term may simply indicate their length (as in one-act plays or plays of one *jornada*); however, they were almost always represented on the site of churches (Lohmann Villena: 45–48). El Inca Garcilaso de la Vega mentions a bilingual dialogue, in Spanish and Quechua, of a *sacramental auto*, which was performed before the Royal Audience in Lima (Parte 1, Lib. II, Cap. XVII). These *autos* were apparently extremely popular and perhaps unseemly in tone—the *cabildos* made repeated injunctions not to permit these performances in churches, especially during Easter and Corpus Christi, without their express permission. Nonetheless, the Jesuit Order incorporated these *autos* into their visual catechism plan (Lohmann Villena: 45), presumably owing to their popularity. In 1579, the *cabildo* took control over these performances, divesting the various theatrical guilds of their creative control over the *autos* (48). Viceroy Toledo similarly ordered changes to the performances of these *autos* on October 10, 1572, coinciding with his victory over the Inqas of Vilcabamba, by arranging the forms in which Corpus Christi in Cuzco would be celebrated in a dignified manner (cf. Ugarte Chamorro).

The colonial Quechua plays, except for the dialogue mentioned by Inca Garcilaso of which there is no extant example, do not belong to the genres of the medieval *auto*, sacramental or farcical. Later, during the 17th century, they became an example of Andean baroque literature: written in Quechua, their themes allude at least in part to the indigenous experience but within a base of literary codes affiliated to Spanish baroque theater (García-Bedoya: 196). These plays are *El Rapto de Prosperpina y sueño de Eudimión, El hijo pródigo, El pobre más rico, Usca Paucar* and *Ollantay*,[33] and their Spanish titles may suggest they were directed to a bilingual audience. All of these plays are structured on literary codes with a strong influence from Calderón de la Barca (García-Bedoya: 207). They all show a tendency toward eight-syllable verse; rhyming schemes, although with frequent irregularities; and a division into three acts or *jornadas*. Further, the *comedias* are constructed around the counterpoint between the protagonist and the *gracioso*, and lyric fragments are distributed throughout the plays. Sacramental *autos* continue to influence these plays in terms of Eucharistic themes and the presence of allegorical characters (García-Bedoya: 200). Because of their calderonian influence, the plays probably date to the mid-17th century but certainly not to the 16th century.

It would probably be safe to conclude that the sacramental and farcical *autos* performed in Lima and in Cuzco during the 16th century would have had a strong influence in the tropes described by Esteve Barba as "priestly" in Manku Inqa's monologues (see note 22). However, the formatting of the *Instrucción* within rubric headings, which sometimes refer to monologues as "documents" or as evidence presented in favor of Titu Kusi Yupanki's legal and historical arguments, render any similarities in the *Instrucción* with Spanish theatrical influences a product of "organic hybridity." This hybridity is intentional in its citations at times when it intends to give its narrative validity to Christian interlocutors, yet is, overall, not systemic to the intended performance projected by the text's format or historical context and to other organizational markers. These intimate instead the Ritual Homage to the Inqa and Quechumara grammatical and syntactical structures as the governing sources behind the dialogic structure that the *Instrucción* displays in the sections mainly set in Cuzco. I will discuss these in reference to the narrative structures examined by Willem Adelaar and Sabine Dedenbach-Salazar Sáenz for the *Huarochirí Manuscript (1607)* and Rosaleen Howard's analysis of discourse structure of oral Quechua narratives from the Huánuco area.

I have also normalized the Spanish, Quechua and Aymara orthography as follows: toponyms receive their modern Spanish spelling for the reader's easy reference. Most of the place names of Peru's highlands and littoral were originally Quechua, Aymara, Puquina, Uru, Culli, Mochica or Quingnam;[34] Quechua and Aymara names and words have been normalized according to the standards set forward by the Peruvian Ministry of Education in 1985; words of Caribbean origin in Spanish have received their modernized Spanish spellings and their etymologies have been noted; Spanish words in the English translation have been italicized. Furthermore, subject/verb and gender/number agreements have been normalized in the interest of greater readability for Spanish readers; readers interested in studying these "anomalies," which are common in Andean Spanish,[35] should refer back to the prior editions of the *Instrucción*.

The signs employed in both my modernization and translation require the following clarifications: omissions and additions have been noted in the modernization within [ ]; writing within < > refers to archaic or alternative spellings which may be of interest; writing within / / preceded by * indicates an original or reconstructed form of a word; and writing within [ ] in my notes indicates a phonetic representation, although within citations of other works it may refer to additions or omissions made to the text.

There are residual problems, however, when Quechua, Aymara and Puquina voices are rephonologized based on the modern orthographic norms set out by the Peruvian Ministry of Education. These problems arise mainly from the differences in dialect, phonology and spelling in colonial texts. For this reason, I have conserved the manuscript's spelling of words belonging to the living, native languages of the Andean area in the Spanish modernization for readers' comparisons with their modern spelling in the English translation. Yet there are some specific decisions I have made, in the rephonologizations, which I would like to address.

Gerald Taylor, among others, has observed that the Spanish first had contact with Quechua and Aymara dialects from the Chinchaysuyu area of the Inqanate, which displayed sonorization of occlusive labials and dentals after nasals (e.g., <condor> */kuntur/, <pamba> */pampa/, <tambo> */tampu/) as well as the complete lack of a post-velar */q/ in a final position (e.g., <topa> */tupaq/), and the frequent replacement of **r** with **l** (ex. the Peruvian capital Lima */rimaq/, 'the speaker') (158). These changes were viewed by the Inca Garcilaso as "corruptions" made by the Spaniards who could not speak the Quechua of Cuzco properly; the intention was to compare the phonetic changes between Latin and the Romance languages, and the Roman Empire with "the general language" of the Inqanate and its dialects, in an attempt to equate both civilizations and thus legitimize his Andean inheritance for Western Renaissance readers. Yet these phonetic features registered in the first colonial texts, and characteristic of the Quechua I dialects, are not typically Iberian.[36] They characterize the first Quechua terms introduced into Spanish, which were often later re-lexified or reintroduced into other Quechua dialects as *hispanismos*. This is especially true of the words the conquistadors were most eager to learn first, including those signifiers referring to the social organization, customs and traditions of the native peoples of Peru and its landscape (cf. Cerrón Palomino 2003: 131).

The morphophonemic reconstruction of the "Southern Quechua common language,"[37] the predecessor of the Cuzco-Collao and Ayacucho-Chanka, has generated some polemic between linguists studying Andean languages.[38] Some unique characteristics displayed by modern Cuzco-Collao, such as fricative consonants in the final position of a syllable, are not represented graphically in the Ministry's orthography in order to facilitate comprehension between writers who are native speakers of different Quechua or Aymara varieties. Even though the Quechua writing system is largely phonetic, it is a modern orthography that is likewise intent on preserving linguistic features of historical value so that the diachronic progressions of certain morphophonemic changes in the language are not lost upon its readers.[39] Thus the intent of my reconstructions of these indigenous voices is not to instill "purity" in the reader's pronunciation of these words, but rather to create an awareness of some of the major differences between these languages and Spanish, the language in which they are embedded in the text.[40]

My spelling of *Inqa* perhaps merits special attention. I am following the spelling proposed for Quechua by Rodolfo Cerrón Palomino. He suggests that this ethnic and hierarchical title of uncertain origin could have perhaps been a Puquina word which survives today in the Quechua words *inqachu~inqaychu*, re-lexified forms meaning "amulet" or "talisman"

(Cerrón Palomino 1998: 435). The more popular version in modern Quechua is written <Inka> and in most modern Spanish texts <Inca>. In the three previous Spanish editions which transcribe the *Instrucción* found in the Escorial Archive, this term is written <Ynga>, <Inga> or alternatively <Ingá>. I have also accepted Cerrón Palomino's etymology and spelling for /Yupanki/, tracing its origin to the Aymara expression *yupa* as defined by Ludovico Bertonio as "something of great esteem," followed by a partially elided verb "to be" that still retains the 3rd person marker *-i*, so that **yupa (ka)nk-i*[41] means "an invaluable person, worthy of esteem" (435).

Throughout this text, I will follow Cerrón Palomino's example by not relying solely on Quechua for my discussion of the Cuzqueño indigenous words within the text.

I have thus included entries from Ludovico Bertonio's *Vocabulario de la lengua aimara* in my annotations of the *Instrucción* as well as the oft-cited colonial Quechua dictionaries.[42] These colonial glosses and renderings of Quechua and Aymara concepts should, however, not be taken at face value. Though any translator always negotiates the references between the cultural codes she has at her command, the linguistic policies of evangelization prior to the III Council of Lima in 1583 stressed cultural equivalencies and literal trans-locations[43] of the European world onto the Andean world. These utopian attempts at cultural trans-locations are evident in the *Instrucción*, where *Wiraqucha* is synonymous with God, "sheep of this land" are llamas and alpacas, and the competition among the members of different *panaqas*, or royal lineages, for the Inqanate is reduced to the European system of primogeniture and regencies.[44] These translations, however, are themselves subverted by the competing voices of the text.

While Quechua is currently the main indigenous language spoken in the Department of Cuzco, the area's very toponymy suggests that the area was originally Aymara speaking and that the Inqa ethnic group may have originated from the Puquina-speaking region of the Lake Titicaca area.[45] In the "Andean Sistine Chapel" of Andahuaylillas, the baptismal niche has the blessing "In the name of the Father, the Son and the Holy Spirit" inscribed in Latin, Spanish, Quechua and Puquina. Furthermore, the Archdiocese of Cuzco ordered its parishes in the *Mandamientos de Prelados*, following the III Ecclesiastic Council in Lima in 1582, to preach in "the general language of the natives, which is called Quechua, or also in Aymara"[46] or in "the native language of their parish: Quechua, Aymara or Puquina"[47] (f. 3v; f. 5; f.36v) and also recognized that "in many of the towns of our archdiocese all of the Indian women, in general, and some

Indian men, do not understand the Quechua language but speak Aymara or Puquina [. . .]"[48] (f. 5).

Ethno-historians and literary theorists often rely heavily on Quechua for their analyses of indigenous voices[49] in the Andean area, often offering apocryphal etymologies which place quite a strain on Quechua semantics and project the contemporary distribution of Andean languages into the pre-Hispanic and colonial past. Harrison, for example, assumes that Wiraqucha, the name for a pan-Andean deity, must be of Quechua origin in the etymology she proposes. While recognizing that *wira* means "fat" and *qucha* means "lake" thus literally signifying "lake of fat," to avoid such an aberrant signification for a deity, Harrison extends the signification of *wira* to "a substance of life and power" so that combined with "lake" *Wiraqucha* could mean "the spreading of life substance" in Quechua (Harrison, 1989: 94). Along a similar vein, Mignolo bases his discussion of Inqa concepts of center in territorial representations on an apocryphal etymology of Cuzco, as "navel of the world"[50] (citing Sullivan), and warns us that "it would be a mistake to think that the coincidence between [similar representations of] Jerusalem and Cuzco [as navels] exemplifies Christian influences in colonial Peru" (Mignolo 1994: 26–27). And though I am inclined to agree with Mignolo that "it would be more satisfactory to think that if both Jerusalem and Cuzco are assigned a central place in territorial representations, it is because there were common features in both Christian and Inca cultures long before European explorers and men of letters changed the image of the world and the mobility of the earth," this would be true if only pre-1532 Inqa projections of center were conceived in terms of "navel"[51] (27).

Instead, in Aymara etymology, the "owl's stone" recalls a variation on the mythical founding of Cuzco by the brothers Ayar (a type of Quinoa) which was registered by the Spanish chronicler Sarmiento de Gamboa (Cerrón Palomino 1997a: 168). Significantly, Sarmiento de Gamboa also incorporates a story about a stone object in the form of a bird that was named *Indi* /Inti/, or "sun," which could speak and was associated symbolically with Inqa aggression and the expansion of the Inqa armies, out of the Cuzco valley after the city had been founded, led by the Inqas who laid a claim to the Sun's very dynastic descent group (Julien: 244–45).

The multiple significations of Cuzco do not always recall the Inqa capital's original etymology. Classen has also noted, for example, that in Inqa cosmology, Cuzco is often compared to a quinoa plant (104), a puma's body (101–102), the sacred place centered by Manku Qhapaq's staff (40), the heart and head of the Inqa empire (99–100) as well as a microcosmic body of the Tawantinsuyu itself (105). Julien's analysis of the ideological changes in Inqa "genres," such as the "life history genre" or the "origins genre," as the power relations between ethnic and kin groups in and out of Cuzco were transformed by Inqa aggression, especially after Pachakutiq's reign, follows the manner in which these structure the evolving projections of Cuzco into the center of the Tawantinsuyu.[52] The metaphors surrounding Cuzco's centrality were embedded in a *corpus* of mythological imagery that negotiated several centers[53] in the Andean world, whereas the imagery surrounding Jerusalem as the navel of the body of Christ (the world) in 16th-century Spain incorporated other known centers of the world within the theological framework of Christianity[54] or rejected them entirely.[55] At the heart of the differing Inqa visions of Cuzco's position is a historical consciousness of its rivalry with other centers of power, both temporal and spiritual, in the Andean world that existed before and during Inqa processes of territorial and ideological expansion.

"Colonial semio[tics]" may prove more fruitful if literary theorists and ethno-historians were to accept that a discussion as to how these "signs from different cultural systems [] interact" should not confuse synchronic linguistic distributions with diachronic phenomena; indeed, their treatment of indigenous semiotics as one monolithic cultural category may obfuscate the multiplicity of voices present in the Tawantinsuyu, replicating within the heuristic categories of "colonial semiosis"[56] the 16th-century European conceptions and perceptions of the "Americas."

The discovery of the missing section of the *Suma y narración de los incas* by Juan Díez de Betanzos, and its subsequent publication in 1987, provided Betanzos's transcription of one of the ritual songs honoring the Inqa that was unintelligible to him even though he was a fluent speaker of the Quechua language. Torero has argued that this "secret language" was Aymara (Cf. Torero 1994: 329), although Cerrón Palomino has given further nuance to this appraisal by recognizing a Puquina subtext to an overall Aymara composition (1998: 440). Any discussion of the historical poems of the Inqas that solely continues to consider Cuzqueño Quechua as their language of composition *per se* is ignoring the literature that Szeminski,[57] Torero and Cerrón Palomino have dedicated to this very subject.

Although it may be difficult to recognize Puquina voices[58] through the many filters of translation in the *Instrucción*—plus the fact that Puquina is no longer spoken and that colonial sources are so few—Aymara should not be overlooked as a potential and major signifier, especially considering that Quechua and Aymara grammatical forms are interchangeable (and lexemes from both languages are often, significantly, combined in the toponymy of the Cuzco region) although the latter's morphophonemic structure is more complex (cf. Cerrón Palomino 2000). While it may still be meaningful to read the *Instrucción* through the lenses of a "ritual homage to the Inqa" or "Cuzqueño literature," as distinct cultural categories within Andean literature, the conflation created by the equivalence between "Cuzqueño" and "Quechua" homogenizes the multiplicity of indigenous voices of 16th-century Cuzco. Our current understanding of this unique form of cultural production, for the preservation of a collective memory of the Inqa rulers within the Tawantinsuyu, should not be limited to a discussion of Quechua as its sole cultural code.[59]

Validating a Son's Vision: Reading for Inqa Ritual within a Spanish Legal Genre

The different terms Lienhard,[60] Jakfalvi-Leiva,[61] Chang-Rodríguez[62] and Mazzotti[63] coined for their readings of the *Instrucción* took their cues from Millones's appraisal that this *Instrucción*, "made and ordered by the aforesaid Father [Marcos García] with the declarations of the aforesaid Don Diego de Castro [. . .]"[64] which "I, Martín de Pando [. . .] wrote with my own hands,"[65] could not help but reveal an indigenous (specifically Quechua) subtext. These authors specified that the "indigenous subtext" was not experienced so much by the presence of indigenous words, but by whether or not their very presence in the *Instrucción* formed part of a Spanish semantic ensemble that denoted "Andeanness" or whether they worked as well within an Andean system of reference:

> The presence of an Andean pattern helps to reinforce the hypothesis that these Mestizo chronicles, that is to say, those in which the Indigenous, Mestizo or European designator places an American referent at the center of the tale and describes it with respect and comprehension, were conceived for a double recipient: the self-evident colonial or metropolitan authorities to whom these were addressed, and the implicit [addressees], the literate Indians or mestizos who were able to identify with this vindicating discourse, as well as those who listened to the telling of these events.[66] (Chang-Rodríguez 1988: 18)

A. Diaz-Rivera has underscored the importance of the multi-ethnic public—formed by "mestizos, natives and Spaniards"[67]—that witnessed "Titu Kusi's oral speech in Quechua"[68] as an important factor in defining the hybridity of the text, which resulted from multiple strands of discourse aimed at the various interlocutors of differing ethnicities gathered to "give faith" to the document addressed to the former governor of Peru (86). Verdesio, in contrast, has contended that unless the authorship of the text, in the strictest sense, is resolved, it is impossible to speak of "appropriation" since one cannot unequivocally establish which referents are being possessed by "whom" to mask or unmask the "other's" referents (404).

Lienhard has claimed that the *Instrucción* belongs to the "Ritual homage to the Inca" genre, in the manner of the ritual songs composed and sung by the *khipukamayuq* upon the death of an Inqa in order to honor and preserve his memory in ceremonies later performed before the mummy. He has defined this "epic genre" through the close reading of Betanzos, Cieza de León, and Titu Kusi Yupanki and recognizing style patterns to define an Inqa literary form (song) whose subject matter was the life history of the Inqa being honored. Julien similarly uncovered a "life history genre" when comparing Spanish historical narratives that drew from "Inca sources [in an] extractive process" to compare genealogical information being transmitted in these narratives (18). As Julien herself concedes, she is using the term "genre" loosely, basing her definitions solely on content[69] in a method aimed at proving an "Inca historical consciousness" evident in an ideology of genealogy contained by these Inca genres *only* in reference to pre-Hispanic events (9). Julien's definition of "Inca genres" based purely on content would not account for the existence of post-1532 Inqa genres, because all of the genres she has recognized refer to pre-1532 subject matter. Could we use Julien's method to argue in favor of an Inqa "life history" genre post-1532 given that there was a post-1532 neo-Inqa state in Vilcabamba? Historical narratives in Spanish which narrate post-1532 events using Inqa sources are difficult to come by. If we were to compare Titu Kusi Yupanki's *Instrucción* with the second part of Inca Garcilaso's *Comentarios Reales,* which narrates the events of the Spanish conquest, we would immediately find conflicting versions (in the content) between two "Inqa" sources.[70] This is one of the main difficulties in basing Inqa "genre" definitions solely on content, in that they necessarily assume a breach in the Inqas' capacity to compose within a "genre" if its subject matter is post-1532 by the scholar's very definition.[71] However, if we use close reading not only to find agreement in content but a pattern in form and style such a possibility would be acceptable within the new heuristic category. Nevertheless, more difficulties arise, as these patterns must be "discovered" in narratives whose main code is Spanish and where the skein of one or more cultural codes may be difficult if not impossible to unravel.

The cultural trans-locations evident in the *Instrucción* are exemplary of situations where indigenous voices[72] are being used to denote "Andeanness" within a Spanish semantic ensemble and makes Lienhard's suggestion that the *Instrucción* can be read as a direct or literal translation of Titu Kusi Yupanki's "ritual homage" to his father, Manku Inqa, highly unlikely (cf. Lienhard: 186–192). Mazzotti, on the other hand, has been careful to emphasize both the "chorality" of the *Instrucción* and its capacity for multiple interpretations from both Spanish and Quechua semantics as well as the "desdoblamiento insuficiente" or the difficulty in attempting to separate or unfold the complex meshing of "different colonial subjects" within the narrative as well as in the monologues themselves (98–99).

> If it is logical to accept the existence of a basic ritual genre ["the ritual homage to the Inqa"] upon which these texts were composed, it is also possible to argue that this kind of Andean "epicity" would take on very unique characteristics in their Spanish transcription.[73] (Mazzotti: 97)

That several of the indigenous words in the *Instrucción* are of Caribbean origin—*chicha, bohío, guazábara*—is more indicative of the words brought to Perú by conquistadors who had been in the Antilles, and so the mere presence of "Cuzqueño Quechua" words could simply betray the acquisition of new indigenous lexemes by the Spanish being spoken in 16th-century Peru.

Having established that an indigenous vocabulary could not, in and of itself, be a marker of Titu Kusi Yupanki's agency in the elaboration of the text, Millones highlighted one of Quechua's syntactic particularities, which could account for the text's dramatic structure (Millones 1985: 10). According to Cerrón Palomino, in Quechua, complementary indicative sentences are constructed by nominalization through the use of the suffix *-sqa* or *-na* which indicate that the action is before, in the former, or after, in the latter, the one implicated by the principal verb. The verbs that accept indicative complements are, among others, *yacha-* (to know), *wiya-* (to hear), *musya-* (to realize), *qunqa-* (to forget); however, verbs like *muna-* (to want) exclude such usage (Cerrón Palomino 1987: 317). These nominalizations usually require a personal reference marker. The nominalization of the subordinate clause functions as a kind of citation of the knowledge being conveyed within the sentence.[74] Millones argued that the long monologues by Manku Inqa, Francisco Pizarro, Wila Uma, Manku Inqa's Captains and his People can be attributed to a literal translation of

Quechua syntax of the narrative because they function as subordinate nominal clauses to the narrative voice; this is made evident by the reiteration of "saying," "says" and "said" which frame these monologues (1985: 10). The verb -ñi "to say," "to consider," "to intend," requires a direct quotation as its complement[75] (Adelaar: 138). Thus the *Instrucción*, like all Spanish legal documents,[76] valued eye-witness testimony over hearsay; yet Titu Kusi Yupanki was not an eye-witness to most of the events narrated in the *Instrucción*, nor was he an interlocutor to the majority of the long speeches that Quechumara syntax would have nevertheless required him to quote, when he reported on their content; these "quotations" left an imprint in the unique style and format of the *Instrucción*.

In the signifying domain of ceremonies honoring the memory of the ancestor, the semantics of validating sources of information may change from that of daily usage:[77] "ritual language usually differs from ordinary discourse in that the system of the ritual often depends on specific verbal forms quoted in a particular sequence. So tightly woven are actions and words that the mere mention of the words serves to connote the symbolic importance of the entire ritual" (Harrison 1989: 75). Dedenbach-Salazar Sáenz has analyzed the switching in use between the -*mi* and the -*si* in the *Huarochirí Manuscript*:

> The suffix -*mi* is typical of a descriptive genre of rituals and ceremonies, as well as eyewitness accounts, and is most often used to show that the narrator has been eyewitness to an event, or, for example, knows places from his own experience. [. . .] Moreover, -*mi* is used in connection with certain supernatural beings, probably marking their integration into human lived experience. [. . .] (164)
>
> As "historical" beings, they may have to be presented in the affirmed knowledge mode, whereas ancient, mythical, supernatural beings, having already disappeared before the last pre-colonial gods, are connected with the hearsay evidential suffix -*si*. (160)

The definition of the "personal experience" of the narrator in reference to the time and space he is describing can be both a reflection of his actual position at the time (and space) of utterance relative to the "historical" or alternatively "mythical" events of the narration. Cummins has suggested that "the forms, designs, and physicality of keros and textiles had a quasi-linguistic function because their presence made them eyewitnesses to an ancient event [. . .]" (207). We know, from Baltasar de Ocampo, that Inqa Titu Kusi Yupanki and later Inqa Thupaq Amaru kept their father's embalmed body with them in Vilcabamba (Markham 1907: 229). Mummies are exemplary of "supernatural beings" which could be known on a "historical," "mythical," and even "quotidian" level. Even if Manku Inqa's mummy were not present in the exact space where Titu Kusi Yupanki recited his story to his multi-ethnic public, the father's body would have formed part of his son's ritual experience in Vilcabamba as well as that of the Inqa members of his audience. Other objects may have "spoken" of the events they had witnessed, and Titu Kusi Yupanki's very body bore the scars of him witnessing his father's murder.[78] Thus the text's dialogic structure eludes Spanish legal forms for validating testimonies which give more authority to eyewitness over hearsay testimonies, likewise stressed by Quechumara[79] grammatical markers; though attaching a similar value to the Spanish dichotomy on the quotidian level, these allow a narrator more mobility to define "personal experience" in relation to historical or mythical characters, time or space in a narrative. Within the genre of "the Ritual Homage to the Inqa," reading for Quechumara syntactical footprints is not enough; it may be worthwhile to explore the *Instrucción* for moments in which Titu Kusi Yupanki's "personal experience" is constructed around artifacts or landscape significant to this Inqa performance.

The presence or absence of objects would have been important to a ritual created by the tactile performance of the *khipukamayuq*, from the readings of the knotted cords (*khipu*) with their hands.[80] That the *khipu*, long multicolored knotted strings, could be read over generations, and were not limited in their signification as mnemonic devices[81] to the *khipukamayuq* who had made them, is made evident by the discovery of what were probably narrative *khipu*, buried with Inqa mummies in the Chachapoyas area of the Peruvian Department of Amazonas, in a cave overlooking the Lago de los Cóndores, near Leimebamba. *Khipu* were also reportedly found on Pachakutiq's mummy. Narrative *khipu* have yet to be deciphered, but Urton has asserted that the *khipu* would not have been a phonological knot alphabet, as the semantic and syntactic structures of Quechua would make it too cumbersome (2002b: 182). Quilter has compared the Inqas' need for narrative *khipu* to the advent of stenography in Europe: resulting from a need to record sermons or parliamentary debates, i.e., to record public speech-acts which hadn't been previously written down (208–209). Quilter has lamented the difficulty in deciphering *khipu*, however, because "*khipu* are *khipu*: the medium and the message appear intertwined in a way in which writing and the surfaces on which it is placed are not. [. . .] Because writing is free to be placed almost anywhere desired, the contexts the hieroglyphics were given when inscribed in books, or monuments, and on walls, have aided in interpreting them" (198). Yet the *khipu* often *do* have a context: their association with mummies indicates a correlation with the song rites to honor their memory (or "life history genre"). In order to seek correlations between signifying units in narrative-accounting type *khipu* and narrative texts in Quechua (Urton 2002b: 191), one would have to recognize their association by the *khipu*'s context and the subject matter of the Quechua narrative text. Following the Third Council of Lima (1581–83), *khipu* were classified as idolatrous objects and were ordered to be burned (Urton 2002a: 10). Although Spaniards initially trusted *khipu* as valid sources of information and a useful method for record keeping, the *khipu* and the *khipukamayuq* increasingly became suspect when legal disputes confronted this native form of record keeping with Spanish written records (Urton 2002a: 4). *Khipukamayuq* testimonies are also considered authorative sources on pre-1532 events for the purposes of Vaca de Castro (in Urteaga 1920: 3–53). Even Viceroy Toledo validated and notarized his *Informaciones* on Inqa history in part on *khipukamayuq* testimonies in Huamanga, Apurimac, and Cuzco (in Urteaga 1920). Spanish friar Diego de Porras thought that the *khipu* might be useful for evangelization and testing the Indians' memory of the commandments, prayers and rules[82] of catechism (Sempat Assadourian: 136–137; Cf. Porras: 27, 28–29). The Inqas of Vilcabamba would most certainly have continued to respect the *khipus* and the *khipukamayuq* as record keepers and as sources of historical knowledge, and should be considered as one of the sources of the *Instrucción*.

Selected passages in the *Instrucción* have received commentary because their sentence structure seems to betray a "Quechua" syntactical footprint, though these anomalies can be present in 16th-century Spanish texts where no Andean origin or influence could be attributed.[83] Legal documents made by notaries from hispanophone testimonies often show a chaining of clauses or list making, most notoriously in colonial documents detailing booty being sent to the Spanish Crown. The high frequency of lists in Manku Inqa's speeches could be illustrative of the Spanish legal format of the *Instrucción*, yet upon close inspection may elucidate the semantics of unrequited reciprocity between the Inqa and the Spanish characters in the text. For example, Manku Inqa, in the "Speech made by the Inqa to all of his Captains and People who were in the Town of Tambo [. . .]" after explaining how he was deceived by the Spaniards, makes a list of things he had given them and how he was repaid:

[. . .] Because they said they were sons of Wiraquchan and sent by
his mandate to enter my land, to whom I gave my consent, and
because of this and many good acts whereby I gave them what I
had—silver and gold, clothes and corn, livestock, subjects,
women, servants and many other innumerable things—they
seized me, insulted and tormented me without my deserving such
treatment. [. . .][84]

This form of listing as a sign of reciprocity between the conqueror and
the conquered can be found in Inqa testimonies referring to pre-1532 and
post-1532 events. If we compare and contrast this passage to the oral testimonies given by Spanish *vecinos* and conquistadors and Hanan and
Lurin Inqas of Cuzco in the *Información dada a pedimento de la Señora
Doña María Manrique Coya Cusiguarcay,* made in January 1567, a significant pattern in list order can be established among the Inqa sources.

In response to the thirteenth question,[85] the Spanish witnesses never
give more information than necessary and tend not to make lists. The
Presbyterian Cristóbal Jiménez responds, "she gives them food to eat and
some things which they take back to their own lands"[86] (f. 143 v.).
Hernando Bachicao says, "the aforesaid feeds them, gives them drink and
other things"[87] (f. 150 v.). The translations (always by the same Interpreter
Juan Calla) from the Inqa testimonies, however, seem to show a list pattern
meant to signify the generosity (and thus political legitimacy) of the giver
in Inqa oral narrative structures. The repetitive "and" found in these testimonies could be attributed to the literal translation of the additive suffix
-pas~-pis, which roughly translates as "even" and "also" (Cerrón Palomino
1987: 216–217) so that a list of "milk, and even bread, and even beans and
even coca" in Cuzqueño Quechua would be: *ñuñupas t'antapas purutupas
kukapas.* <Don Garcia Quispe Guara> testifies that the Indians

stay there and are in [her house] and [Doña María Kusi Warkay]
harbors them and gives them to drink and to eat and he has seen
her give sheep of this land and calves and cloaks and sandals and
other things of wealth and value which he has seen with the sight
of his eyes and this he knows. (f. 153)[88]

Similarly, <Don Felipe Ojea Malta> of Lurin Cuzco affirms,

and she gives them food and drink and more and he has seen sheep
and calves and things of silver for the ears and nose and wrists

being given and if this were not done she [Doña María Manrique Quya Kusi Warkay] would not be following the customs of the Ladies of this kingdom.[89]

Likewise, <Don Juan Paucar Guamani> of Hanan Cuzco says in his testimony,

she receives them in her home and gives them food and drink and other clothes and things of gold and silver for the nose, ears and arms and that this is the custom of all the lords of this kingdom.[90]

<Don Juan Sona Indio de los Principales de esta ciudad> goes even further to establish Doña María's generosity by contrasting the reciprocal exchange in gifts: the Indians who arrive from the Andes "bring feathers and other little trinkets of minor value"[91] whereas the "the Lady gives them to eat and drink and cloaks and calves of this land and things in gold and silver for the nose and ears and arms and other things from Castilla."[92] (f. 173). The political legitimacy of post-1532 Inqas, such as María Kusi Warkay, is symbolized by the obligations founded upon their acts of "generosity" in these Inqa testimonies.

In the *Declaración de los quipocamayos a Vaca de Castro,*[93] the Inqa sources, specifically *khipukamayuq*, narrate the Inqas' history of conquest of other peoples of the Andean region. In the passage dealing with a major Inqa victory over the Chimu Empire of the Northern Coast of Peru, the text reads as follows:

[Once Chimo Capac recognized Viracocha Inga as his lord] Chimo Capac [. . .] then acknowledged his lordship, giving him obeisance and sent him his ambassadors with his gifts and presents, and he sent him twenty young maidens, and necklaces of precious stones of emeralds and turquoise *chaquiras*[94] of shells and clothes and things which were of his land, making himself vassal of the son of the Sun.[95]

The *new* vassal of Wiraqucha Inqa shows his obeisance in an act of asymmetrical reciprocity. The *Relación de los señores indios que sirvieron a Tupac Yupanqui y Huayna Capac*[96] gives a similar account of the victory over the Chimu, showing a similar chaining of clauses to signify an asymmetrical reciprocal exchange:

> It was the custom of he who subjugated his subjects to make *chakra* of corn and *coca* and *ají* and to take it to him; and in this manner many were conquered, such as the lord of the valley of Trujillo, whose name is Chimo Capac [...][97]

In this exchange, the Inqa bestows upon his new subject lands for growing corn, *ají*, and *coca*, all of which are crops of important ritual significance in the Andes. The asymmetrical reciprocal exchange between the Inqa Empire and the conquered Chimu Empire is evident in the archaeological record of *tumis*, or sacrificial knives, of the Northern Coast region of Peru. One of the measures the Inqas took to establish their hegemony in this area of Chinchaysuyu was to prohibit the local production of *tumis* in native Chimu bronzes (i.e., arsenical bronze) and to impose their replacement through the import and production of tin bronzes native to the Southern altiplano (Cf. Lechtman 1987). These two distinctive processes of *tumi* production and the forced reception of the tin bronze *tumis* was a powerful symbol of Chimu subordination to the Inqas, within a relationship created by asymmetrical reciprocity.

Further down the Inqa's dynastic line, those who peacefully entered into the dominion of the Inqa's Tawantinsuyu also received gifts, but they were required to build "a house" for the Inqa *to commemorate the obedience they had shown him*:

> [Capac Yupangui] graced all of the lords who came to him in peace, ordering the entire province to build him a house, in memory of the obedience they had shown him, and he gave them gold and textiles from Cuzco.[98]

The same structure is repeated for Inqa Yupanki or Pachakutiq:

> And as they witnessed the strength of Inga Yupangui and the good manner, way and form in which he attracted people, which was with gifts [...] When this Inga and Lord had returned to Cuzco, the natives then built him a house and named lands to grow corn, *coca* and *ají* and other plants, and they were not forced to do so but did so voluntarily, and they took half of the harvest to Cuzco and the other half they left in the Inga's warehouse [...] and the Inga graced them and gave them *gold, silver, women* and other things.[99]

The asymmetrical relationship of reciprocity between the Inqa and his subjects, symbolized in the exchange of gifts,[100] and in the parallel listing of these gifts—creating a comparison, structurally, between the ruler's "gifts" and the subject's "obligations"—highlights an important cultural sign in the pre-1532 Tawantinsuyu. When the Inqa gave silver, gold or women to another lord or people of the Andean region, this was a sign to reinforce their obligation to him; it was not a ransom that the Inqa paid for his liberty, nor a levy paid to a foreign lord to signify his subjugation. The underlying ideology of these *khipukamayuq* narratives, in the parallel structure of "gift" lists, places the receiver of the most munificent gifts in obligation to the giver, in direct opposition to the Spanish manner of conquest.

The *Relación de los señores indios que sirvieron a Tupac Yupanqui y Huayna Capac* summarizes the Inqas' manner of conquest.

> The Inqas sometimes had the custom of making *fiestas* in order to gain the good will of their vassals [. . .] and there, with his hand, the Inqa gave the *caciques matis* or cups of *chicha* to drink, which was a great favor, and gave them his very own clothes for them to wear and silver cups and some other things.[101]

In the *Instrucción*, Ataw Wallpa twice shows the Spanish Wiraquchas much favor when he offers them *chicha* to drink, which the Spaniards despised both times in a derisive manner:

> *Among these Wiraquchas two were brought by some Yungas before my uncle. Ataw Wallpa (who happened to be in Cajamarca) who cordially received them and gave them each to drink, a drink that we drink, from a golden cup.*[102] *The Spaniard, upon receiving the drink in his hand, spilled it which greatly angered my uncle. And after that, the two Spaniards showed my uncle a letter, a book or something, saying that this was the* Qillqa *of God and the King and my uncle, as he felt offended by the spilling of the* chicha, *took the letter (or whatever it was) and knocked it to the ground, saying:*
> I don't know what you have given me. Go on, leave.[103]

The scene has been interpreted as mutual signs of disrespect signifying parallel forms of conquest: the Spaniards first offend Ataw Wallpa by spilling the *chicha*, and Ataw Wallpa shows disrespect for the Holy Book by throwing it to the ground (cf. Salomon 1982; Seed 1991: 21). The misunderstanding is more pronounced, however. Ataw Wallpa asks the Spaniards to leave: they had rejected an invitation to enter into a relationship of asymmetrical reciprocity, or to be the vassals of Ataw Wallpa. The second encounter directly leads to the slaughter of the Indians in Cajamarca:

> *And having arrived, he asked them why they had come and they replied under the mandate of the Wiraqucha to tell them how they were to know Him. And my uncle, as he heard what they told them he started and was silent and offered them to drink in the same way the others had, and so they did, because they didn't drink or listen. And my uncle seeing that they respected little, said:*
> Since you don't respect me I won't respect you either.
> *And angry, he stood and shouted for the death of the Spaniards and the Spaniards, who were on guard, seized the four entrances of the plaza so that the Indians were surrounded on all sides.*[104]

Ataw Wallpa here makes one more overture to the Spaniards to be his vassals through peaceful means. Their rejection of the *chicha* was an affront to the ideology of the supremacy of the Inqas, as reflected in the testimonies of the *khipukamayuq*, and an invitation to war; "he shouted for the death of the Spaniards," yet the Spaniards had already prepared the scene of the encounter for an ambush. Their slaughter of the "Indians" at Cajamarca has prevailed in the collective memory of the Andean peoples to the present day as the Spanish manner of conquest.

Throughout the *Instrucción*, Manku Inqa, Wila Uma and other members of the Inqa nobility recite long lists of things they bestowed upon the Spaniards and are encountered by silence where one might expect a parallel list on the Spaniards' behalf, or at the very least one enumerating things of lesser value as in the contrasting testimony of <Don Juan Sona Indio> or in the *khipukamayuq* testimony detailing the gifts of <Chimo Capac> or the exchange between the powerful Inqa Yupanki and his new vassals. This silence or gap of the *Instrucción* in what should be a parallel structure of lists in Inqa testimony, which are offered to an interlocutor to compare and contrast characters in social relations, reflects the inability of the Spaniards and the Inqas to engage in a true dialogue of asymmetrical reciprocal exchange. The silencing of traditional narrative structure thus formally incorporates the very disintegration of the Inqa social fabric unraveled by the conquistadors. The confusion arises from a realization that these *guests* of the Inqa do not wish to be his vassals or to be integrated with the Tawantinsuyu but rather to become its possessors. The list-making in the narrative structure is replaced with the lamentations in the monologue of the Inqa's Captains when they reprimand the Spaniards for their unacceptable behavior:

And you said that you came to serve the Inqa, to love him, to treat him and his people as your very selves. [. . .] What should [Manku Inqa] give you now that you have imprisoned him? Where is he supposed to find what you ask for when he has nothing to give? **All the people of this land are so distressed and disconcerted by your actions** that they do not know what to say nor where to go, **because they see themselves dispossessed of their king**, their women, their children, their homes, their lands, their fields, and all they possess, and their tribulation leaves them no choice but to hang themselves or to risk everything and they have told me this many times.[105]

How does a subject possess a king? Through the system of obligations signified by the asymmetrical gift-giving described in the Inqa sources recounting pre-1532 events. This system is undermined by the Spanish refusal to engage on these terms and so "dispossesses" Tawantinsuyu subjects of their "king." In the *Instrucción*, Wila Uma berates Manku Inqa for his tragic-like *hubris*, his inability to recognize the Spaniards for what they were: foreigners to the Tawantinsuyu who felt no obligation to its mores and were convinced of their superiority to the Inqas and had lied to them, pretending to be Wiraquchas:

> I told you when we heard the news that they had landed, that I would go with ten or twelve thousand Indians, and would make piecemeal out of them and you never let me, instead, "calm down, calm down, these are Wiraquchas or their sons," as if we would not be bothered with **this type of people who come to command and not to obey** from such a far away place.[106]

The assumption underlying Wila Uma's speech is that had the Spanish truly been Wiraquchas they would have come to obey the Inqa, not to rule over them. Manku Inqa is charged, in the text, for continuing to give signs of peaceful conquest when open war was already being waged over the Tawantinsuyu, in his complete failure to comprehend Spanish signs of invasion. Yet it is Manku Inqa himself who finds and outlines the system to replace the asymmetrical reciprocal exchange for Inqa and Spanish social relations: rather than reciprocal gift-giving, "an economy of lies"[107] would repay the Spaniards for their deceptive words. Signs of obeisance, on the Spanish terms of conquest, would never give the Spaniards security of their own position in the Andean world as "lords" over "subjects" who

would simply silence the foreign invaders from their native forms of reciprocal exchange, "because [the others] would not listen." He orders his
Indian subjects to bow their heads to the Spaniards but reminds them of
their obligations to his dynastic descent line, thus creating a narrative
space for both submission and dissent within the *Instrucción*:

> Look well on what I command; do not forget what I have told you.
> I mean to tell you now to remember all the time that my forefathers
> and their forefathers and I have nourished and kept you, favored
> and governed your homes, providing for them in the way you
> needed, so that all of you are obliged not to forget us, my forefa-
> thers and myself, during your lives nor the lives of your descen-
> dants, and to respect and obey my son and brother Titu Kusi
> Yupanki and the rest of my sons who may follow him. For in this,
> you will greatly please me and they will thank you as I command.
> Enough has been said.[108]

The obligation to remember, to this very day in Andean communities,
ensures the renewal of relations among the powers that animate the souls of
the dead, the landscape, the animals and human society. Crop failure, sickness, or death is the retribution for the failure to remember (cf. Howard: 30).
The obligation "not to forget," within the new rites of possession of the
Spanish Conquest, transforms the asymmetrical reciprocity of the "giver"
and the "receiver," between "ruler" and "subject" in the Tawantinsuyu of the
Inqas, to the new reciprocity between "ruler" and "subject" in colonial Peru:
silence and lies as "the gift" for feigned submission to the Spaniards by the
native population, and "memory" as "the gift" for the "defeated" Inqa; thus
two parallel forms of social relations coexist and are circumscribed within
the same territory, known either as colonial Peru or the Tawantinsuyu. The
Tawantinsuyu is continually recast in the gifts of Andean peoples who have
not forgotten their obligation to remember.

   The progression from descriptive to dramatic structure, from narrative to theatrical formats, in the *Instrucción*, seems to obey Quechumara
grammatical devices that position Titu Kusi Yupanki's locus of utterance
(Vilcabamba) in relation to the events described in Cajamarca, Cuzco,
Jauja and later in the Cordillera Vilcabamba. Both Rosaleen Howard and
Willem Adelaar have analyzed the relationship between Quechua texts,
oral and written, and the relationship created between the narrator's
position and the events narrated or to the landscapes described within
and his actual location without the narrative. Howard has commented,

"it is as if the landscape were being constructed as a human-like system of relationships, produced through human discourse in the very act of speaking about it" (35). The grammatical devices described by Howard are the following:

(i) The use of verbal subordination or switch referring on the verb, enabling parallelism in the sequencing of events.

(ii) The use of directional suffixes indicating centrifugal or centripetal movement (*-mu*), or movement in, out, up and down, locating action in space and relating protagonists to each other and the world around them.

(iii) The use of deictic markers that connect the event of the story told with the event of the storytelling.

(iv) The use of the possessive construction to relate spatial coordinates one to the other.[109]

(v) The use of *chaymanta* 'after that' to sequence events.

(vi) The use of reported speech.

I have already analyzed the footprints of (iii) and (vi) grammatical devices on the *Instrucción*. I will now analyze the influence of (i), (ii), and (vi) in creating the transitions between descriptive narrative passages to parallel dialogic encounters in the *Instrucción* because of their settings' relative positions to Titu Kusi Yupanki in Vilcabamba.

The different locations in the Cordillera Vilcabamba, mentioned by Titu Kusi Yupanki in the *Instrucción*, will be described more in depth in the next section but it will be helpful to emphasize some characteristics of the region's rough topography for the purposes of this discussion. The main territory controlled by Inqa Titu Kusi Yupanki spans the modern-day departments of Apurimac and Cuzco, is dominated by snow-capped mountains, cloud forest, and jungle and is bounded by the rivers Apurimac [Apu Rimaq 'Great Speaker'] and Vilcanota [Willka-n-uta 'House of the Sun'[110]]. Dominating features of the Cordillera Vilcabamba are the "wall" of mountains that separate the Vilcabamba region from the altiplano area of Chinchero, the Vilcanota valley, and the great depth and span of the Apurimac river which defines the boundary between Apurimac and Ayacucho. Titu Kusi Yupanki speaks of events that occur beyond and within these topographic walls and defines his relation to them by the imagined landscape created by the language of the *Instrucción*.

In the oral narrative of a native Quechua speaker of Huánuco registered by Howard, the narrative took a dramatic turn once the events occurred in places beyond a mountain behind which the speaker could no longer "see," in the most literal sense, where the mythological events were taking place in her narrative. Adelaar and Salazar-Saenz have described a similar pattern for the *Huarochirí Manuscript (1607)*. Within a landscape void, "the narrative is constructed entirely through the use of direct speech and verbal subordination: when a change of actor is indicated, switch reference comes into play as a means of leading on to the next action, leading to the dialogic structure of the narratives" (Howard: 36). This is true of the dramatic passages of the *Instrucción* which "narrate" the encounters between the Spaniards, Manku Inqa and the Inqa captains in Cuzco, in a space that cannot seem to be visualized by Titu Kusi Yupanki, thus accounting for its dialogic structure based on the juxtaposition of their monologues. These monologues are in turn separated by Spanish rubrics or chapter headings, which give them a narrative format within the legal genre of the Spanish *relación*. The monologues are written with no direct reference to the setting in which they occur, emptying the narrative landscape, in striking contrast to the theatrical tradition of the medieval *auto* or *comedia* of the Spanish Golden Age in which the opening monologue or soliloquy of an act or the initial exchange between characters in a scene often serve to create the setting for the public.

Yet there are moments in the scenes set in Cuzco where the narration switches back from the parallel monologues and is suddenly rooted in landscape; the toponymy of Cuzco comes to the fore in the passages under the headings: "Response Given to Manku Inqa by the Indians about the Treasure Hunt when he was in Prison" (1), "Speech of the Inqa to his Captains about the Siege of Cuzco" (2), "Entrance of the People into the Enclosure" (3):

> 1. *As all the people of the land searched its four corners, one thousand two hundred leagues long and almost three hundred leagues wide, which were distributed in this way throughout the world (it is convenient to know): in the east and west, north and south, what we call Antisuyu, Chinchaysuyu, Kuntisuyu, Qullasuyu; Antisuyu to the east, Kuntisuyu to the north and Chinchaysuyu to the west, and Qullasuyu to the south. This we said from Cuzco, which is the center and head of all the earth. And for this reason, because we were at the center, my ancestors, who had been placed there by their ancestors, were called Lords of the Tawantinsuyu, which means Lords of the Four Quadrants of the world for they thought there was no world beyond our own.*[111]

2. *And without delay they started to work, sending their own to each quarter of the earth: to Chinchaysuyu Wila Uma sent Quyllas and Uskay and Quri Ataw and Taypi to bring the people from that quarter; and to Qullasuyu, Liqlis went with many other captains to bring people from that quarter; to Kuntisuyu, Suranwaman, Kikana and Suri Wallpa and many other captains went; and to Antisuyu, Rampa Yupanki and many other captains, so that each and every suyu would unite the necessary people. Note that these four suyus that are named here, it is good to know, as I have said above, are the four quarters in which the earth is divided and spread, as I have declared more extensively above.*[112]

3. *By Carmenca, going towards Chinchaysuyu, Quri Ataw and Quyllas and Taypi and many others closed that entrance with the people they brought. By Coacachi, going towards Kuntisuyu, Wamani, Kikana and Quri Wallpa and many others closed off a large mile, more than half a voice league, all well-equipped for war; going towards Qullasuyu, Liqlis and many other captains with many people, the largest number found in this siege, entered; and going towards Antisuyu, Anta Allka and Rampa Yupanki and many others finished off the enclosure that had been placed on the Spaniards that day.*[113]

The centripetal and centrifugal movements in and out of Cuzco respond to the insertion of mythological time in the narrative, and reflect the usage of the directional verbal modifier in the subtext:[114] the idea of the Tawantinsuyu radiating out of Cuzco on four axes follows the same narrative pattern that creates the landscape of conquest in the *Suma y narración* of Betanzos wherein the clockwise and counterclockwise movements of Pachakutiq's armies center Cuzco relative to the rising and setting of the Sun. Mazzotti's comparison[115] of the inner and outer spiral movements of the Inqa's calls to his people and armies in the *Instrucción* contends that order and chaos were conceived in terms of centripetal and centrifugal forces radiating from Cuzco (94). In the first excerpt, the narrator is conscious of this citation of mythological time and space, saying, "this we said from Cuzco, which is the center and head of all the earth." Moreover, as a direct result of this speech-act in mythological time and space, Cuzco is re-centered in a landscape of conquest: "and for this reason, because we were at the center, my ancestors, who had been placed there by their ancestors, were called Lords of the Tawantinsuyu, which means Lords of the Four Quadrants of the world." The second excerpt forms part of a descriptive passage contained under the heading for a "Speech," as it immediately follows the orders the Inqa gives to his Captains. It is not until the counterclockwise enclosure of the third excerpt that this narrative movement over a ritual landscape is actually rooted in Cuzco's toponymy, with the mention of "Carmenca" and "Coacachi." The narrative sequences following this last excerpt are dedicated to the siege of Cuzco by the Inqa armies and their eventual defeat by the Spaniards. This historical event had taken on mythic proportions in Spanish histories— the intervention of the Virgin Mary and Santiago *matamoros* turned *mataindios* was a matter of fact—and the increasing frequency of Cuzco's toponymy responds to its prominence in the Spanish landscape of conquest. Yet this vision of Cuzco is darkened or covered by " a great darkness" under the titles "The Siege of Cuzco" (4) and "Battle of the Spaniards against the Indians at the Fortress" (5):

> 4. *The next afternoon a throng of people arrived and did not enter because they thought it was too dark and that they could not use the night against their enemies because of the great darkness.*[116]

> 5. *And this encounter lasted for a day and in the black night the very darkness impeded them from startling their enemies and so they pulled back to their encampments.*[117]

The name of "the fortress," Sacsahuaman, where the Spaniards finally defeat the Inqas, is silenced, or covered, by the narrative despite the increased naming of places in Cuzco in this narrative sequence. This temple was conceived by Betanzos' Inqa sources as the "puma's head" of Cuzco following its refoundation as 'the center and head' of the Inqa empire by Pachakutiq; the place name intimately associated with an Inqa landscape of conquest is literally silenced from the Spanish landscape of conquest in the *Instrucción*.

Millones has argued that these images of darkness recall the chaotic "beginnings" of Inqa origin stories (Millones 1985: 13). Thus the narrative in the *Instrucción* weaves a landscape of conquest in mythological time and space and then unravels it into the landscape of chaos; Titu Kusi Yupanki's narrative sight is literally overtaken by night as he "sees" Cuzco as it was *before* the Inqas had centered it in the Andean world, *after* the Spaniards' victory over the Inqas. This seemingly paradoxical shift in mythological space and time, visualized in the darkening of the landscape of conquest into a landscape of chaos, responds to Andean cyclical histories of destruction and renewal rather than Western linear histories of cause and effect, of origin and evolution.

The narrative's reference to landscape following "The Inqa's Arrival in Vitcos" shows more of the markers described by Howard, which create the inter-relationships between the narrator and the setting:

> *And it so happens that when my aunt Kura Uqllu, my father's sister, stepped outside, she saw the people coming from afar and heard the clattering of the hooves and ran to my father, in his bed, to warn him in a clamor that his enemies were coming, to please wake up and arm himself. My father, seeing her so terrified, was calm, and dressed quickly to see for himself whether what his sister told him was true. And he quickly returned home and had his horse readied to speedily warn his people to make haste so that his enemies would not take them by surprise. And when he was armed he ordered his horse to be saddled for the enemy was near, and when they were sighted he had the women line the hillside, spears in hand, so that the Spaniards would think they were men. And having done this, with great ease upon his horse, spear in hand, he alone surrounded his people so that they would not flee before the enemy until the runners had crossed through the fields. When they arrived, in the nick of time, and saw my father, their master, in dire straits, though tired from running up above, they were eager to fight their enemies down below.*[118]

Immediately before this excerpt, the narrator sets the scene in "Oroncoy, a town near Rabantu," within the Vilcabamba area. The movement between the characters and within the landscape is quick, jumping from Kura Uqllu (outside) seeing the Spanish soldiers arriving to her warning cries to Manku Inqa (inside) who is in bed; he, in turn, is calm and arms himself (inside); "he dressed quickly to see for himself whether what his sister told him was true." We can also visualize the entire scene: the arrangement of the women on the hillside, spears in hand, Manku Inqa circling them with his horse as they await the arrival of their enemy from the valley, and of the runners "though tired from running up above, [ ] were eager to fight their enemies down below." The text creates a chain of events that occur inside and outside Manku Inqa's house, down in the valley and up on the mountainside, that is terminated with a description of the runners which unites their past action (running) with their present action (eagerness to fight) and thus reconciles the runners' opposing locations in the narrative, above and below. The protagonists and their actions in space and time relate them to one another and to the Vilcabamba setting consistently. The narrator has been able to locate them within his narrative vision, which does not belong to a mythological time and space, rather to a topography he knew well. The changing relationships between narrative and landscape of the *Instrucción* seem to obey Titu Kusi Yupanki's vision of these events from his position in Vilcabamba, which in turn were darkened or illuminated in relation to where the center of power of the Inqas had been dismembered and where a new center continued to incorporate its people, its language, and its landscape.

A Bid for Qhapaq Status from the New Inqa Center of Vilcabamba: Performances of Possession and a Reading of the *Instrucción* as a *Waka*

The *Instrucción* was written in February 1570, following more than a decade of negotiations and skirmishes between the Inqa rebels in Vilcabamba and the Spanish officials who, in Cuzco and Lima, were receiving their orders from Spain to find a diplomatic, or alternatively violent, solution to integrate these independently governed territories under colonial rule. In 1572, Viceroy Toledo sent an army of "Cañaris, Chachapoyas, etc." led by Martín Hurtado de Arbieto to capture Inqa Titu Kusi Yupanki and the other Inqa rebels and their followers (Don Francisco de Toledo, *A fabor de Don Francisco Chilichi*: f. 187). By then, Inqa Titu Kusi Yupanki had already died and his younger brother, Thupaq Amaru, reigned in his stead along with Inqa "captains" who had served his elder brother and Kispi Titu, the son of Titu Kusi Yupanki.

Following the death of Manku Inqa Yupanki in 1545, it is not clear who assumed the *maska paycha* among the Inqa rebels, but by 1556 it seems the Inqas of Vilcabamba had a clear strategy for combating the Spaniards from their vast territorial holdings which bordered Huamanga, Cuzco, Apurimac and areas of Puno (Guillén Guillén, 1994: 135). Along the Southern border of Vilcabamba, Spanish caravans were attacked on the Chinchaysuyu road between Lima and Cuzco (Beauclerk: 19). When Sayri Thupaq and his wife and sister Kusi Warkay left Vilcabamba and submitted to colonial rule, the Spanish negotiators had assumed they would gain control over their territory and their followers (Hemming: 294). Instead, they found that the rebellion continued and Kusi Warkay openly[119] supported the rebels with the rents from the rich estates she inherited from her husband in Yucay, Chinchero and Jaquijahuana, which were also strategically located near Cuzco. From the information given by Felipe

Kispi Titu about his sisters who were living in Cuzco, when he wrote his will prior to his death in Lima in 1579, Nowack and Julien have indicated that Titu Kusi Yupanki may have had daughters living in Cuzco during the period of his rebellion (33), suggesting that he may have had several female sources of information on Spanish colonial affairs in Cuzco, in addition to María Kusi Warkay, within a generalized colonial perception that did not view the presence of Inqa women from Vilcabamba as a threat to Spanish colonial society in Cuzco.

Negotiations with Governor Lope García de Castro began from the moment he arrived in Lima in 1564 and culminated in the treaty of Acobamba signed by the Inqa and the Governor's representative, the Treasurer García de Melo, in 1566. The treaty required of the Inqas the entrance of priests for the purpose of evangelization, the conversion of the Inqa and his followers and their eventual exit from Vilcabamba to Cuzco. It also provided for the marriage between Beatriz Clara Quya, the only child of Kusi Warkay and Sayri Thupaq, to Kispi Titu, Titu Kusi Yupanki's son, to ensure that her estates would be kept within control of the Inqas of Vilcabamba. The epistolary record underscores the importance of this marriage, to both the Spanish authorities and the Inqas of Vilcabamba, following the new governor's arrival (Dunbar Temple: 615; Nowack: 139). Spanish authorities viewed the marriage as the only way to achieve Titu Kusi Yupanki's exit from Vilcabamba without having to offer more lands and privileges than those conceded to Sayri Thupaq for his capitulation to the Spanish Crown in 1558. In every missive sent, by the Spanish colonial authorities or Crown and the Inqas of Vilcabamba, one of the stipulations for a peaceful incorporation into colonial society is the marriage between Beatriz Clara Quya and Felipe Kispi Titu.

Beatriz Clara Quya's estates in Yucay made her a rich heiress and a tempting prospect for the Spanish *vecinos* of Cuzco. Indeed, at the age of seven, she was kidnapped by the Maldonado brothers and married to Christóbal Maldonado in December 1565. María Kusi Warkay aided her daughter's kidnappers by removing her from the Santa Clara monastery in Cuzco but later stated that the marriage had taken place without her knowledge or consent (Nowack: 142–143). The worries of Spanish authorities in Cuzco that the marriage might result in a serious impediment for the peace negotiations with Titu Kusi Yupanki are indicated by the *corregidor's* swift intervention: Beatriz Clara Quya was immediately returned to the Santa Clara monastery in Cuzco[120] and Arias and Christóbal Maldonado were charged by the *corregidor* for endangering the peace negotiations with Vilcabamba (Nowack: 142–143). Though marriage was normally a matter pertaining to the Church's jurisdiction, clergy members did not protest when trial was brought before the Audiencia of Charcas; the *corregidor*'s allegation that the continued viability of Beatriz Clara Quya's marriage to her cousin Felipe Kispi Titu was a public affair, because the peace process with Vilcabamba was at stake, seemed to have obtained a consensus between ecclesiastic and civil authorities alike. The Maldonado brothers defended themselves, charging negotiations with Titu Kusi Yupanki were already broken and that the Inqa's recent attacks on neighboring *encomiendas* proved he had no intention to reach a peace agreement with the Spanish colonial authority. Both Felipe Kispi Titu and Beatriz Clara Quya would have reached twelve years of age, the Church's requirement for marital union, between 1570 and 1571 (Cf. Nowack and Julien: 31), and the former was only baptized in July 1567 (Nowack: Cuadro 1). Titu Kusi was to become Beatriz Clara Quya's tutor, pending her marriage with his son, and her rich *encomiendas* certainly would have ensured a comfortable position in Spanish colonial society.

The importance of this marriage to Titu Kusi Yupanki may not have been limited to Beatriz Clara Quya's rich inheritance from her father Sayri Thupaq, his brother; rather Titu Kusi Yupanki wished to make a strong claim to Qhapaq status for the male child such a union would produce,[121] as he had already signaled Felipe Kispi Titu, his son, as his successor to the Inqanate; Beatriz Clara Quya was the only daughter of Sayri Thupaq and Kusi Warkay, who were both children of Manku Inqa. Titu Kusi Yupanki could have been ensuring the centrality of Vilcabamba and of his dynastic line several generations in the future through the marriage of Kispi Titu, the son he had signaled as his heir, and Beatriz Clara Quya, whose concentration of Qhapaq status in her lineage would have legitimated Kispi Titu's claim to the *maska paycha* (cf. Nowack and Julien: 32). María Kusi Warkay's initial rejection of Kispi Titu as a candidate for her daughter's hand could be an indication of her inclination for a Spanish suitor, as her initial involvement in the Maldonado affair would seem to suggest. Yet her rejection of Kispi Titu could likewise have been on Inqa terms; as a mother she may have felt Beatriz Clara Quya would be the sole legitimating factor in Kispi Titu's accession and that in such an alliance with Vilcabamba she would not be receiving much in return. D'Altroy writes of the power of prospective Quyas and their mothers in marriage negotiations with the Inqa ruler or with Inqa males who had aspirations to the *maska paycha*:

> The *qoya* brought a *great* deal into the marriage [with the Inqa], including counsel, status, legitimacy for offspring, and wealth.

Once in the alliance, she wielded some independent power and was also a persuasive political adviser for her husband and son who succeeded him. Even though she may well have been voicing the interests of her kin group, a *qoya* mother could also impede the marriage of her daughter to the king. Similarly, a prospective *qoya* could reject the proposal. [. . .](D'Altroy: 103–104)

María Kusi Warkay later had a change of heart with respect to Felipe Kispi Titu and to the situation of the Inqas of Vilcabamba, apparently sending them supplies to aid their rebellion against the Spanish (see note 119). The great importance placed on the marriage, by both Spanish authorities and Vilcabamba Inqas, in the peace negotiations could have also led María Kusi Warkay to believe that her daughter's prestige would indeed increase through this marriage; she could have visualized her own greater involvement as the Quya's mother both on the Spanish Colonial and Vilcabamba Inqa political scenes. Inqa men typically married between their late teens and mid-twenties, while the girls married somewhat younger (D'Altroy: 191). Kispi Titu would have been an initiate in the Inqa male rite of passage, which was celebrated during the December solstice festival, or Qhapaq Raymi, lasting into January, at around the age of fourteen[122] (cf. D'Altroy: 190).

Following the reign of Pachakutiq Inqa, an Inqa ruler's claim to Qhapaq status was based on affiliation to the dynastic descent line through the father and the mother[123] (Julien: 248). This concentration of Qhapaq status resulted from pairing individuals who were closest in dynastic terms, to the dynastic descent line from the mythical progenitors, Manku Qhapaq and his sister (296); the first ruler born to the union of a brother and a sister from a preceding dynastic generation was Wayna Qhapaq (30). The Inqas of Vilcabamba were not alone in their dynastic claims and would have felt rivalry even with the Inqas who had incorporated themselves into Cuzco's society of colonial elites (cf. Dunbar Temple: 619: Nowack and Julien: 35–39). This is evident in the genealogical aspirations of Carlos Inqa, the son of Christóbal Pawllu Inqa; the grandson of Christóbal Pawllu Inqa, Melchor Carlos, was sworn as Qhapaq[124] on the day of his Christian baptism in 1571 by Felipe Sayri Thupaq, the child's uncle, "and others," ostensibly members of the Inqa elite in Cuzco (Nowack and Julien: 20). The claims of Titu Kusi Yupanki and of his son, Kispi Titu, to Qhapaq status were poor on their mothers' side; the latter gives contradictory information in his will as to his mother's identity (Nowack and Julien: 31). Even the claims of Manku Inqa had been highly contested by other Inqas who felt their claims to the dynastic descent line were greater. The Spanish Crown, however, recognized the Inqas of Vilcabamba as the "legitimate" heirs of the dynasty of Wayna Qhapaq; this pushed the territorial center of Qhapaq status, on Spanish terms, to Vilcabamba even though their claims, on Inqa terms, may have been weaker by comparison.[125] Titu Kusi Yupanki's perseverance in ensuring the marriage between Felipe Kispi Titu and Beatriz Clara Quya is a clear demonstration of his desire to concentrate Qhapaq status in Vilcabamba *for future generations*. His negotiations with the Spanish Crown and authorities may not have been focused on the immediate future, or a peaceful exit from Vilcabamba into Spanish colonial society, rather—paradoxically—how to preserve a parallel Inqanate in Vilcabamba through his negotiations with the Spanish officials, when Cuzco was increasingly being transformed into a Spanish center of colonial authority.

Significantly, Punchaw, or "sun idol," was central to the rites performed at the Temple of the Sun in Vilcabamba, the neo-Inqa city constructed by Manku Inqa following his retreat into the Cordillera Vilcabamba. It was not found in Cuzco's Quri Kancha when it was sacked by the Spaniards (Duviols 1976: 165). Pachakutiq Inqa had ordered Punchaw to be made during the restructuring of Imperial Cuzco; Punchaw was thus coupled with the Inqas' sacred powers to conquer out of Cuzco. It symbolized Cuzco's sacrality, and the new ideology of marriage stressing alliances within the Inqa's dynastic descent line, in a reversal of the prior exogamic marital unions which were a part of the Inqa negotiation or alliance process with other ethnic groups for the purposes of territorial expansion (cf. Julien: 248–256). Punchaw embodied the belief that the Inqas were descended from Inti: a child's figure cast in gold, which contained an interior box filled with the ashes of the burnt hearts and livers of earlier Inqa rulers (cf. Duviols 1976: 166, 170–1). The retrieval of Punchaw from Vilcabamba was a major symbol of Viceroy Toledo's military victory over the neo-Inqanate. According to the *Instrucción*, Manku Inqa Yupanki had also intended to maintain the ancestor worship of the mummies of Wayna Kawri, Wiraquchan Inqa, Pachakutiq Inqa, Thupaq Inqa Yupanki and Wayna Qhapaq in Vilcabamba, but they were stolen from him during his retreat to Vitcos. Yet the presence of Punchaw, and its heart of ashes, symbolically centered Vilcabamba as the legacy of Inqa aggression, and grounded these Inqas' claims to a new territorial center of Qhapaq status, as a parallel Inqa dominion during the first forty years of the Spanish colonial presence in Peru.

The marriage between Beatriz Clara Quya and Felipe Kispi Titu never came to pass. This may be one of the reasons why, following Titu Kusi

Yupanki's death in 1570, Thupaq Amaru took up the *maska paycha* and governed Vilcabamba until the Spaniards invaded and defeated the Inqas in 1572. The invasion of Vilcabamba and its incorporation into Spanish territorial domains was indeed later consummated by the marriage of Beatriz Clara Quya to Martín García de Loyola,[126] the Spaniard who captured Inqa Thupaq Amaru and Kispi Titu in 1572 and was rewarded by Viceroy Toledo with the dowry of his rich Inqa bride. Her mother, María Kusi Warkay, was also married to a Spaniard. Toledo was thus able to incorporate Inqa lands into the Spanish colonial economy and society through rich Inqa women by either marrying them to Spaniards or by forcing them into religious life, thus giving the Church ownership of these lands (Nowack and Julien: 34). Accusations of conspiracy with the Inqas of Vilcabamba, warranted or not, were leveled at the descendents of Pawllu Inqa and other prominent Inqas of Cuzco in order to strip them of their titles and property (40). Felipe Kispi Titu died in Lima, the City of Kings, in 1579 awaiting his exile to New Spain; in his will, he makes an allowance for a non-Inqa indigenous woman named "Francisca Soco" of Abancay who was to bear his child (in Dunbar Temple: 629). Viceroy Toledo's *reformas* envisioned an absence of Inqa *encomiendas* in the new colonial landscape, and the silencing of any dynastic descent claims for Inqa elites whether on Inqa or Spanish terms of Qhapaq or *mayorazgo*.

How could the Inqas of Vilcabamba have performed Qhapaq Raymi for their male initiates in a landscape so divorced from the mythological center of Cuzco? The violence of the trans-location of these Inqas into the inner reaches of the Antisuyu is rendered in the language of the *Instrucción*, in Inqa Titu Kusi Yupanki's attempt to re-center the dynastic descent line within the boundaries of Vilcabamba. The violent rupture that the Spanish conquest entailed for the de(con)struction of a cohesive collective memory of Cuzco is rendered in the *Instrucción* in the passage entitled "How Gonzalo Pizarro received the Treasure and Quya in Hand and how Manku Inqa, in a Sign of Friendship, shared a Meal with Him." It follows the scene where Manku Inqa is forced to give Inkill to one of the Pizarro brothers to gain his release from a Spanish prison.

In the *Instrucción*, Inkill is portrayed as a successful proxy decoy for the "real" Quya, Kura Uqllu. Yet the Inqa's "deceit" in the text may in fact veil a deeper humiliation; Inkill or Ynguill may be a character of the *Instrucción* constructed in reference to Francisca Ynguill, who, according to Inqa sources, was affiliated to the *panaqa* of Inqa Ruqa, and was being kept in seclusion by Manku Inqa because he intended to make her Quya, once she reached a proper age, as an important factor in his bid for the *maska paycha* (Julien: 40–42; 305, note 13). Instead, she was forced into marriage with Juan Pizarro. The Spaniards were aware of the importance of these Inqa women to Inqa men's aspirations to power; miscegenation between Spanish conquistadors and Inqa women would have been a powerful weapon to limit the genealogical aspirations of Inqa men.[127] In the *Instrucción*, the scene is even more devastating because the violation of the "Quya" by a Spaniard is made public, before Inqa and Spanish witnesses, in what would have been a terrible *deshonra* of Manku Inqa for the Spaniards and a desecration of the *yanasa*, or promised woman, to the Inqas (cf. Diaz-Rivera: 246). Her very identity is "deflowered" by this Spanish violation, as Inkill means "orchid flower" in Quechua, and the signification of her name is glossed in the text as "flower." Yet the *Instrucción* portrays the incident as an Inqa victory over the shameless Spaniard, who accepts the possession of a fraud, rather than the "real" Quya, a vessel of Qhapaq status. In the *Instrucción*, the Inqas have the last laugh by making use of what Manku Inqa perceives as the fundamentals of Spanish discourse, lies and deception.

It is significant that the narrative sequence of the *Instrucción* associates a Spaniard's public rape of "the flower" with the Spanish violation of Qhapaq Raymi, in the description of the initiation rite for the male members of the Inqa dynastic group, which immediately follows. The underlying theme uniting both passages is the violent possession by the Spaniards of Inqa referents that were central to the construction of Inqa identity as descendants of the Sun and "natural" rulers of the Tawantinsuyu. Specifically, the passage narrates the Spaniards' attempted theft of Manku Inqa's gold and silver *yawri* during "a large feast in which we pierce our ears and amongst we Inqas this is our foremost feast of the year, for this is when we are given our names and change old names for new ones."[128] The name-giving ceremony of *warachikuy* was a puberty rite for boys in which the initiates took on the names of the animals they hunted on the hills (Millones 1985: 13). *Warachikuy* also marked the first wearing of the breechcloth, which had been woven by their mothers (D'Altroy: 190), and was only one of the many ceremonies involved in Qhapaq Raymi.

> The piercing of the ears to receive golden spools was only part of the rite of male initiation. [...] The rite also involved three pilgrimages by the initiates to different mountains around the Cuzco valley, each followed by an assembly in the main plaza at which the ruling Inca, the images of the major supernaturals, the residents of

the city, and the initiates were present. The mountains visited were Huanacauri, Anahuarqui and Apo Yavira. (Julien: 278)

During the assemblies in the plazas, the "life history" genre or "Ritual Homage to the Inqa" was performed before the mummies, who were gathered with their descendants, to receive the initiates. Both Huanacauri and Anahuarqui were *wakas* that had iconic and animistic facets; they were both mountains and mummies; their powers were at once fixed and mobile in the sacred landscape and ritual processions of Inqa Cuzco. Like the various ceremonies and pilgrimages involved in Qhapaq Raymi, the passage in the *Instrucción* renders homage to the mythical founding of Cuzco by the Ayar brothers and its naming. Qhapaq Raymi recalled the mythical creation of center and possession by the Inqa's ancestors, whereby the Inqas metaphorically relived and reinitiated the naming of their *wakas* as they reinforced their own collective and individual identities as rulers of the Tawantinsuyu through Cuzco. In one of the variants of the origin myth of Cuzco, Ayar Uchu, upon reaching the hill of Huanacauri, tells his brother and sisters to remember him in all of their ceremonies, especially in the initiation rites (Classen: 42; Julien: 276), and Ayar Awka, "who had grown a pair of wings," flew into the valley, obeying the orders of his brother Qhapaq.

And sitting there he was converted into stone and stayed there as a rock of possession, which in the ancient language of this valley is called cozco, whereby the name of Cuzco remained till this day.[129]

Yet in the *Instrucción*, the Spanish desecration of Qhapaq Raymi occurs not at Huanacauri but at Anahuarqui, who was associated with the mummy of Pachakutiq's Quya (Bauer: 25), and thus with the consecration of Cuzco, as center of the Tawantinsuyu, and the endogamic shift in the ideology of Inqa marriage for the greater concentration of Qhapaq in subsequent Inqa rulers. The Spanish penetration of the rites at Anahuarqui thus mirrors the earlier violation of the "Quya" in the *Instrucción*, both female vessels of Qhapaq status, and the later theft of the mummy Wayna Kawri (i.e., Huanacauri)—the foundation stone of Inqa memory—foreshadows the physical and spiritual disintegration of the Tawantinsuyu from its very center. Although the festivities are later completed in this section of the *Instrucción*, the violent intrusion of the foreigners into the ceremony—and their desecration of *wakas* that centered Cuzco in the

Andean landscape—initiates a memory of fragmentation for an entire generation, the post-1532 Inqas.

The possible relationship between a messianic movement called Takiy Unquy, centered in Huamanga, and the rebellion of the Inqas in Vilcabamba caught the attention of the Spanish authorities in Lima, Huamanga and Cuzco in 1564, and the activities of Cristóbal de Albornoz and other extirpators of idolatries continued until 1584. The activities of the Takiy Unquy movement coincided with the height of the guerrilla campaign waged against colonial urban centers by the Inqa rebels. Researchers such as Guillén Guillén (1994: 137) and Varón Gabai (1990: 365), arguing in favor of a connection or at least some coordination between the Takiy Unquy movement and the Inqa rebels, highlight the colonial sources which themselves attribute some kind of connection. On the other hand, Millones (1990: 11–18 and 1995: 155–166) and Lemlij et al. (1990: 426) have argued that the ideologies and goals of the Takiy Unquy movement and the Inqas were so contradictory that the attempt of the former to revive the *wakas* of local cults would not have been favored by the Inqas seeking to recuperate their territorial control over the Tawantinsuyu, whose cohesion had been maintained by the official religion, the worship of the Sun, the Moon, Wiraqucha, and Illapa (Millones 1990: 14).

González Holguín glosses <huacca> in Quechua as "Ydolos, figurillas de hombres y animales que trayan consigo; quando tiene seis dedos en manos y pies como león" (idol, human and animal figurines they bring with them; when a man has six fingers on his hands and feet like a lion)[130] (165). Santo Tomás notes as well that <guaca> can be a "templo de ydolos, o el mismo ydolo" (a temple of idols or the idol itself) (279). Classen writes, "huacas, requiring the services of a vast number of priests, also manifested a split nature, existing on both the material and spiritual levels at once. Huacas were conceptualized as bodies—and, in fact, some actually were mummified bodies—that had to be ritually fed in order for them [the Inqas] to use their powers in support of, rather than against, the state" (67). As we saw above, the animating forces of *wakas* could ubiquitously possess mountains and mummified bodies, as in the case of Anahuarqui and Huanacauri. *Wakas* could also be killed (Julien: 266); in the *Instrucción*, Manku Inqa avenges himself for the Wanka ethnic group's treachery (allying themselves with the Spaniards) by killing their principal *waka*, Wari Willka. The animating force of *wakas* is described by Duviols as a fluid, or an ethereal element, possessing the ability to reside in a physical envelope and to leave it (Duviols 1978: 134). The <camaquen>, or the soul of the ancestral mummy, could abandon its container and possess the heart "sunqu" of the medium through his prayers.

Wakas can be understood as formations or containers of uncanny powers with multifaceted expressions in the Andean landscape and ancestor: a mountain, a rock which has taken the form of an animal, an adobe pyramid, an idol or a mummy can be *waka*. *Willka* is the Aymara word for *waka* and it was glossed in the following manner by Ludovico Bertonio: "it meant sun in ancient times although now *inti* is used; a shrine dedicated to the sun or other idols; it is also a medicine, or a drink given to purge, or to sleep, and when sleeping it is said that the robber came to rob the sleeper of his lands; they were the lies of sorcerers" (emphasis mine: 386). One of the entries of *willka* is thus associated with the temporal world of dreams and with the imagery and speech produced and experienced by shamanic practices, involving the use of hallucinogens, in those who possess or consume *willka*. Significantly, Manku Inqa and his descendants chose a landscape animated by *waka* to recenter the Inqanate: Vilcabamba, "the plains of the Sun," bounded by two "speaking" rivers, the Apurimac "the Great Speaker" and the Vilcanota "River of the Sun Temple,"[131] which symbolically separated the colonial territories from the territory possessed by the Inqas, a landscape which spoke to the Inqas of the possibility of reconstructing collective memory through renewed ceremonies of possession.

The *wakas* that were important to the Takiy Unquy movement were those that had defined and rooted the landscape with significance. In order to revive the *waka*s for their final battle against Christ when the Spaniards would finally be swept from the Tawantinsuyu into the Western Sea, followers of the sect offered their own bodies as vessels through which the *waka*s could speak (Millones 1990: 15; Millones 1995: 115–166). Takiy Unquy means "singing sickness," and its believers would sing and dance ecstatically, trembling and shaking, until they slipped into a lethargic state. Those who witnessed the *wakas* entering the living persons would later take them to a predetermined spot where a shrine of cloth and straw had been prepared, and community members would honor them and bring them offerings. It was believed that in these living persons the *wakas* would recuperate their strength; in the meantime, believers could hear them speak, recalling the millenarian tradition of ancestor worship in the Andes[132] and the significance of layering mummies with textiles for the creation of territorial and narrative spaces which linked landscape and the collective memory of its inhabitants, the living and the speaking dead. Thus the Inqa tradition of honoring their mummies with songs composed in *khipu* and sung to revitalize cohesion within the *panaqas*, or royal lineages, is understood within a greater Andean tradition.

The Takiy Unquy movement arose in response to a rupture in the cycle of signification between the living, the dead, their narratives and their landscapes. After the warfare between Ataw Wallpa and Waskar over who would be the successor to Wayna Qhapaq, the war between Manku Inqa and his followers and the Spaniards, the civil wars fought between the almagristas, the pizarristas and those loyal to the Crown and thousands of indigenous peoples whose souls had been *encomendadas* (placed in the care of) these bellicose *encomenderos*, those who had not been killed or died from a new disease were left to wander the land seeking to escape the bloodshed and the forced labor in the mines, or alternatively search for work in the newly ordered colonial cities that mapped an otherwise chaotic territory according to Renaissance ideals[133] (Varón Gabai 1990: 380). Alternatively, <mitimaes>, those local communities that had been uprooted and relocated by the Inqas, flooded the Spanish courts to be relocated to their homelands (cf. Torero 1987). The social fabric of memory and land woven by each generation was being unraveled and torn apart, and it may have become increasingly difficult to glean "speech" from the dead and the abandoned local *wakas* (Millones 1990: 15). Thus, Juan Chocne, the leader of the Takiy Unquy movement, claimed that the Spaniards and their god had defeated the Inqa gods and the *waka*s of the landscape were "dying," that they no longer "incorporated themselves in the stones, clouds and rivers to speak" (in Millones 1995: 115) and could no longer be heard, thus the importance in relocating the *wakas*, signifiers of local memory to the living and not to the dead, in a messianic movement that performed the reconquest of lost territories at the intimate and most local level, the very self (Lemlij et al. : 434).

Notwithstanding the (im)possibility of military and ideological coordination between the Takiy Unquy and Vilcabamba movements, some of the phrases in the *Instrucción* seem to echo Takiy Unquy precepts. For instance, in one of Manku Inqa's speeches, he gives his final orders in a "document" to his people before retiring to Antisuyu :

> You must do this: if there should come a time when they tell you to adore what they adore—what they say is Wiraquchan are but painted clothes—and when they say to adore them as a *waka*, which is but cloth, do not obey. Instead, adore what we hold dear, for, as you can see, the *willkas* speak to us; and the Sun and the Moon, see them through our own eyes and what they speak of we do not see well.[134]

In this passage, the *wakas* and the *willkas* "speak" and the Sun and the Moon are "seen," perhaps denoting an important difference in local and Inqa cosmologies. Likewise, the local and official cults have a capacity for synesthesia—sight and hearing—similar to the synesthesia involved in *khipu* reading or palpable poetry (cf. Robert Ascher: 112)—sight, hearing, speech—which does not form a part of the European religion as experienced here by Manku Inqa; "their" speech is separated from "our" sight: "what they speak of we do not see well." Moreover, the *wakas* are associated with the messengers of the Inqa who will come to his people when he "calls for them," some lines before. Thus the Sun and the Moon, though important, are secondary to the *wakas* and the *willkas*, in this passage, for the construction of collective memory and the Inqa's "calling" or heralding of his return.

Prior to the entrance of Friar Marcos García and Friar Diego Ortiz into Vilcabamba in 1568, Titu Kusi Yupanki and Martín de Pando were able to rehearse several images and referents which would later be reiterated in the envisioned performance of the *Instrucción* in early 1570; these ideological strands of the *Instrucción* text began to take shape in the *Memorias* to the Licentiate Matienzo and in the letters addressed to the Augustine friar Juan de San Pedro and to the Licentiate Lope García de Castro. In Martín de Pando's letter dated November 7, 1567, written in Talawara and addressed to the Governor, we can hear the foreshadowing echoes of the *Instrucción* narrators' reiterated assertions that the devil had influenced the Spaniards' actions or the accusation that the words and letters of men can be deceiving:

> They would have been happy to heed their governor and to be merry among themselves with their bounty, but their joy, as we will see later, did not outlast them, *because the devil, being as evil as he is, is the friend of differences and dissidence and never sleeps.* (emphasis mine)[135]

In the letter, Pando, describing the "mestizo and Indian" traitors, like María Kusi Warkay, who he said were trying to convince Titu Kusi Yupanki that the Spanish peace negotiations were a farce, writes:

> As a Christian I have always advised him and told him how good it is to be in the faith of our lord Jesus Christ and how good peace is and he would have understood it all *but for the devil who is so subtle that even in the best of times there was no lack of mestizos and*

Indians with letters and words who would come to deceive him.
(emphasis mine)[136]

Errors in gender and number agreement are also evident in this letter, and these types of anomalies in the Spanish of the *Instrucción* could be attributed to Martín de Pando's transcription. Furthermore, it could be that Suta Yupanki[137] and Rimachi Yupanki and Sullka Waraq who are only presented as witnesses to the composition of the *Instrucción* may have had some input in its overall elaboration because, in the *Segunda memoria*[138] to the Oidor Matienzo, it is written,

> The Lord Sapa Inqa and Llanki Mayta and Rimachi Yupanki after having agreed amongst themselves [the] best method and way to achieve peace and the exit of the Lord Sapay Inqa and his knowledge of the holy gospel, came to an agreement, today 16 of June, in the following manner and order [. . .][139]

Perhaps this kind of recognition of a collective authorship was stifled when the *Instrucción* was written in February 1570, although their presence as "witnesses" give "faith" or authority to the narrative.

In the *Primera memoria* addressed to Oidor Matienzo, "Sapa Inqa Titu Kusi Yupanki" used a similar narrative strategy to describe his father's plight and humiliation and how the Spaniards misled him:

> When the **Christians** entered this land my father Manku Inqa was imprisoned, under the pretense and accusation that he wanted to revolt with the kingdom, after the death of Ataw Wallpa, only so that he would give them a *bohío* full of silver and gold. In prison they treated him badly, in actions as well as words, placing a collar at his gullet, like a dog, and weighing his feet down with irons, taking him by the collar from one part to the next among his vassals, asking him questions at every hour [. . .]. (emphases mine)[140]

The passage reveals some basic imagery which would later be reiterated throughout the *Instrucción*: the recurring comparison between his father's plight with the life of a dog, the repeated detail of his father's shackled feet and the iron collar at his throat, the rhetoric of coherence or incoherence between actions and words, the presence of the Antillean word *bohío*, suggesting that it may have formed part of Martín de Pando's vocabulary, and the rhetoric for justifying his father's revolt, mainly that the Spaniards abused the Inqa's hospitality.

Absent, however, is the complexity of the lascasian discourse in the *Instrucción* which often makes the multiple voices of the text contradict themselves; here, there is no distinction made between "Spaniards" and "Christians"—Bartolomé de las Casas had made such a distinction,[141] arguing that the conquistadors were more idolatrous than the Indians in their lust for gold and indigenous women, and an obstruction to the evangelization of the Americas. The accusation in the *Segunda Memoria* that the **Christians** had committed these atrocities does not embrace the theological framework for discussing the Americas within the dichotomy, Christian and Pagan, which defined the players according to whose Iberian interests were being defended, and may have been one of the major changes introduced by the two Augustine Friars, Marcos García and Diego Ortiz, when the *Instrucción* was later composed in 1570.

Titu Kusi Yupanki's signature underwent several changes as well. In the *Memorias* to Oidor Matienzo he simply signs, "Sapa Inqa Titu Kusi Yupanki," with no reference whatsoever to a Christian name, and thus displays no manipulation of any Christian referents. It is only when he directs himself to the Augustine Friar Juan de San Pedro on December 23 and 24, 1568, that he signs as "Santiago de Castro Titu Kusi Yupanki"[142] once the evangelization of Vilcabamba was already underway (Apéndice B, 1916 Edition: 302). These letters were written after his baptism in Rayangalla on August 29th of that same year, so Hemming's assertion, that Titu Kusi Yupanki had adopted the name "Diego de Castro" upon his baptism because the Governor Lope García de Castro was his godfather,[143] seems unfounded (Hemming: 109). Instead, the "de Castro" could have been strategically used to establish a relationship of prestige with the governor when addressing this ecclesiastical authority, to signify that he had signed the treaty of Acobamba with the Spanish governor on August 24, 1566, and that they were on an equal and reciprocal relationship. Titu Kusi Yupanki used Spanish names like enclitics, added or subtracted to signify relative rank with his interlocutors, and probably did not ascribe to the Christian idea of the baptismal name as an "imprint" on the person (cf. Lemlij et al.: 427–28).

Father Antonio de Vera, Augustine Friar of Cuzco, was purportedly the first to give Titu Kusi Yupanki catechism and baptize him in Vilcabamba in 1566, though Rodríguez de Figueroa brought to the Inqa's attention, when he was opening the negotiations for the Oidor Matienzo in 1565, that he had "seen in the baptismal book of the principal church (in Cuzco) that the Inca had been baptized and named Diego" (192). Titu Kusi Yupanki's pious response almost suggests a performance: "He told me that it was true, and that he was a Christian, and he confessed it before the Indians." If Titu Kusi Yupanki had indeed "confessed" to Rodríguez de Figueroa in 1565 that his baptismal name was "Diego," why did he switch to "Santiago" when writing to Juan de San Pedro in 1568? "Diego" and "Santiago" are related, although it is not clear whether their cognate status would have been known to Titu Kusi Yupanki, Martín de Pando or the Augustine friars to whom these letters were addressed. Sebastián de Covarrubias wrote that "Diego" was a "corruption" of "Santiago"; his entry for "Santiago," on the other hand, is lengthy, and begins by noting how unnecessary it is for him to refer to the Apostle's history and legend which was well known to all Spaniards who acknowledged him as their patron saint; "Santiago" is the final destination of Christian pilgrimage in Europe; the Augustine order is also viewed by Covarrubias as a main player in the events leading to the canonization of the apostle and patron saint of Spain.[144] Furthermore, the importance of Santiago, the apostle, in the Andes was such that had the cognate status between "Diego" and "Santiago" been recognized, it probably would have been treated in the same manner of the entries in the *Tesoro de la lengua castellana o española*, which viewed the former as a "corruption" of the latter. Indeed, the Augustine friars may have been wary of Titu Kusi Yupanki's prior appropriation of "Santiago" as his Christian name in his previous letters and have suggested or imposed the cognate "Diego" of lesser prestige in its stead.[145]

Santiago, to any Spaniard, would have been an obvious reference to the Patron Saint of Spain who was the standard of the Spanish reconquest and whose transformation from *Santiago matamoros* (Santiago Moor killer) to *Santiago mataindios* (Santiago Indian killer), projecting the conquest of the Americas as an extension of the reconquest of Spain, has been amply discussed. But the use of "Santiago," in Titu Kusi Yupanki's letters to the Augustine friar, may not have only been a way of pandering to the nationalist and religious sensibilities of this Spanish ecclesiastic authority but may also have included a reference to Inqa cosmogony. Following the advent of Catholicism, by 1570, Inqa belief had converted *Santiago matamoros* into the patron of livestock, an invincible warrior whose attributes recalled the traits of *Illapa* (Millones 1995: 115). Indeed, *Inqa* may have been left out from Titu Kusi Yupanki's signature in his 1568 letter to Juan de San Pedro because of the implicit association Santiago could have had to *Illapa*.[146] Though this letter simply discusses the number of priests that should be sent to Vilcabamba—two and not three, perhaps showing an Andean preference for pairs[147]—it displays, just in the choice of name, the "chorality" of referents to which Titu Kusi Yupanki and Martín de Pando could ascribe.

This strategic use of Christian names, in Andean struggles for independence, recalls a similar usage by the Takiy Unquy movement whereby Juan Chocne compared himself to John the Baptist, and two of his female followers were called María and María Magdalena (Lemlij et al.: 427–28). At first glance, the names of Titu Kusi Yupanki and those of the Takiy Unquy leader and his followers may look like an example of acculturation, syncretism or "mestizaje"; nonetheless, these names allowed them to assume messianic roles in a war that had taken on a ritual character from the first major encounter between the Spaniards and Ataw Wallpa in Cajamarca (cf. Seed 1995: 69–99; Cornejo Polar 1994: 25–50).

The performance of conquests in the "New World" had acquired the character of a notarized High Mass by 1531, the time the Spaniards had arrived off the northernmost coasts of modern Peruvian territory (cf. Seed 1995: 70–72). The document called the *Requerimiento* provided indigenous peoples with the opportunity to repent and submit to the sovereignty of the Crown and Pope or else the conquistadors would kill them and their children.[148] The conquest was legalized because the document was read aloud and the notary, who witnessed the performance, gave faith that this act of conquest had been completed in due order.

These acts of orality, based on the authority of the written word, are not comparable to the lexical confluence Zumthor observed in the medieval world between "reading," "saying," and "singing" due to the practice of reading aloud to the literate and illiterate in Europe (1987: 41–46). The homilies, where the first sketches of the Romance languages are found on the margins of the Holy Book, belong to this confluence of the oral and the written. The liturgy and the gospel, read and sung in a language unintelligible to the majority of believers in the medieval world, was a ritual based purely on the authority of the written word—"as the anchor of knowledge and understanding"[149]—but not on its actual comprehension to the majority of the faithful (Mignolo 1995: 82). So many of the conquistadors were themselves illiterate, or literate only in the Spanish vernacular, but not the Latin of the Holy Book.

The "act of faith" provided by the notary in the *requerimiento* became indispensable to the metropolitan powers intent on confirming its authority over vast territories, so that legality took on the religious zeal of other exclusionary "acts of faith" based on the belief in the manifestation of these "new" invisible lands—which produced vast amounts of wealth—in maps, testimonies, relations, instructions and chronicles (Rama: 3–4). It is significant that Betanzos and Cieza de León compared the "ritual homage to the Inqa," which was an exclusionary Inqa performance of political legitimation, to the *romanceros, cantares* and *villancicos* of the medieval Spanish oral poetic tradition[150] or to the more harmonic confluence of the oral and the written that Zumthor discusses for medieval Europe. Though the *khipus* could be grudgingly recognized by the Spanish as something similar to writing,[151] they did not possess the power or authority which *the* book, and later the document, had to the Europeans and which Cornejo Polar has likened to a "fetish" or a "magical object" of an expanding colonial bureaucracy (1994: 47).

In the *Instrucción*, the conquistadors liken the "possession of faith" to the possession of the treasures that Manku Inqa has just given them for his own ransom:

> May our Lord the almighty God [...] repay you with the revelation of his Sacred Majesty so that knowing him, you will love Him and possess Him, and by possessing Him enjoy with Him his Kingdom forever, as we enjoy the possession of the gifts Your Majesty has given us.[152]

The first encounter of the Andean world with the Spanish written word was with a performance of possession;[153] the *orality* of this performance was intended to be unintelligible, exclusionary and authoritative[154] because it was based on a document whose bureaucratic function was equivalent to the act of faith implied in the wielding of the Holy Book before the sword for the possession of unknown lands and its peoples' souls.

The Chuquichaca bridge created a dramatic space for the encounter between the Inqas and the Spanish on the threshold of a territory in resistance:[155] the exchange of documents, the interpretation of translators, the blandishing of weapons and the pageantry of the Vilcabamba court, and was a reminder to the Spanish that there was still a vast territory which they could only imagine but not "ignore" or consider "empty" in their maps of conquered territories[156] because it was still unknown to them, its saliency heightened because it was hidden all the while it made its existence painfully manifest to the metropolis in the Inqas' violent incursions into "colonial" territory. Fray Martín de Murúa imagined a Vilcabamba so bounteous and rich that the Inqas in this separated land, or, better said, this land of exile, did not miss the presents, grandeur and sumptuousness of Cuzco, because everything that could be had outside was brought to them by the Indians for their delight and pleasure and they were happy to be there.[157]

Vilcabamba had the attributes of the uncanny,[158] if understood as the manifestation of the hidden as hidden. The experience of reading the *Instrucción* is an experience with the uncanny, forcing us to search for innumerable categories to describe these strands of referents knotted into signifiers that speak to some and remain hidden to others.

The *Instrucción* read as a *khipu* of palpable poetry and political legitimacy, a memory aide for Lope García de Castro when he came before the King Felipe of Spain to recite Titu Kusi Yupanki's grievances[159] and to honor the memory of his father Manku Inqa (Mazzotti: 271), is an exercise in deciphering intentions; and in the expression of these intentions there is no other text quite like it in the Andean world,[160] in that its purpose visualized a performance of political legitimation on Inqa terms, as though the written word could function as a *khipu*, though framed in a Spanish legal document, following the Spanish formula to request an audience for written memories: "because the memory of men is weak and thin and if we do not turn to the written word to benefit from it in our hour of need [. . .]."[161] Thus the "harmonies" or discords, choralities, and counterpoints created by this juncture between the written word and the *khipu* tradition cannot be experienced adequately within the category of "oral texts" elaborated by Zumthor for Medieval Europe.[162]

It may be revealing, instead, to articulate the experience of the *Instrucción* as a "contradictory whole,"[163] as that of a speaking *waka*, as explored by the contemporaneous Takiy Unquy movement, that paradox of a fractured collective memory disembodying the dying Andean landscape and possessing the bodies of the living led by John the Baptist, the Virgin Mary and Mary Magdalene for the final expulsion of Christianity. The conflicting voices of the *Instrucción,* elaborated for the purpose of speaking and remembering the unity of the Tawantinsuyu from the new Inqa center in Vilcabamba, through the body of a Spaniard in the metropolis, engages in a reversal of the Spanish ritual possessions of territory in the Americas. Yet there is no evidence that such a performance—the former Governor Licentiate Lope García de Castro reciting the *Instrucción* before the King of Spain—ever transpired; though they may never have been actually fulfilled, the *Instrucción* continues to display its intentions to possess the Spanish interlocutor for a performance on Inqa terms on the Iberian Peninsula.

There were limitations to Titu Kusi Yupanki's agency in the elaboration of these *waka* texts. The fact that Titu Kusi Yupanki was dependent on Martín de Pando and Friar Marcos García for his correspondence with the colonial world is made particularly poignant in the apology he sent in his second letter to Juan de San Pedro where he expressed regret that he could not have responded sooner: though "two weeks ago I received your [letter] from Your Preeminence, and in it the accustomed honors, I did not respond sooner because Martín de Pando was in Carco, in the company of Father Friar Marcos"[164] (121).

Soon after the *Instrucción* was written, Friar Marcos García was expelled from Vilcabamba for desecrating the local *wakas*, Titu Kusi Yupanki fell ill, perhaps poisoned, and Martín de Pando and Friar Diego Ortiz were blamed for his death and were killed in retribution. Viceroy Toledo, hearing of their deaths, sent Titu Kusi Yupanki his own personal *requerimiento* dated October 16, 1572, chastising the Inqa for his absence from a display of Spain's might in the former capital of the Tawantinsuyu when the attendance of "his son, the Inqa" was compulsory:

> Understanding what must have been an oversight on your part at not having come to see me on parade, when I came to this city [Cuzco], nor after I had been here awhile, and recognizing what you owed to the service of God and his majesty of the King my lord, complying with the obligation of a father which I owe you because of the faith you have in God and the King my lord [. . .] you can see what is expected of you in this business, to execute what I say with the obedience that you owe to that which involves you, and to your security and that of your children, brothers and captains; as your father, for your good and benefit I warn and tell you this.[165]

In this letter he refers to other letters sent earlier and which had never received any response. The Viceroy sent this letter with Tilano de Anaya to legalize his belligerent intentions, though he knew there were no longer any readers and interpreters of Spanish in Vilcabamba who could translate his *requirements* before waging war on the neo-Inqanate. The messenger, Tilano de Anaya, was killed on the Chuquichaca bridge when he tried to gain entrance to Vilcabamba for the delivery of the Viceroy's silent declaration of war; the bridge itself was later burned by the Inqas to stall the advance of Toledo's armies. The death of Tilano de Anaya, the destruction of the Chuquichaca bridge and the invasion of the uncanny Vilcabamba brought an end to the creation of frontier spaces for parallel performances of power and the elaboration of *waka* texts.

The last Inqa of Vilcabamba, Thupaq Amaru, was brought through the gate of Carmenca in Cuzco, where the Plaza Mayor would be the setting for his beheading (Baltasar de Ocampo in Markham 1907: 223). In the *Instrucción*, the siege of Cuzco begins with the entrance of Manku Inqa's armies into Cuzco through Carmenca. Thupaq Amaru's return to the center of the Tawantinsuyu thus mirrors the entrance of the Inqa's armies and their defeat, from their very center, which had taken on mythic proportions to both the Spaniards and the Inqas by 1572. Inqa Thupaq Amaru's death would also leave its imprint on the collective memory of Cuzco. Ocampo, who witnessed the execution, wrote, "when the head was cut off, it was put on a spike, and set up on the same scaffold in the great square, where the execution had taken place. There it became each day more beautiful, the Inca having had a plain face in life" (229). He adds that the Inqa's head had to be buried soon after because the "Indians" would bow before it, rather than accept it as a symbol meant to dissuade all resistance to the Spanish colonial authorities. The decapitation of Inqa Thupaq Amaru continues to live in the memories of the peoples of Cuzco and the Andes in the narrative of Inqa Rey (or *Inkarrí*): when the Inqa finds his head, and his body is restored, he will reorder the Tawantinsuyu and expel the Spaniards from the Andes. Vilcabamba was finally incorporated into the Spanish colonial dominions of Peru, and there were attempts to maintain a colonial outpost there, in San Salvador de Vilcabamba, although settlers soon lost interest when there were not many riches to be found in the area.

Yet Vilcabamba continues to surprise us. This Cordillera and jungle continues to be rediscovered and remapped by explorers intent on finding the Paititi, or the "lost city of the Incas." In the 18th century, a *memorial* described the location of four "completely deserted ancient cities" between the rivers Apurimac and Urubamba, including Choquequirao "which in the Inqa language means cradle of gold," Chuquitiray "which means spilled gold," and Vilcabamba la Grande, "*tierra adentro*, which was the Inqa's main quarters" and "another city where the Inqa's silversmiths lived" (Huertas Vallejos: 203–204). Cosme Bueno in 1768, later the French Count Sartiges in 1834, and the Italian explorer and cartographer Antonio Raimondi also rediscovered Vilcabamba in the 18th and 19th centuries, to name a few who braved the area's difficult terrain. Choquequirao, situated midway up Huiracochan Mountain, and perched above the Apurimac, was an original favorite for the location of the "last refuge" of the Inqas. Hiram Bingham explored the Cordillera Vilcabamba in 1909 and 1911, armed with the maps made by previous explorers, the *Instrucción*, Captain Martín García de Loyola's *relación* of his deeds during the invasion of Vilcabamba, and Calancha's narrative of the events leading to fray Diego Ortiz's martyr-dom, trying to pinpoint the locations mentioned in these narratives and the Inqa ruins he encountered during his incursion, and more specifically, to "discover" the "Last Inca Capital." He passed through Choquequirao, but defined it as "a frontier fortress that defended the upper valley of the Apurimac, one of the natural approaches to Cuzco, from the country occu-pied by the Chancas and the Amazonian Antis" (100). He located "Vitcos," where Manku Inqa was murdered, at Rosaspata, and the "Last Inca Capital" or "Vilcabamba" at Machu Picchu. Paul Fejos "retraced the Inca Road explored by Bingham, examined the sites mentioned by him, and was also fortunate enough to discover a number of new sites" between the Urubamba (or Vilcanota) river and its tributary, the Acobamba. These include many of the sites visited by tourists who hike the Inca Trail to Machu Picchu to the present day: Phuyu Pata Marka, Sayac Marka, Inti Pata, Chacha Bamba, Choquesuysuy and Wiñay Wayna (19). Later explor-ers in the 1960s and 1970s, such as Gene Savoy, and Edmundo Guillén Guillén questioned Bingham's identification of Machu Picchu as Vilcabamba; Savoy identified Espíritu Pampa as Vilcabamba because it occupies a lower jungle terrain than Machu Picchu, in the northwestern reaches of the Cordillera Vilcabamba, and there he found five Inqa palaces and three hundred common houses. Both Savoy and Guillén Guillén agreed with Bingham in his identification of Rosaspata as Vitcos. John Beauclerk asserted that he had identified the location of Acobamba, where Inqa Titu Kusi Yupanki signed the capitulation treaty in 1566, as well as the location of the Chuquichaca Bridge, at the confluence of the Vilcabamba and the Urubamba (Vilcanota) rivers (19–20).

The work of explorers and archaeologists[166] in the Cordillera Vilcabamba is to be commended. Many of these Antisuyu Inqa sites have now been mapped and cleared and can be visited. The Peruvian govern-ment has recently rediscovered the importance of Choquequirao, and the number of tourists that visit the site increases yearly. The beauty of the area's green cloud forests punctuated by the immense snow-capped Panta, Salcantay, Ampay, and Suyrucocha mountains is not lost upon its visitors.

Nonetheless, Vilcabamba's difficult terrain and the changes in the toponymy of these various Inqa sites over the years seem to resist identifi-cation. Perhaps Quilter's tautology, "khipu are khipu" (to describe the knotted-string narratives' resistance to being deciphered), can be said of the uncanny Vilcabamba. No method seems to adequately link the places named in the colonial chronicles with the archaeological sites in the Cordillera Vilcabamba. The legend of the Paititi lives on, as does the myth of *Inkarrí*, and Vilcabamba remains uncanny, as our attempts to unequivocally fix the location of these historical encounters, which occurred in the 16th century, seem to escape us; they remain hidden, or darkened, from our narrative sight.

The Last Capital of the Incas remains "hidden"; its location has tracked a mobile trajectory on our maps over the centuries, following the Spanish invasion of the last Inqa-dominated territory in 1572. We circle around Vilcabamba, as the center of Inqa resistance; we may visit, but cannot possess it. Vilcabamba, in the Quechua of Peru's Southern highlands today, can also be understood as "The Land of Descendants"[167] or of the indigenous peoples of Peru who have not forgotten their obligation to remember and so continue to "possess their king." Titu Kusi Yupanki's intention to create a parallel Inqa center to the Spanish colonial authority survives in the living landscape of the Inqas, the languages of the Tawantinsuyu, the living culture of its peoples, and the *wakas* that continue speaking with them.

Endnotes

1. Relation of the Conquest of Peru and the life of Inca Manco II.

2. I am following the spelling proposed for Quechua in Cerrón Palomino 1998: 435.

3. Relation of the manner whence the Spaniards entered Peru and how Mango Inga faired whilst he lived among them.

4. "las humillaciones del 79"

5. "una unidad étnica y la conciencia nacional"

6. "conciencia mestiza"

7. "Indio ignorante"

8. "Fiestas de la Patria de 1916"

9. "al Perú que en su pasado encuentra su porvenir escrito, porque la raza que fundó el Imperio de los Incas, vive: Sólo que está sujeta é inmovilizada por nuestro egoísmo: ¡desatadla y dejadla ir!"

10. "más bárbaros que los mismos indios"

11. Relation of the Conquest of Peru.

12. "su punto de vista es indio [. . .] la historia de un aspecto de la conquista que nadie sino él vio"

13. "ya en pleno mestizaje"

14. "el alma, la palabra y sonoridad indios"

15. Emphasis in *italics* are Temple's, emphases in **bold** are mine. "*Si bien no hay que perder de vista, en ningún momento, el hecho incontrovertible de que los Incas de Vilcabamba defendían, con justicia y con heroicidad admirables que les hace honor frente a la historia, sus derechos a una tierra y a un Imperio que era el suyo*, es precisio a un tiempo mismo tener presente que Titu Cusi y sus capitanes habían prestado ya sumisión a la Corona, **que la autoridad de España se había impuesto por la fuerza de la Conquista**, que había sido reconocida por los mismos indios, **y arraigado aún biológicamente porque se sustentaba en el naciente pero no menos poderoso mestizaje.**"

16. When I use the term "hybrid" or "hybridity" in a text, I am referring to Bakhtin's definition: "a mixture of two social languages within the limits of a single utterance, an encounter, within the arena of an utterance, between two different linguistic consciousnesses, separated from one another by an epoch, by social differentiation or by some other factor" (358). Bakhtin also refers to the ability of a word (or voice) to mask another word (or voice) within the same utterance as "intentional" or "non-organic" hybridity. Generally, the terms "hybrid," "mestizo" or "acculturated, " when applied loosely to texts, tend to assume the assimilation of one linguistic conscious-ness by another rather than an "encounter" between one or more conscious-nesses within an utterance.

17. "una traducción escrita más bien en circunstancias más bien precarias"

18. "que siendo expresados como episódicos parecen ser estructurales de la sociedad andina"

19. "criterios de verdad"

20. "apuntaban más bien a la reconstrucción de conductas que a la certeza cronológica o geográfica de los hechos"

21. See Cornejo Polar 1997 for his discussion of the problems caused by using "mestizo" or "hybrid" as a category for literary analysis because of its racist connotations.

22. Previous literary studies such as those by Esteve Barba focused on the "forma externa católica y hasta sacerdotal" (external catholic and even priestly form) of the *Instrucción*, especially in the homily structure of Manku Inqa's speeches, though noting the presence of Titu Kusi Yupanki's narrative footprint (LIX).

23. "memoria dirigida a Felipe II"

24. For a critique on her treatment of Andean words in her edition of *La Suma y narración de los Incas* by Juan de Betanzos, see Cerrón Palomino 1998.

25. "crítico o no del sistema, Martín de Pando fue, como era frecuente entre los de su grupo social [mestizo], un oportunista"

26. "no proclama como propio, sino en todo caso heredado de su padre Manco Inca, recado que disimula de mala manera en los imaginarios discursos de su progenitor [. . .]"

27. Although her edition is based on microfilm copies of the same manuscript (in the library of El Escorial), like the Millones edition, Regalado de Hurtado seems to have left out entire sentences, and her punctuation often makes little sense of the text's meaning. I have made note of these differences in the modernization of the *Instrucción* where I have deemed necessary.

28. In Spanish *lengua* has several entries, alternatively understood as "language," "tongue" and "interpreter." My literal translation of *lengua* into English will, I hope, emphasize the visceral and metaphoric overlapping that this word embodies in Spanish in the context of a conquest, as the subjugation of a people (their language, their bodies, and their speech).

29. I am indebted to Antonio Cornejo Polar's reading of Father Vicente Valverde's death by "mouth" and "voice," as a fitting retribution for the priest who presented the bible to Ataw Wallpa in the encounter of Cajamarca (1994: 48).

30. For Harrison's discussion of the sorry deaths of Martín and Felipillo, the indigenous "tongues" who notoriously served the Spanish conquistadors and were likewise accused of and punished for several "betrayals" cf. Harrison 1989: 40–41. Their "poor translations" became the scapegoat for the Cajamarca massacre once the Spanish Crown chastised the conquistadors for Ataw Wallpa's execution.

31. In Spanish the word *voz* or "voice" can be used as a synonym for "word." In English, the phrase "Andean voices" or "indigenous voices" can be used to reinforce a reference to Andean speaking subjects. Glossing the indigenous words in the *Instrucción* can be understood within the juncture between the distinctive Spanish and English significations of "voice" as such an undertaking seeks to reveal the partially obscured subjects (voices), in part though the careful scrutiny of particular words. My thanks to Dr. Mary Gaylord for her suggestions in this matter.

32. One-act Play on Gluttony

33. *La Tragedia del fin de Atahualpa* (The Tragedy of Ataw Wallpa's End) is not included because the extant versions of this play date to Peru's modern Republic though the Colonial Quechua in these copies suggests that prior colonial versions of the play existed. Most editions of these plays are in Spanish and their titles in English are the following: *Persephone's Abduction and Eudemon's Dream, The Prodigal Son, The Poorest Rich Man, Usca Paucar* (whose title in Quechua suggests it may have been a 'remake' of *The Poorest Rich Man*), and *Ollantay*. Cf. Meneses; Vargas Ugarte.

34. Extensive onomastic studies have yet to be developed in Andean linguistics and are beyond the scope of this essay. For example, Cajamarca, a city nestled in the northern highlands of Peru, was spelled as <Caxamarca> or <Caxamalaca> in the 16th century and seems to have both a Quechua and an Aymara component. See Torero 1995. I have kept the traditional Spanish spelling of Cuzco, following Cerrón Palomino's appraisal of the controversy in Cerrón Palomino 1997a.

35. See De Granda and Escobar for socio-linguistic studies of the Spanish and Quechua spoken in the Andes; see also Rivarola for his edition of colonial legal documents and the characteristic "anomalies" presented by Quechua-Spanish speakers in these texts.

36. Notwithstanding el Inca Garcilaso's insistence to the contrary, the toponymy of the Cuzco-Apurimac area and early chronicles with Cuzco sources indicate that these phenomena of Chinchaysuyu Quechua were also being experienced by the Quechua spoken in Southern Peru prior to the Spanish presence in the Andes.

37. A hypothetical proto-language, reconstructed by linguists. Cf. Cerrón Palomino 1994b for his unified dictionary of the Southern Quechua group, which proposes a unified orthography for writing purposes, for the varieties spoken from the Peruvian regions of Huancavelica and the highlands of Ica to Puno and Moquegua.

38. The process of prothesis of the **h**, which is a synchronic rule in the modern Cuzco-Collao dialect, is an example of such changes. The rule is as follows: when a word beginning with a vowel acquires a glottal occlusive consonant, it automatically acquires an **h** as a prothesis to accommodate the speaker's pronunciation. Mannheim rejects Cerrón Palomino's thesis that should a

word lose the glottal occlusive consonant, the **h** prothesis would also be lost (145). The rule is particularly salient for the modern Ayacucho-Chanka varieties, which no longer register glottal occlusive consonants, in contrast with Cuzco-Collao Quechua, which do.

39. Where I have seen evidence of a contrast being made between the lateral consonants in the manuscript (i.e., **l** and **ll** [λ]), a contrast which has been largely neturalized in modern Southern Quechua dialects (Mannheim: 148), I have preserved it.

40. Most English and Spanish speakers would be unable to pronounce [q], which is a phoneme in Cuzqueño Quechua. Moreover many Quechua speakers of dialects other than Cuzco-Collao and Bolivian varieties no longer pronounce [q] and have replaced it with [x] or with the elongation of the vowel that would have preceded the now absent */q/.

41. See Cerrón Palomino 1997b for his analysis of the copulative verb in Quechua and Cerrón Palomino 1994a for his discussion of parallel grammatical structures in Quechua and Aymara.

42. Cf. Domingo de Santo Tomás, *Lexicon o vocabulario de la lengua general del Perú* (1560) and González Holguín, *Vocabulario de la lengua general de todo el Perú llamada Lengua Quechua o del Inca* (1608). Domingo de Santo Tomás registers Coastal, Chinchaysuyu Quechua ten years prior to the elaboration of the *Instrucción*. González Holguín was interested in registering the morphonemic singularities of Cuzqueño Quechua in the early 17th century, which were not evident in other dialects at the time and are no longer extant in the modern Cuzco-Collao dialect. Through the careful analysis and comparison of his grapheme choices (including <ç, ss, z, s>) to represent sibilant consonants in Quechua and Spanish, Cerrón Palomino was able to prove the existence of two sibilant phonemes in early 17th century Cuzco Quechua, whereas modern dialects display only one. González Holguín's dictionary also differs from the Santo Tomás dictionary in that it belongs to the period of the extirpation of idolatries based on Viceroy Toledo's reforms and the evangelization program of the Third Lima Council.

43. I am indebted to Walter Mignolo and his meaningful etymological play on "translate" (Mignolo 1995: 82).

44. Yet Julien has demonstrated that the Inqas "also preserved a knowledge of the line of dynastic descent through a form of geneaology" (4).

45. See also Cerrón Palomino 1987: Capítulo X for a discussion of the origin and spread of Quechua; Cerrón Palomino 2000: Capítulo VII for a discussion of the origin and spread of Aymara; Cerrón Palomino 1994 for his analysis of the parallel grammatical and syntactical structures of these two main Andean languages. See also Torero 1987.

46. "la lengua general delos naturales que llaman Quichua, o la aimara"

47. "la lengua propia de su Curato quichua, o Aymara o Puquina"

48. "en muchos pueblos deste nuestro obispado generalmente todas las Indias, o las mas y algunos Indios no entienden la lengua quichua sino la Aymara o Puquina"

49. Cf. note 39.

50. The origin of this apocryphal etymology can be attributed to the Inca Garcilaso, a native Cuzqueño of "mestizo" descent who was familiar with European medieval and renaissance literature, as well as the history and literature of his native Cuzco; his etymology should not be dismissed, nonetheless, as it specifically refers to the "secret language" of the Inqas and it has become an integral part of Cuzqueño nationalism. Indeed, this rhetoric that negotiates between European and Andean representations of center could be understood within Mignolo's concept of "colonial semiosis."

51. The word in Quechua for "navel" is *pupu* or *puputi* (Classen: 169; Cerrón Palomino 1994b: 60). "Cuzco" in Quechua is pronounced [Qosqo] and is written <Qusqu> (Cerrón Palomino 1997a: 166).

52. "The transformation of Cuzco, as described by Betanzos and Sarmiento, follows the revelation that the Incas were descended from a solar supernatural and that a special status passed through the dynastic line that explained their success at achieving power in the Cuzco region and beyond" (267).

53. The "origins genre" registered by Betanzos and Sarmiento de Gamboa involves several "centers" in the trajectory of Wiraqucha: the Lake Titicaca basin to Tiahuanaco, then to Cachas in Canas territory, then to the Urcos lakes near Cuzco, and from there crossing the Andes mountains and disappearing off the coast of the Ecuadorian sea (cf. Julien: 287).

54. Where the beginning is always "the word" or Christ. This tautological map of Christianity should not be confused with Spain's own bids for centrality within the Christian world. The body of the Apostle Santiago, in Compostela, for example, provided another "rock" on which the Church could be built with respect to Rome, especially in its relative position to the "New" World.

55. Thus the great debate between fray Bartolomé de las Casas and Juan Ginés de Sepúlveda [1550–1551] over whether New World natives had souls. In a sense, the "Indians" were either on or off the Christian map. Were they potential converts or natural slaves? Las Casas extends the Body of Christ to the New World and positions the Indians as *innate* rather than *potential* Christians in their defense; they were included in the unity of mankind, formed in the image and likeness of God; moreover, their ways of life prepared them for the coming of Christianity. He creates a vision of purity for the margins of the Christian World in opposition to the corruption at the "core" of the "known" world, in his descriptions of the conquistadors, which reverts the dichotomy Christian/Pagan: the Indians are more Christian than the Spaniards. This inversion, nonetheless, is still conceived within the imagery of the world as the Body of Christ.

56. Cf. Mignolo 1994: 16.

57. Cf. Szeminski 1990 and 1998.

58. Cf. note 31.

59. See Ferrell for a discussion of Aymara in Waman Puma's *Corónica y buen gobierno*, a text not considered as "cuzqueño" because of the Chinchaysuyu provenance of the author and his non-Inqa status.

60. "Homenaje Ritual al Inca" (Ritual Homage to the Inqa) (Lienhard: 171–192).

61. "Crónica oralizante" (oralizing chronicle) (Jakfalvi-Leyva: 149).

62. "Crónica mestiza" (mestizo chronicle) (Chang-Rodríguez 1988: 18).

63. "Una escritura coral" (choral writing) (Mazzotti: 98–99).

64. "Fue hecho y ordenado todo lo arriba escrito dando aviso de todo el Ilustre señor don Diego de Castro Titu Cusi Yupangui [. . .] por el reverendo padre fray Marcos García."

65. "Yo, Martín de Pando [. . .] doy fe que todo lo arriba escrito lo relató y ordenó el dicho padre a insistencia del dicho don Diego de Castro, lo cual *yo escribí por mis manos propias* de la manera que el dicho padre me lo relataba." The fragment which has been quoted has been italicized.

66. La presencia del patrón andino ayuda a reforzar la hipótesis de que las crónicas mestizas, es decir, aquellas en que el designador indígena, mestizo o europeo, coloca en el centro del relato al referente americano y lo describe con respeto y comprensión, fueron concebidos para un doble destinatario: el evidente, vale decir, las autoridades coloniales, o metropolitanas a quienes iban dirigidas, y el implícito, o sea, los indios y mestizos alfabetizados capaces de identificarse con el punto de vista ofrecido por este discurso reivindicatorio, y también aquellos que escuchaban el relato de estos acontecimientos.

67. Martín de Pando, mestizo; Fray Marcos García and Fray Diego Ortiz, Spaniards; and three of Titu Kusi Yupanki's captains: Suta Yupanki, Rimachi Yupanki and Sullka Waraq.

68. "Discurso oral en quechua" (86).

69. 'Genre' is a cetegory used to divide all kinds of artistic works on the basis of form, style, or subject matter. For example, detective novels can be said to be a 'genre' of fiction.

70. The conflicts arise in the subject matter simply because the Hispanic presence in the Spanish narrative is no longer that of "filters of language and culture" (Cf. Julien: 4); they have become protagonists in a conflict that involved ruptures in native loyalties and ideologies as well as their own complex alliances and betrayals between Almagristas and Pizarristas, the conquistadors' grievances with the Crown and its officials in Peru, etc. Inca Garcilaso and Titu

Kusi Yupanki come into direct conflict over the figure of Manku Inqa—one which involves alliances and betrayals between Almagrista and Pizarrista factions of the conquistadors and perceived loyalties to the Spanish Crown—in what can be reduced to their similar desires to honor the memory of their fathers. In Inca Garcilaso's situation he is defending the memory of his Spanish conquistador father, while at the same time responding to the *panaqa* rivalry to which he belonged through his Inqa mother.

71. I would like to underscore the clarity of Julien's approach for defining Inqa "genres" in the narratives of pre-1532 events. Her analysis of the changing ideology of "Capac status," in the construction of the Inqas' self-projected identity as descendants of the Sun in the Andean territory which they conquered out of Cuzco, and the struggles to privilege some descent lines over others within the Inqa ethnic group, is central to my own discussion of Titu Kusi Yupanki's position with relation to Cuzco as seen in the *Instrucción*.

72. Cf. note 31.

73. "Si es lógico aceptar la existencia de un género ritual base ['el homenaje ritual al Inca'] sobre el que se redactaron dichos textos, también es posible postular que aquel tipo de 'epicidad' andina asume en su trascripción castellana características muy particulares".

74. The following examples are given by Cerrón Palomino: [tusu-šqa-n]-*ta* musya- (I know that he danced); [aywa-šqa-yki]-*ta* wiya-rqa-n (he heard that you left) (Cerrón Palomino, 1987: 317). In both of these sentences, the brackets connote the subordinating clause; the suffix -*ta* (emphasis mine) is the marker of the direct object, i.e., the knowledge (that he danced or that you left) becomes a nominal phrase and functions as the direct object of the main clause. The validating suffixes (-*mi* "first-hand information", -*si* "second-hand information", -*chu* "interrogative-negative", -*chi* "conjectural"), sometimes known as "enclitics" (Cf. Harrison: 73) because of their formal similarities to the enclitic markers in Romance languages, are normally used to qualify the speaker's relationship to his/her information, establishing certainty or doubt (Cerrón Palomino 1987: 287–88). The relationship of the speaker to the subordinated nominal phrase, in the second example, changes if we add the validators: [aywa-šqa-yki]-**mi**-ta wiya-rqa-n "He heard that you left" (the speaker knows this because he/she was there when "he" received the news); [aywa-šqa-yki]- **si**-ta wiya-rqa-n "He heard that you left (so they say)"; [aywa-šqa-yki]- **chu**-ta wiya-rqa-n "He (really) heard that you left(?)"; [aywa-sqa-yki]- **chi**-ta wiya-rqa-n "(It seems) he heard that you left."

75. Adelaar is referring specifically to the *Huarochirí Manuscript*, written in colonial Quechua, and the development of a written tradition: "When a written tradition is about to develop, grammatical markers referring to the speaker's involvement in the event are either likely to disappear, to become merely decorative or fixed" (147).

76. Mazzotti recalls the third of the Siete Partidas of Alfonso X as the foundation for eye witness validation in Spanish legal testimonies (54).

77. The examples in note 74 refer to quotidian uses for qualifying sources of information in Quechua.

78. Which he later showed to Diego Rodríguez de Figueroa: "[the Spaniards], however, succeeded in giving him a stab in the leg, the mark of which he afterwards showed me" (178).

79. Cf. Cerrón Palomino 1994a.

80. Urton has observed, "according to Inca Garcilaso, the stories and poems memorized by the *khipukamayuq* were memory aids for knowing how to read/interpret the full narrative tradition, the latter of which were recorded in the knots and strings of the khipu"; yet the traditional view has viewed the *khipu* as a mnemonic device, or the exact opposite of the *khipu*'s purpose as described by Inca Garcilaso (Urton 2002b: 180).

81. In the way Parry has broached the subject, comparing the *khipu* to the string instruments held by Slav singers who could not recite their poems without them (Parry 1987: 442). See Maria Ascher and Robert Ascher, for their discussions of the coding capabilities of the *khipu* and their own experiments enciphering and deciphering *khipu*. It is possible for someone familiar with *khipu* signifiers to decipher the *khipus* made by another person and to add, correct, or subtract from a *khipu* by detaching strings or knots. For a recent approach to the *khipus* as a form of binary codification, see Urton 2002c.

82. Fray Diego de Porras' *Instrucción para los sacerdotes* bears no date. However, his instructions to others clergy to rely on *khipus* and *khipukamayuq* for the purposes of evangelization would indicate a date prior to the Third Council of Lima.

83. For a discussion of Quechua sub-syntax in the *Instrucción* that follows Subject-object-verb orders, see Mazzotti: 65–66.

84. "[. . .] Por decir que eran hijos del Wiraquchan y enviados por su mandado habían entrado en mi tierra, a lo cual yo les di consentimiento. Y por esto y por otras muchas y muy buenas obras que les hice dándoles lo que yo tenía en ella: plata y oro, ropas y maíz, ganados, vasallos, criados y otras muchas cosas sin número, me prendieron, ultrajaron y maltrataron sin yo merecérmelo [. . .]"

85. "Sisauen Señoría que ordinariamente salen delos Andes dejunto deonde esta el dicho Tito Ynga retirado muchos Indios, losquales bienen acasa deladicha Doña María porquelatienen portal Señora y posan ebiben ensu casa, queda alimentos y desbestir y todo lonecesario Digan lo que sauen" (f.139).

"Whether they know that from the Andes, where the aforesaid Tito Inga [Titu Kusi Yupanki] keeps many Indians in captivity who then go to the house of Doña María [his sister who married his brother Sayri Thupaq] because they respect her as their Mistress and they rest and live in her house where she gives them food, clothing and everything necessary."

86. "ella les da decomer y algunas cosas que lleban asus tierras".

87. "quela suso dicha les da decomer y beber y otras cosas".

88. "posan y estan en [su casa] y [Doña María Kusi Warkay] los recoje y da decomer y beber y le habisto darles obejas delatierra y carneros y vestido y ojotas y otras cosas deprecio y balor lo qual a bisto por bista de ojos y esto sabe".

89. "y ella lesda de comer y beber y lo mas quees necesario para Su comida y les habisto dar obejas y carneros y cosa deplata paralas orejas e Narices y muñecas y que siesto no hiciese seria no hacer loque las Señoras suelen y acostumbran hacer eneste Reino" (f. 161).

90. "ella los Recibe ensu casa y lesdá decomer y beber y otras cosas de ropa eganado y cosas deoro y plata paralas Narices y orejas y brazos y que esto es costumbre según todos los señores deeste Reino" (f. 169).

91. "letraen plumas y otras cosillas depoco balor".

92. "Señora lesda decomer ybeber y vestidos y carneros delatierra y cosas de oro y plata para las Narices y orejas y los brazos y otras cosas de Castilla".

93. "Testimony of the *khipukamayuq* given to Vaca de Castro"

94. The DRAE 2001 does not specifiy this word's American origin but gives *chaquira* three entries: *f.* "rosaries, beaded necklaces made of different materials which the Spanish took to sell to the American aborigines. 2 Chain, necklace, bracelet made with beads or shells and used as decoration. 3. Neckplate, as in a feminine ornament, made of different colored beads." "*f.* Cuentas, abalorios, etc., de distintas materias que llevaban los españoles para vender a los indígenas americanos. 2. Sarta, collar, brazalete, hecho con cuentas abalorios, conchas, etc, usado como adorno. 3. *Pan.* Cuello postizo, como adorno femenino, hecho con abalorios de diversos colores." Significantly, *chaquira* is being used in this passage describing gift-giving in contexts of conquest, and the first entry for this word in Spanish describes the Spaniards 'selling' beads or trinkets to the indigenous peoples of America.

95. "[Cuando Chimo Capac reconoce como señor a Viracocha Inga] El Chimo Capac [. . .] luego le reconoció por Señor, dándole la obediencia y le envió sus embajadores con sus dones y presentes, y le envió veinte mujeres doncellas, y collares de piedras finas de esmeraldas y de turquesas y chaquiras de almejas y ropa y cosas que en su tierra había, haciéndose su vasallo como a hijo del Sol" (Urteaga 1920:16).

96. "Relation of the Indian lords who served Tupac Yupanqui and Huayna Capac." These testimonies belong to the Toledan period.

97. "Era uso que el que subjetaba los subjetos le habían de hacer chácara de maíz y coca y ají y llevársela; y desta manera hubo muchos que conquistaron,

como fue el señor del valle de Truxillo, que se llamaba Chimo Capac [. . .]" (Urteaga 1920: 57).

98. "[Capac Yupangui] a todos los señores que le salían de paz hacía mercedes, mandando que en memoria de aquella obediencia que le habían dado, le hiciese toda la provincia una casa junto donde edificasen para él, y él les daba vasos de oro y ropa de la del Cuzco" (Urteaga 1920: 65).

99. "Y como ellos vieron la pujanza del Inga Yupangui y el buen medio y modo y forma con que los atraía a la gente, que era con dádivas [. . .] Vuelto este inga y señor al Cuzco, y los naturales que edificasen luego casa y le nombrasen tierras para sembrar maíz, coca y ají y otras legumbres, y esto no forzados sino de su voluntad, y los frutos, parte dellos le llevaban al Cuzco, y parte ponían en los depósitos del Inga [. . .] y el Inga les hacía Mercedes y les daba oro, plata, ropa, mujeres y otras cosas" (Urteaga 1920: 65). The emphases in the translation are mine.

100. In 1924, Marcel Mauss published his important essay on "the gift" and its function in power relations of archaic societies. He wrote that parties to a relationship of gift exchange were obligated to give gifts, to receive them and to repay them in the appropriate manners. The gift, in these specific social relationships, bore the identity of the giver. Upon receipt of the gift, the recipient not only received the object in question but the association of that object with the identity of the giver. The gift's nature could be economic, political, kinship oriented, legal, mythological, personal and social. The gift-giver rearranged the fabric of social relations by the movement of the gift-object through the social landscape; this relationship is the basis of the gift's power. Mauss did not write specifically in reference to Andean societies.

101. "Tenían costumbre los Ingas para ganar las voluntades de sus vasallos hacer fiestas algunas veces [. . .] y allí con su mano el Inga a los caciques les daba mates o vasos de chicha que bebiesen, que era un gran favor, y dábales ansimismo ropa de la propia suya para vestir y vasos de plata y algunas otras cosas" (81).

102. Or /qiru/ in Quechua.

103. *De estos viracochas trajeron dos de ellos unos yungas a mi tío Ataguallpa que a la sazón estaba en Cajamarca, el cual les recibió muy bien y dando de beber a uno de ellos con un vaso de oro de la bebida que nosotros usamos; el español en recibiéndolo de su mano lo derramó, de lo cual se enojó mucho mi tío. Y después de esto, aquellos dos españoles le mostraron al dicho mi tío una carta o libro o no sé qué, diciendo que aquella era la quillca de Dios y del rey, y mi tío, como se sintió afrentado del derramar de la chicha, que así se llama nuestra bebida, tomó la carta o lo que era y la arrojó por ahí diciendo:*

Qué sé yo qué me dais ahí, anda vete.

104. [. . .] *y llegados que fueron les preguntó [que] a qué venían. Los cuales les dijeron que venían por mandado del Viracocha a decirles cómo le han de cono-*

cer. Y mi tío, como les oyó lo que decían, atendió a ello y calló y dio de beber a uno de ellos de la manera que arriba dije para ver si se lo derramaban como los otros dos y fue de la misma manera que ni lo bebieron ni hicieron caso. Y visto por mi tío que tan poco caso hacían de sus cosas [dijo],

Pues vosotros no hacéis caso de mi ni yo lo quiero hacer de vosotros.

Y así se levantó enojado y alzó grita y guisa de querer matar a los españoles, y los españoles que estaban sobre aviso tomaron cuatro puertas que había en la plaza donde estaban, la cual era cercada por todas partes.

105. Y decíais que veníais a servir al Ynga, a quererle mucho, a tratarle como a vuestras personas mismas a él y a toda su gente.[. . .]¿De dónde pensáis que ha de sacar tanto oro y plata como vosotros le pedís? Pues os ha dado hasta quitarnos a nosotros nuestras joyas, todo cuanto en su tierra tenía. ¿Qué pensáis que os ha de dar ahora por la prisión en que le tenéis preso? ¿De dónde ha de sacar esto que le pedís ni aun nada si no lo tiene ni tiene qué daros? **Toda la gente de esta tierra está muy escandalizada y amedrentada de tal manera de ver vuestras cosas** que no saben ya qué decir ni a donde se pueden ir, porque lo uno, **se ven desposeídos de su rey**, lo otro, de sus mujeres, de sus hijos, de sus casas, de sus haciendas, de sus tierras, finalmente de todo cuanto poseían, que cierto están en tanta tribulación que no les resta sino ahorcarse o dar al través con todo y aun me lo han dicho a mí muchas veces. (Emphases are mine.)

106. Yo te fui a la mano muchas veces sobre que no les metieses en tu tierra y aún si se te acuerda, te dije cuando tuvimos nueva que habían llegado a la tierra, que yo iría por la posta con diez o doce mil indios y los haría pedazos a todos y tú nunca me dejaste, sino antes, "calla, calla que son viracochas o sus hijos", como si no barruntáramos nosotros que gente de esta manera, **que venía de tan lejos tierra, que antes venía a mandar que a obedecer.** (Emphases are mine.)

107. Diaz-Rivera: 197.

108. Mirad que os mando que no se os olvide lo que os he dicho. Pienso decir ahora que es que miréis cuánto tiempo ha que mis abuelos y bisabuelos y yo hemos sustentado y guardado, favorecido y gobernado todas vuestras casas, proveyéndolas de la manera que habéis habido menester, por lo cual tenéis todos obligación de no nos olvidar en toda vuestra vida vosotros y vuestros descendientes, así a mí como a mis abuelos y bisabuelos, y tener mucho respeto y hacer mucho caso de mi hijo y hermano Titu Cusi Yupangui y de todos los demás mis hijos que de él descendieren. Pues en ello me daréis a mí mucho contento y ellos os lo agradecerán como yo se lo dejo mandado, por tanto bastaos esto acerca de lo dicho.

109. Adelaar has outlined the role of the comparison and contrast of proximal demonstrative pronouns in passages of the *Huarochirí Manuscript* that are not quotations (138). These are the following: *kay* 'this' and 'this place' vs.

chay 'that' and 'that place'; their combination with the locative suffix *-pi* in the absence of adverbial forms, thus *kaypi* 'here' vs. *chaypi* 'there'; and the use of directional case markers *kayman* 'hither,' *chayman* 'thither,' *kaymanta* 'hence': *chaymanta* 'thence' (137). Yet the main cultural code of the *Instrucción* is Spanish and these grammatical markers in translation would be difficult to recognize or "discover" because these markers translate more readily to the Spanish grammatical devices used to locate narrative positions within a text. Since we do admit the possibility for "confluence" or "chorality" between Quechua and Spanish grammatical markers and semantic fields, it would not be farfetched to examine the *Instrucción* for the instances where the speaker orientation of *kay* ('aquí' 'this place') is preserved when there is a reference to the geographical point at which the writing of the text occurs, as in the *Huarochirí Manuscript* (cf. Adelaar: 138). The main focus of this piece, however, is to analyze the moments where the subtext of the "ritual homage to the Inqa" causes a counterpoint to the Spanish legal format in the *Instrucción*.

110. The Vilcanota is also known as the Urubamba river. The roots of the word "Vilcanota" are Aymara but its grammatical structure is Puquina. Bertonio glossed <Villcanuta> as the following, "a famous shrine found between Sicuana and Chungara; it means house of the sun, according to the barbarian Indians" "Adoratorio muy célebre entre Sicuana, y Chungara; significa casa del sol, según los indios barbaros" (386).

111. *Como toda la gente de la tierra juntada de las cuatro partes de ella, en las cuales está repartida toda ella más de mil y doscientas leguas de largo y otras casi trescientas de ancho, repartida en esta manera a la discreción del mundo, conviene a saber: en oriente y poniente y norte y sur, en nuestro uso llamamos Andesuyu, Chinchaysuyu, Condesuyu, Collasuyu, rodeando de esta manera: Andesuyu al oriente, Chinchaysuyu al norte, Condesuyu al poniente, Collasuyu al sur. Esto hacíamos puestos en el Cuzco, que es el centro y cabeza de toda la tierra, y por esto y por estar en el medio se nombraban mis antepasados puestos allí por ser su cepa, señores de Tahuantinsuyu, que quiere decir señores de las cuatro partidas del mundo, porque pensaban de cierto que no había más mundo que éste [. . .]*

112. *Y así sin ninguna dilación luego lo pusieron por la obra y enviaron por sus parcialidades cada uno como le cabía: la vez de los Chinchaysuyo envió Vila Oma, a Coyllas y a Ozca y a Cori Atao y a Taipi; que trajesen la gente de aquella parcialidad de los Collasuyo fue Lliclli y otros muchos capitanes para que trajesen la gente de aquella parcialidad; a Condesuyo, Suranvaman, Quicana y Suri Vallpa y otros muchos capitanes; y los de Andesuyo Ronpa Yupangui y otros muchos capitanes, para que todos éstos cada suyo por sí juntasen la gente necesaria para el efecto. Nota que estos cuatro suyos que aquí son nombrados, conviene a saber como arriba tengo dicho, son las cuatro partes en que toda esta tierra está divisa y repartida, como más por extenso arriba está declarado.*

113. *Por la parte de Carmenca, que es hacia Chinchaysuyo, entraron Cori Atao y Coyllas y Taipi y otros muchos que cerraron aquel postigo con la gente que traían, por la parte del Condesuyo, que es hacia Caocachi, entraron Vamani, Quicana y Curi Guallpa y otros muchos que cerraron una gran milla de más de media legua de voz, todos muy bien aderezados en orden de guerra. Por la parte de Collasuyo, entraron Liclli y otros muchos capitanes con grandísima suma de gente, la mayor cantidad que se halló en este cerco, por la parte de Andesuyo, entraron Anta Allca y Ranpa Yupangui y otros muchos, los cuales acabaron de cercar el cerco que a los españoles pusieron este día.*

114. *-mu* in Quechua.

115. The context Mazzotti establishes for his discussion of "Cuzqueño Quechua" concepts of center considers the theology of world unity elaborated by Bartolomé de las Casas through the imagery surrounding the body of Christ (cf. Mazzotti: 54–55). See note 55.

116. *[. . .] esa tarde llegó a vista del Cuzco el tumulto de la gente, los cuales no entraron entonces porque les parecía que era muy [de] noche y no se podría aprovechar, siendo noche, de sus enemigos por la oscuridad grande que hacía.*

117. *Y ya que la noche les sobrevenía por la mucha oscuridad que en ella hacía, no se pudiendo aprovechar de sus enemigos, se retrajeron a sus sitios [. . .]*

118. *Y acaso saliéndose a proveer mi tía Cura Ocllo, hermana de mi padre, vio la gente que venía desde lejos y hubo el tropel de los caballos y vino corriendo donde mi padre estaba en la cama y le dijo con gran alboroto que venían enemigos, que se levantase y fuese a ellos. Mi padre, como la vio tan despavorida, sin hacer caso de nada se levantó con gran prisa para ir a reconocer si era así lo que su hermana le decía y desde que se asomó al viso vio ser así lo que le había dicho y volvió a casa con gran prisa y mandó que le echasen el freno al caballo para de presto, así como estaba, poner cobro en su gente por que no le tomasen los enemigos de sobresalto, sino estar apercibido. Y ya que lo tuvo puesto a punto de guerra, mandó que le echasen la silla al caballo porque estaban ya cerca los enemigos, a la vista de los cuales puso en un cerro muchas mujeres en rengleras, todas con lanzas en las manos para que pensasen que eran hombres. Y hecho esto, con gran ligereza encima de su caballo, con su lanza en la mano, cercaba él solo toda la gente por que no pudiese ser empecida de sus enemigos hasta en tanto que llegasen los corredores que habían ido a correr al campo, los cuales que así llegaron a una con los españoles al viso a tiempo que mi padre solo lo traía a mal andar. Y como llegaron y vieron a su amo que andaba de aquella suerte, tan fatigados aunque cansados de la cuesta arriba, cobraron nuevo esfuerzo para pelear contra sus enemigos que de la parte de abajo estaban [. . .]*

119. At least to the extent that both Inqa and Spanish witnesses, in 1568, used the fact that María Kusi Warkay had to supply those Indians who came out of Vilcabamba and returned with her provisions, as one of the main arguments supporting her claim that she should once again receive her pension of 3,000 pesos and not 1,000 pesos (which had been severed because of the debts she

had to pay off after Sayri Thupaq's death). She also was in constant communication with her brother, ostensibly trying to convince him to live among the Spanish in Cuzco, according to these witnesses (Cf. *Información dada a pedimento)*. Martín de Pando, in his letter to the Governor Lope García de Castro, accused her of sending letters and supplies to her brother, Titu Kusi Yupanki, and inciting him to revolt (Pando: 255). At any rate, the legal rule María Kusi Warkay exercised over these lands outside of Cuzco would have allowed the rebels three safe entries into the city as well as control over the trading routes from Huamanga and Huancavelica to Cuzco and to Sicuani (Hemming: 294). Sayri Thupaq died less than three years after his exit from Vilcabamba.

120. The Church's position on marriage had been recently ratified by the Council of Trent. The marriage between Christóbal Maldonado and Beatriz Clara Quya was illegal on three counts: the young age of Beatriz, that her mother and tutor had been forced to give their consent to the marriage and the secrecy of the marriage (Nowack: 143).

121. "In the transmission of *capac* status, an argument was made that the Incas were affiliated through the male line, an ideology of descent is clearly present. The dynastic line became a conduit for this status; once the dynasty recognized its importance, the status was preserved through marriage to a woman who was also descended from Manco Capac, even a sister [. . .]" (Julien: 243).

122. His Qhapaq Raymi would have been celebrated in Vilcabamba either from December 1568 to January 1569, December 1569 to January 1570, or December 1570 to January 1571.

123. Through the mother's affiliation through her father's dynastic descent. Inqa dynastic descent was a patrilineage. Beatriz Clara Quya was doubly affiliated to the dynastic descent line, through the descent lines of her father, Sayri Thupaq, and through her mother, Kusi Warkay, who was also her father's sister.

124. Viceroy Toledo interpreted this claim to Qhapaq status as a claim to Kingship or treason against the Spanish Crown as a part of his campaign to disinherit the Inqa elites of their *encomiendas*. Claims to the dynastic descent line continued to be important in colonial society, prior to Viceroy Toledo's rule and the invasion of Vilcabamba, because the Crown would recognize "noble status" to these descendants with all of the associated benefits.

125. Titu Kusi Yupanki was conscious of the limitations of his genealogical claims to rule the Inqanate. Titu Kusi Yupanki clarified Inqa succession to Diego Rodríguez de Figueroa in the following manner: "I then observed that the report was that he was an illegitimate son. He then told me that among them, when there was no legitimate son, the custom was that a bastard succeeded. He was, therefore, high priest in what we call spiritual things. This

was in default of another brother, at least one who was older than himself. He thus inherited the temporal lordship. He was in possession and was recognized by the other Incas. They all obeyed him, and if he had not the right they would not obey him. For the rest the question had better be settled by arms and not by talking" (Markham Translation 1913: 189).

126. One of the captains in the expedition led by Martín Hurtado de Arbieto.

127. Inca Garcilaso de la Vega is the child of such a marriage. Betanzos married Angelina Añas Yupanki, herself the niece of Wayna Qhapaq and wife to Ataw Wallpa.

128. *"una fiesta muy principal en la cual se horadaba las orejas y en esta fiesta nosotros los Ingas solemos hacer la mayor fiesta que hacemos en todo el año porque entonces nos dan mucho nombre y nuevo nombre del que teníamos antes"*

129. *"y sentándose allí luego se convirtió en piedra y quedó hecho mojón de pos-esión, que en la lengua Antigua de este valle se llama cozco, de donde le quedó el nombre del Cuzco al tal sitio hasta hoy"* (Sarmiento de Gamboa 1965: 217). I am indebted to Cerrón Palomino 1997a for directing me to this specific passage in Sarmiento de Gamboa's *Historia índica*.

130. Cuzqueño Quechua distinguishes between the homonyms *waka* and *wak'a* with the latter's glottal stop. The former means deity or sacred place whereas the latter signifies a crevice, crack, cleft or flaw as in a hare lip (Cerrón Palomino 1994b: 80).

131. See note 110.

132. Care for and festivities surrounding mummies and cemeteries predate the Inqa Empire and were not limited to Quechua, Aymara and Puquina speaking cultures (cf. Isbell: 284–315).

133. Cf. Rama 1994: Chapter 1.

134. *"Lo que más habéis de hacer es que por ventura éstos os dirán que adoréis lo que ellos adoran, que son unos paños pintados, los cuales dicen que es Wiraquchan, y que le adoréis como a waka, el cual no es sino paño, no lo hagáis sino lo que nosotros tenemos eso tened, porque como veis las willkas hablan con nosotros y al sol y a la luna vémoslos por nuestros ojos y lo que esos dicen no lo vemos bien".*

135. *"De creer es que irían acompañados al gobernador y que allá se regocijarían entre sí cada uno con lo que llevaban, el cual regocijo, según adelante se verá, no les duró mucho porque como el demonio sea tan malo como es, y amigo de disensiones y diferencias, nunca para"* (emphasis mine).

136. *"Yo como cristiano siempre le he aconsejado y dicho cuan buena cosa es estar debajo de la fe de nuestro Señor Jesucristo y cuán buena cosa es la paz y él así lo tienen [sic] entendido sino como el diablo es tan sotil siempre al mejor tiempo que no faltaban mestizos e indios que con cartas y palabras le venían a engañar".* (énfasis mío; Pando: 255)

137. Wallpa Yupanki was later Thupaq Amaru's "captain-general" during the war against Francisco Toledo's troops in 1572 (Guillén Guillén: 161).

138. The *Memorias* are both dated to the day the Oidor Matienzo received them on the Chuquichaca bridge, June 18, 1565.

139. "El señor capa ynga y yanque mayta y rimache yupangui Despues de auer tratado entre ellos [el] major modo y medio que se tendrá en la paz y salida del señor capa ynga y conocimiento Del sancto evangelio acordaron oydiez y seis de Junyo la horden y manera siguiente [. . .]"(in Guillén Guillén 1994: 260).

140. "Al tiempo que los **cristianos** entraron en esta tierra fue preso mi padre Mango Inga, so color y achaque que se quería alzar con el Reino, después de la muerte de Atagualipa, sólo a fin que les diese un *bohío* lleno de plata y oro. En la prisión le hicieron muchos malos tratamientos, así de obra como de palabra, echándole una collera al pescuezo, como a perro, y cargándole de hierros los pies, y trayéndole de la collera de una parte a otra entre sus vasallos, poniéndole a quistión a cada hora [. . .]" (énfasis mío; Titu Kusi Yupanki in Matienzo: 301–302)

141. See note 115. Domingo de Santo Tomás formed part of the Bishop of Chiapas's network of advocates for indigenous "self-rule" organized in Christian communities, specifically in the Mantaro Valley, as a Christian replacement for the contemporaneous *encomienda* system of land distribution for the sustenance of the Indian "souls" who had been placed in the "care" of the Spanish conquistadors as rewards for their services to the Crown in expanding the territory of the Spanish empire.

142. <Titu Cusi Yupanqui>.

143. Especially considering that Titu Kusi Yupanki says in the *Instrucción* that his godfather for his baptism in Rayangalla had been González Pérez de Vivero.

144. Although Covarrubias viewed "Diego" merely as a "corruption" of Santiago, a relatively new saint, San Diego of Alcalá, a monk of the Franciscan order who lived in Spain during the 15th century, would soon be canonized (in 1588). Though Covarrubias makes no mention of him under his entry for Diego, San Diego famously provided a life-saving miracle for Felipe II beyond his grave: Prince Carlos was saved from death when the Spanish Monarch summoned the curative powers of Diego of Alcalá to his son's aid. His powers were later extolled by Lope Félix de Vega Carpio (1562–1635) in *San Diego de Alcalá*, one of his many *comedias* dedicated to the lives of Saints (cf. Sánchez Romeralo: 357–360). San Diego bay in California was named by the expedition of Sebastián Viscaino because the Saint's feast day was closest to that of the landing; it was also the name of the flagship. A Franciscan mission was not founded there until 1769. The veneration of San Diego de Alcalá probably did not have many followers among the Augustine missionaries in Peru, who were Titu Kusi Yupanki's main contact with the Catholic religion.

145. Especially if we consider that one of the Augustine friars was also named Diego, Friar Diego Ortiz.

146. Santiago makes his appearance in the *Instrucción* in the symbolism of the white horse that enters Sacsahuaman, leading the Spaniards to victory. *Illapa* is the deity of lightning.

147. Cf. Harrison 1989: 103.

148. Seed has suggested that this ritual of conquest has its origin in Muslim Spain and that the Catholic Monarchs used this legitimating tradition of *jihad* without showing the tolerance of Muslim sovereigns towards the religions of the peoples they conquered (81–84).

149. Mignolo 1995: 105.

150. Cf. Lienhard: 180.

151. Cf. Mignolo 1995: 125–170; Robert Ascher: 103–104.

152. "Plega a nuestro Señor, Dios todopoderoso [. . .] le pague trayéndole a conocimiento de quien su Sacratísima Majestad es, para que conociéndole le ame y amándole le posee y poseyéndole se goce con él en su reino para siempre, así como nosotros nos gozamos poseyendo la merced que Vuestra Merced nos hace".

153. I am indebted for the phrases "rituals of possession" and "rituals of power" (Cf. Seed 1995; Cornejo Polar 1994: 48).

154. Cf. Cornejo Polar 1994: 47, for his discussion of the relationship between this intentionality in the Americas and the Counter-Reformation in Europe.

155. Rodríguez describes the Inqa's entrance into such a scene of encounter on the Chuquichaca bridge: "Many lances were drawn up on a hill, and messengers arrived to say that the Inca was coming. Presently the escort of the Inca began to appear. The Inca came in front of all, with a head-dress of plumes of many colours, a silver plate on his breast, a golden shield in one hand, and a lance all of gold. He wore garters of feathers and fastened to them were small wooden bells. On his head was a diadem and another round the neck. In one hand he had a gilded dagger, and he came in a mask of several colours" (Markham 1913: 179).

156. Cf. Mignolo 1995: 121.

157. "No echaban de menos los ingas en aquella tierra apartada, o por mejor decir, desterradero, los regalos, grandeza y suntuosidad de Cuzco, porque allí todo cuanto podía haber de fuera les traían los indios para sus contentos y placeres y ellos estaban allí con gusto" (*Historia General del Perú*: 64).

158. I am referring to Freud's discussion of the "uncanny" in relationship to the shared meaning of "hidden" between the *heimlich* and the *unheimlich* (195).

159. Though Martín Rubio ignores the language of the *Instrucción*, "you may favor me before his Majesty in all things" ("me ha de hacer merced de favorecerme

ante su Majestad") preferring to assert instead that it was directly addressed to Felipe II of Spain (1988 Edition: 41).

160. Other colonial "mestizo" texts of the Andean area manifest different approaches to the Spanish written word. The intentions of Guamán Poma de Ayala to be published, for example, in his *Nueva crónica y buen gobierno*, are evident in the pagination, rather than foliation, and formatting of the manuscript, as well as his expressed desire for it to be distributed amongst the officials within the colonial bureaucracy in order to incite change in colonial Peru, whose social fabric, he argued, had been destroyed by Viceroy Toledo's reforms *(Adorno 2001)*. He was clearly conscious of Western Historical tradition and showed a clear intention to present an Andean vision within it. *The Huarochirí Manuscipt*, on the other hand, was never intended to be published when it was written in 1607 (Dedenbach-Salazar Sáenz: 165 note 1). This transcription, redaction and ordering of Quechua and Aymara testimonies of the Yauyos area in Lima, which narrate native customs and beliefs, was found among Francisco de Avila's papers as source material for his *Tratado* in Spanish on the extirpation of idolatries; the presentation of the *Tratado* (clear calligraphy and title page) may be evidence of an intention to publish. Comparative graphological analysis of the two manuscript texts attributed to Avila is still outstanding, so it is difficult to pinpoint the exact relationship between *The Huarochirí Manuscript* and Avila in terms of the manuscript's authorship, redaction and transcription, although defining its authorship in relation to the native oral testimonies and their transcription and ordering into written colonial Quechua is a highly complex enterprise. By avoiding comfortable heuristic categories such as "mestizo texts," or strict dichotomies, such as Spanish/ indigenous, written word/orality, scholars may articulate new readings which underscore the distinctive relationships between the plurality of indigenous voices and their relationship to the Spanish written word in colonial Peru.

161. "y porque la memoria de los hombres es débil y flaca y si no acudimos a las letras para aprovecharnos de ellas"

162. But see Mazzotti: 272.

163. Cf. Cornejo Polar 1983.

164. "Avra 14 días, recibí la de V.P. y con ella la merced acostumbrada y no respondí luego a ella, por haber estado Martín de Pando, en Carco, en compañía de P. Fr. Marcos".

165. "Entendiendo el descuido que había habido de vuestra parte en no salir a verme al camino, cuando vine a esta ciudad, ni después de haber estado en ella, y a reconocer lo que debiades al servicio de Dios y de la Majestad del Rey mi señor, cumpliendo con la obligación de padre que os debo por la fe que tenéis prestada a Dios y al Rey mi señor, [. . .] Y así, podéis ver lo que os va en este negocio, y ejecutar lo que os digo con la obediencia que debéis a lo que os importe, y a vuestra seguridad y de vuestros hijos, hermanos y capitanes;

que como padre, de vuestro bien y remedio se os advierte y dice esto" (Apéndice C of the 1916 Edition: 123–4).

166. Cf. Lee; Dougall de Zileri.

167. Willka, the homonym for 'sun' or 'deity,' means 'grandchild' or 'great-grand-child' (Cerrón Palomino 1994b: 83).

Instrucción del Inga Don Diego de Castro Titu Cusi Yupangui para el muy ilustre Señor el Licenciado Lope García de Castro (1570)

(Modernized Spanish Version)

Instrucción del Inga Don Diego de Castro Titu Cusi Yupangui para el muy ilustre Señor el Licenciado Lope García de Castro, Gobernador que fue de estos reinos del Perú, tocante a los negocios que con su Majestad, en su nombre, por su poder, ha de tratar; la cual es ésta que sigue:

Por cuanto yo, don Diego de Castro Titu Cusi Yupangui, nieto de Guaina Capac¹ e hijo de Mango Inga Yupangui, señores naturales que fueron de los reinos y provincias del Perú, he recibido muchas mercedes y favor del muy Ilustre Señor el licenciado Lope García de Castro por su Majestad el rey Felipe nuestro señor, me ha parecido que, pues su Señoría va de estos reinos a los de España y es persona de valor y gran cristiandad, no podría hallar quien con mejor título y voluntad me favoreciese en todos mis negocios que ante su Majestad haya de presentar y tratar, así en cosas a mí necesarias como a mis hijos y descendientes, para lo cual, por el gran crédito que de su Señoría tengo, no dejaré de ponerlos todos en su mano para que así en uno como en otro (pues en todo hasta aquí me ha hecho tanta merced) en ésta tan principal me la haga como yo espero de su Ilustre persona.

Y porque la memoria de los hombres es débil y flaca y si no [] acudimos a las letras para aprovecharnos de ellas en nuestras necesidades, era casi imposible podernos acordar por extenso de todos los negocios largos y de importancia que se nos ofreciese y por eso, usando de la brevedad posible, me será necesario hacer recopilación de algunas cosas necesarias en las cuales, su Señoría llevando mi poder para ello, me ha de hacer merced de favorecerme ante su Majestad en todas ellas, como a la clara de ayuso irá declarado y relatado; la recopilación de las cuales cosas es ésta que se sigue:

Primeramente, que su Señoría me haga merced, llegado que sea con bien a los reinos de España, de dar a entender a su Majestad del rey Felipe nuestro señor, debajo de cuyo amparo yo me he puesto, quién soy y la necesidad que, a causa de poseer su Majestad y sus vasallos la tierra que fue de mis antepasados, en estos montes padezco. Y podría su Señoría dar la dicha relación siendo de ello servido por esta vía, comenzando por quién soy y cúyo hijo, para que le conste a su Majestad más por extensión la razón que arriba he dicho para gratificarme.

Bien creo que por nuevas de muchas personas se habrá publicado quiénes fueron los señores naturales antiguos de esta tierra y de dónde y cómo procedieron y por eso no me quiero detener acerca de esto. Sólo me hará su Señoría merced de avisar a su Majestad de cómo yo soy el hijo legítimo, digo el primero y mayorazgo que mi padre Mango Inga Yupangui dejó entre otros muchos, de los cuales me mandó tuviese cargo y mirase por ellos como por mi propia persona, lo cual yo he hecho, desde que él falleció hasta hoy, y lo hago y haré mientras Dios me diere vida, pues es cosa tan justa que los hijos hagan lo que sus padres les mandan, en especial en sus postrimeros días.

También que su Majestad sepa que mi padre Mango Inga Yupangui, hijo que fue de Guaina Capac y nieto de Topa Inga Yupangui² y así por sus abolengos descendiendo por línea recta, fue el señor principal de todos los reinos del Perú, señalado para ello por su padre Guaina Capac y tenido y obedecido por tal en toda la tierra después de sus días como yo lo fui, soy y he sido en ésta después que el dicho mi padre falleció.

Y también dar a entender a su Majestad la razón por donde yo ahora estoy con tanta necesidad en estos montes en los cuales me dejó mi padre con ella al tiempo que reinaba y gobernaba el Perú y toda su tierra, que fue en el tiempo que los españoles le desbarataron y mataron.

Y también que sepa su Majestad por extensión, como abajo irá declarado, la manera [] y en qué tiempo los españoles entraron en esta tierra del Perú y el tratamiento que hicieron al dicho mi padre todo el tiempo que en ella vivió hasta darle la muerte en ésta que yo ahora poseo, que es la que se sigue:

Relación de cómo los españoles entraron en el Perú y el suceso que tuvo Mango Inga en el tiempo que entre ellos vivió, que es ésta que se sigue:

En el tiempo que los españoles aportaron a esta tierra del Perú que llegaron al pueblo de Cajamarca, ciento y noventa leguas poco más o menos de aquí, mi padre Mango Inga estaba en la ciudad del Cuzco; en ésa era con todo su poderío y mando como su padre Guaina Capac se lo había dejado, donde tuvo una nueva por ciertos mensajeros que vinieron de allá de un hermano suyo mayor (aunque bastardo) llamado Ataguallpa[3] y por unos indios yungas tallanas que residen a la orilla del Mar del Sur, quince o veinte leguas del dicho Cajamarca, los cuales decían que habían visto llegar a su tierra ciertas personas muy diferentes de nuestro hábito y traje que parecían viracochas, que es nombre con el cual nosotros nombramos antiguamente al criador de todas las cosas diciendo Tecsi Viracochan, que quiere decir principio y hacedor de todo. Y nombraron de esta manera a aquellas personas que habían visto, lo uno porque diferenciaban mucho en nuestro traje y semblante y lo otro, porque veían que andaban en unos animales muy grandes, los cuales tenían los pies de plata y esto decían por el relumbrar de las herraduras, y también les llamaban así porque les habían visto hablar a solas en unos paños blancos como una persona hablaba con otra y esto por el leer en libros y cartas, y aun les llamaban viracochas por la excelencia y parecer de sus personas y la mucha diferencia entre unos y otros, porque unos eran de barbas negras y otras bermejas, y porque les veían comer en plata, y también porque tenían illapas, nombre que nosotros tenemos para los truenos, y esto decían por los arcabuces porque pensaban que eran truenos del cielo.

De estos viracochas trajeron dos de ellos unos yungas a mi tío Ataguallpa que a la sazón estaba en Cajamarca, el cual les recibió muy bien y dando de beber a uno de ellos con un vaso de oro de la bebida que nosotros usamos; el español en recibiéndolo de su mano lo derramó, de lo cual se enojó mucho mi tío. Y después de esto, aquellos dos españoles le mostraron al dicho mi tío una carta o libro o no sé qué, diciendo que aquella era la quillca de Dios y del rey, y mi tío, como se sintió afrentado del derramar de la chicha, que así se llama nuestra bebida, tomó la carta o lo que era y la arrojó por ahí diciendo:

Qué sé yo qué me dais ahí, anda vete.

Y los españoles se volvieron a sus compañeros, los cuales irían por ventura a dar relación de lo que habían visto y les había pasado con mi tío Ataguallpa.

De ahí a muchos días, estando mi tío Ataguallpa en guerra y diferencias con un hermano suyo Guascar Inga[4] sobre cuál de ellos era el rey verdadero de esta tierra, no lo siendo ninguno de ellos por haberle usurpado a mi padre el reino a causa de ser muchacho en aquella sazón y querérsele levantar con él, por los muchos tíos y parientes que tenían el uno y el otro, los cuales decían que por qué había de ser rey un muchacho aunque su padre en sus postrimeros días le hubiese nombrado por tal, que más razón era lo fueron los grandes y no el chico, la cual razón no se pudo llamar tal sino pasión de codicia y ambición porque ellos descendían aunque hijos de Guaina Capac de parte de las madres de sangre soez y baja, y mi padre fue hijo legítimo de sangre real, como lo fue Pachacuti Inga, abuelo de Guaina Capac. Y estando éstos en estas diferencias como dicho tengo, uno contra otro, aunque hermanos en diferentes asientos, llegaron a Cajamarca, pueblo arriba nombrado, dicen que cuarenta a cincuenta españoles en sus caballos bien aderezados, y sabido por mi tío Ataguallpa, que cerca de allí estaba en un pueblo llamado Huamachuco haciendo cierta fiesta, luego levantó su real, no con armas para pelear ni arneses para defenderse sino con tumis[5] y lazos, que así llamamos los cuchillos nuestros para cazar aquel género de nuevas llamas, que así llamamos el ganado nuestro, y ellos lo decían por los caballos que nuevamente habían aparecido, y llevaban los tumis y cuchillos para los desollar y descuartizar no haciendo caso de tan poca gente ni de lo que era.

Y como mi tío llegase al pueblo de Cajamarca con toda su gente, los españoles les recibieron en los baños de Conoc, legua y media de Cajamarca, y así se fueron con él hasta Cajamarca, y llegados que fueron les preguntó [que] a qué venían. Los cuales les dijeron que venían por mandado del Viracocha a decirles cómo le han de conocer. Y mi tío, como les oyó lo que decían, atendió a ello y calló y dio de beber a uno de ellos de la manera que arriba dije para ver si se lo derramaban como los otros dos y fue de la misma manera que ni lo bebieron ni hicieron caso. Y visto por mi tío que tan poco caso hacían de sus cosas [dijo],

Pues vosotros no hacéis caso de mí ni yo lo quiero hacer de vosotros.

Y así se levantó enojado y alzó grita y guisa de querer matar a los españoles, y los españoles que estaban sobre aviso tomaron cuatro puertas que había en la plaza donde estaban, la cual era cercada por todas partes.

Desde que aquella plaza estuvo cercada y los indios todos dentro como ovejas, los cuales eran muchos y no se podían rodear a ninguna parte ni tampoco tenían armas porque no las habían traído por el poco caso que hicieron de los españoles, sino lazos y tumis como arriba dije. Los españoles con gran furia arremetieron al medio de la plaza donde había un asiento del Inga en alto a manera de fortaleza que nosotros llamamos usnu, los cuales se apoderaron de él y no dejaron subir allá a mi tío, mas antes al pie de él le derrocaron de sus andas por fuerza y se las trastornaron y quitaron lo que tenía y la borla, que entre nosotros es corona, y quitado todo lo dicho le prendieron, y porque los indios daban grita los mataron a todos con los caballos, con espadas, con arcabuces, como quien mata a ovejas, sin hacerles nadie resistencia, que no se escaparon [] más de diez mil doscientos. Y desde que fueron todos muertos, llevaron mi tío Ataguallpa a una cárcel de noche, donde le tuvieron toda una noche en cueros, atada una cadena al pescuezo. Y otro día por la mañana le dieron su ropa y su borla diciendo:

¿Eres tú el rey de esta tierra?

Y él respondió que sí, y ellos dijeron:

¿No hay otro ninguno que lo sea sino tú? Porque nosotros sabemos que hay otro que se llama Mango Inga, ¿dónde está éste?

Y mi tío respondió:

En el Cuzco.

Y ellos replicaron:

Pues, ¿[ ]dónde es el Cuzco?

A ésta respondió mi tío:

Doscientas leguas de aquí está el Cuzco.

Y más tornaron a decir los españoles:

Pues luego ése que está en el Cuzco, porque nosotros tenemos por nueva [que] es la cabeza y principal de esta tierra, debe de ser el rey.

Y mi tío dijo:

De ser sí es, porque mi padre mandó que lo fuere, pero porque es muy mozo, gobierno yo la tierra por él.

Y los españoles dijeron:

Pues aunque sea mozo será justo que sepa nuestra llegada y cómo venimos por mandado del Viracochan, por eso avísaselo.

Y mi tío dijo:

¿A quién queréis que envíe pues me habéis muerto a toda mi gente y yo estoy de esta manera?

Y esto decía porque no estaba bien con mi padre y temía que si le avisaba de la llegada de los viracochas por ventura terminarían con él porque le parecían gente poderosa y aún pensaban que eran viracochas por lo que arriba dije.

Los españoles como vieron que mi tío Ataguallpa se detenía de dar aviso a mi padre de su llegada, acordaron entre sí de hacer mensajeros. Y en este medio tiempo que los españoles enviaban o no, lo entendieron los tallanas yungas, y porque temían mucho a mi padre, porque le conocían por su rey, acordaron entre sí sin dar aviso a los españoles ni a mi tío, de ir ellos a dar la nueva a mi padre y así lo hicieron y se partieron luego para el Cuzco, y llegados que fueron allá, dijeron a mi padre estas palabras:

Sapay Inga[6] —*que quiere decir tú solo señor*— te venimos a decir cómo ha llegado a tu tierra un género de gente no oída ni vista en nuestras naciones, que al parecer, sin duda, son viracochas —*como dicen dioses*— han llegado a Cajamarca donde está tu hermano, el cual les ha dicho y certificado que él es el señor y rey de esta tierra, de lo cual nosotros como tus vasallos recibimos gran pena y con ello, por no poder sufrir a nuestros oídos semejante injuria sin darle parte, te venimos a dar aviso de lo que pasa porque no seamos tenidos ante ti por rebeldes ni descuidados a lo que toca a tu servicio.

Y mi padre, oída su embajada, quedó fuera de sí diciendo:

Pues ¿cómo en mi tierra ha sido osada a entrar semejante gente sin mi mandado ni consentimiento? ¿Qué ser y manera tiene esa gente?

Y respondiendo los mensajeros dijeron:

Señor, es una gente que sin duda no se puede ser menos que no sean viracochas porque dicen que vienen por el viento y es gente barbuda, muy hermosa y muy blanc[a]. Comen en platos de plata y las mismas ovejas que los traen a cuestas, l[a]s cuales son grandes, tienen zapatos de plata. Echan illapas como el cielo. Mira tú si semejante gente y que de esta manera se rige y gobierna si serán viracochas. Y aún nosotros les habemos visto por nuestros ojos a solas hablar en paños blancos y nombrar a algunos de nosotros por nuestros nombres sin se los decir nadie, nomás de por mirar al paño que tienen delante, y más que es gente que no se les aparecen otra cosa sino las manos y la cara, y las ropas que traen son mejores que las tuyas porque traen oro y plata, y gente de esta manera y suerte ¿qué pueden ser sino viracochas?

A esto mi padre, como hombre que de hecho se deseaba certificar de lo que era, tornó a amenazar a los mensajeros, diciéndoles así:

Mirad no me mintáis en lo que me habéis dicho que ya sabéis y habréis entendido cuáles, mis antepasados y yo, solemos para los mentirosos.

Y ellos, tornando a replicar, con algún temor y grima, dijeron:

Sapay Inga, si no lo hubiéramos visto por nuestros ojos y te tuviéramos el temor que tenemos por ser como tus vasallos, no te osáramos ver ni venir a ti con semejantes nuevas. Si no nos queréis creer, envía tú a quien tú quisieres a Cajamarca y allí verán a esta gente que te hemos dicho, que esperando[] están la respuesta de nuestro mensaje.

Y viendo mi padre que aquellos tan de veras se certificaban en lo que decían y dándoles en ello algún crédito les dijo:

Pues que tanto me hincáis en certificarme la llegada de esta gente, andad y traedme aquí algunos de ellos para que viéndolos yo lo crea a ojos vistos.

Y los mensajeros hicieron lo que les mandaba mi padre y volvieron a Cajamarca con no sé cuántos indios que mi padre envió a la certificación de lo dicho y a rogar a los españoles [que] llegase alguno de ellos donde él estaba porque deseaba en extremo ver a tan buena gente, que con tanto ahínco los yungas tallanas le habían certificado que era. Y finalmente todos los mensajeros, unos y otros, se partieron del Cuzco por mandado de mi padre para Cajamarca a ver la gente que eran aquellos viracochas.

Y llegados que fueron al marqués don Francisco Pizarro, los recibió muy bien y se holgó con saber de mi padre y con no sé qué cosillas que les envió, el cual, como dicho tengo, les enviaba a rogar se viniesen con él algunos de ellos, los cuales lo tuvieron por bien y acordaron de enviar dos españoles a besarle las manos, llamados el uno fulano Villegas y el otro, Antano, que no le supieron los indios dar otro nombre. Y salieron de Cajamarca por mandado del marqués y consentimiento de los demás y llegaron al Cuzco sin temor ni embarazo ninguno, mas antes mi padre desde que supo mucho antes que llegase[] su venida, les envió al camino mucho refresco y aún había mandado a los mensajeros que fueron del Cuzco a llamarl[e]s, que los trajesen en hamacas, los cuales lo hicieron así. Y llegados que fueron al Cuzco y presentados delante de mi padre, él los recibió muy honradamente y los mandó aposentar y proveer de todo lo necesario.

Y otro día, les hizo venir a donde estaba y haciendo una gran fiesta con mucha gente y aparato de vajillas de oro y plata en que había muchos cántaros y vasos y librillos, y barrañones de lo mismo. Y los españoles, como vieron tanto oro y plata, dijeron a mi padre que les diese algo de aquello para llevarlo a enseñar al marqués y sus compañeros y les significar la grandeza de su poderío, y mi padre lo tuvo por bien y les dio muchos cántaros y vasos de oro y otras joyas y piezas ricas que llevasen para sí y sus compañeros. Y los despachó con mucha gente al gobernador, diciéndoles que pues le habían venido a ver y venían de parte del Viracochan,[7] que entrasen en su tierra y si querían venir a donde él estaba, viniesen mucho en hora buena.

Entre tanto que estos dos españoles fueron a besar las manos [de] mi padre y a verse con él en el Cuzco, mi tío Ataguallpa, lo uno por temores que le pusieron aquellos viracochas y lo otro de su grado, por tenerles de su mano para que le favoreciesen contra Mango Inga, mi padre, y Guascar Inga, su hermano, les dio gran suma de tesoro de oro y plata, que todo pertenecía al dicho mi padre, y por recelo que tenía aún de mi tío Guascar Inga, desde el lugar donde estaba, envió ciertos mensajeros a que se confederasen con su gente y le matasen para tener por aquella parte las espaldas seguras, pensando que las tenía por la parte de los españoles, como digo, por el tesoro que, sin ser suyo sino de mi padre, les había dado, los cuales mensajeros lo hicieron tan bien que mataron a Guascar Inga en una refriega que tuvieron en un pueblo llamado Huánuco Pampa.

Y sabido por el Ataguallpa la muerte de Guascar Inga, su hermano, recibió de ello sumo contento por parecerle que ya no tenía a quién temer y que lo tenía todo seguro, porque por la una parte ya al mayor enemigo tenía destruido y muerto y por la otra, por el cohecho que había hecho a los viracochas, pensaba que no había más que temer; y le salió al revés de su pensamiento, porque llegados que fueron los dos españoles adonde estaba el marqués don Francisco Pizarro y sus compañeros con la empresa que mi padre les enviaba

y con las nuevas de mi padre, fue certificado el marqués —que nosotros llamamos Machu Capitu— de cómo mi padre Mango Inga Yupangui era el rey
verdadero de toda la tierra, a quien todos respetaban, tenían y acataban por
señor, y que Ataguallpa, su hermano mayor, poseía el reino tiránicamente, de
lo cual, lo uno por saber tan buenas nuevas de mi padre y que era persona tan
principal, y lo otro por tan buen presente como le enviaban y tan de voluntad,
recibió mucho contento y gran pena de ver que su hermano tan sin justicia le
procurase de vejar y molestar, usurpándole su reino sin justicia, el cual, según
después pareció, no quedó sin castigo, porque fue castigado según su merecido.

Ya que fueron llegados, como arriba dicho tengo, los españoles mensajeros
que fueron a mi padre a su real y los demás indios que mi padre enviaba con
el presente de oro y plata, que fue más de dos millones arriba dicho, represen-
taron su embajada los españoles por sí y los indios por la suya, según que por
mi padre Mango Inga Yupangui les fuera mandado, al gobernador diciendo
que mi padre Mango Inga se había holgado mucho con la llegada de tan
buena gente a su tierra, que le rogaba que si lo tuviese por bien se llegasen al
Cuzco a donde él estaba y porque él l[e]s recibiría muy honradamente y les
daba su palabra de hacer todo lo que le rogasen pues venían por mandado del
Viracochan [y] que les hacía saber cómo, por aquellas partes donde ellos
habían aportado, estaba un hermano suyo llamado Ataguallpa, el cual se
nombraba rey de toda la tierra, que no le tuviesen por tal porque él era el rey
y señor natural de ella, señalado para ello en sus postrimeros días por su
padre Guaina Capac, y que el Ataguallpa se le había levantado con el reino
contra su voluntad.

Sabido todo esto, lo uno y lo otro, por el gobernador y toda su gente, recibió
a los mensajeros de mi padre con gran alegría juntamente con el presente
arriba dicho y mandó que los hospedasen y honrasen como a mensajeros de
tal señor. Y de ahí a algunos días los indios mensajeros de mi padre se
volvieron con la respuesta. Y se quedó en Cajamarca el marqués, teniendo
como tenía todavía preso a Ataguallpa desde que llegaron él y sus compañeros
a la tierra por la sospecha que tenía de él, porque le parecía que si le soltaba
se alzaría contra él, y lo otro porque tuvo siempre sospecha diciendo que no
era él el rey natural de aquella tierra y se quería certificar de ello con la
respuesta que de mi padre viniese y por esto le tuvo tanto tiempo preso hasta
que por mi padre le fuese mandado otra cosa.

Y visto por mi tío Ataguallpa que mi padre había enviado mensajeros y
tanto oro y plata a los españoles, recibió de ello gran pena, lo uno por ver que
con tanta brevedad se había confederado con ellos y ellos recibiéndole por rey
y señor, y lo otro porque sospechaba que de aquella confederación le había de
venir algún daño. Y estando con esta sospecha y temor de una parte y otra le

cercaba, determinó de hacer juntar toda la gente y capitanes suyos que por ahí a la redonda estuviesen para significarles la aflicción en que estaba puesto y desde que los tuvo juntos les dijo estas palabras:

Apoes —*que quiere decir señores*— esta gente que ha venido a nuestras tierras es muy contraria a nuestra opinión y se ha confederado y tienen mucha paz con mi hermano Mango Inga, si os parece démosles en la cabeza y muertos todos estos, porque me parece que, aunque es poca gente, es valerosa. No dejaremos de tener la suprema[cía] en toda la tierra como antes teníamos, pues ya es muerto mi hermano Guascar Inga, y si no los matamos y estos se hacen con mi hermano Mango Inga, a causa de ser gente tan valerosa y que al parecer son viracochas, podría ser que nos fuese mal el negocio porque mi hermano está muy enojado contra mí y si hace llamamiento de toda la tierra hará capitanes a éstos y él y ellos no podrían dejar de matarnos, por eso si os pareciese ganémosle nosotros por la mano.

Los capitanes y gente como oyeron el razonamiento de mi tío Ataguallpa, les pareció muy bien lo que les decía[8] *y dijeron todos a una voz:*

Hu [hu] Sapay Inga —*que quiere decir: muy bien has dicho, señor*— bueno será que matemos a éstos porque ¿qué gente es ésta para con nosotros?, [¿]no tenemos en todos ellos un almuerzo[?]

Y ya que entre todos ellos estuvo concertado el día y la hora en que los habían de matar, no tardó mucho que no sé por qué vía lo supo el marqués: y sabido por el marqués la traición que estaba armada para matarles, antes que [lo] comiesen lo[s] almorzó él porque mandó poner espías por todas partes y que estuviesen a punto. Sin dilación ninguna mandó sacar a la plaza a Ataguallpa, mi tío, y en medio de la plaza, en un palo, sin ninguna contradicción le dio garrote, y desde que se le hubo dado levantó su real para venirse a ver a mi padre, y por presto que lo quiso levantar, no dejaron de venir sobre él indios como llovidos, porque un indio capitán general de Ataguallpa llamado Challco Chima[9] *y otro llamado Quisquis, su compañero, ambos de gran valor y poderío, juntaron gran suma de gente para vengar la muerte de su señor, de tal manera que le fue forzado al marqués y a toda su gente venir con gran aviso por su camino, porque era tanta la gente que los perseguía que venían por el camino con gran trabajo y detrimento, recibiendo siempre grandes guazábaras de los perseguidores.*

Lo cual, sabido por mi padre que así venía con tanto aprieto, determinó de hacer gente para irle a ayudar. Y así [] salió del Cuzco con más de cien mil hombres y llegó hasta Vilcacunga, adonde [se] encontró con el marqués que ya traía preso a Challco Chima, el cual marqués viéndolo recibió muy gran contento, y mi padre yendo que iba en sus andas de oro y cristal y [con su] corona real, se apeó de ella y abrazó al marqués que ya se había apeado de su caballo y ambos, mi padre y el marqués, se confederaron en uno, y mandaron a sus gentes que nadie se desmandase, salvo que atendiesen a Quisquis, que aún andaba por allí barloventeando con mucha gente, porque no se desmandase a querer quitar al Challco Chima.

Recibidos que fueron [como] uno, mi padre y el marqués se salieron juntos de Vilcacunga y durmieron aquella noche en Jaquijahuana, []donde se le entregó el marqués a mi padre el Challco Chima, diciendo:

Veis aquí, señor Mango Inga, os traigo preso a vuestro enemigo capital, Challco Chima —*diciendo*[10]— *veis lo que mandáis se haga de él.*

Y mi padre como lo vio, mandó que fuese quemado a vista de todos porque fuese la nueva a Quisquis, su compañero, y fuese este castigo y a los demás ejemplo.

Hecho este castigo de tan mal indio como era aquél, se fueron de allí para el Cuzco juntos, aunque iba mi padre con gran pena por ver la desvergüenza de aquel indio Quisquis. Y llegados que fueron al Cuzco, mandó mi padre a toda su gente que respetase[] y tuviese[] en mucho al marqués y a los suyos y los proveyesen de todo lo necesario hasta que él volviese, diciendo que quería ir a matar a aquel bellaco de Quisquis y destruir a toda su generación, pues tanto se le desvergonzaba así a él como a los españoles, que tanto por entonces quería, a causa de haberle parecido tan bien el marqués don Francisco Pizarro.

Alcance de Mango Inga y el Capitán Antonio de Soto[11] contra Quisquis, traidor a la Persona Real y a su Rey Mango Inga

Otro día después que mi padre hubo hecho aposentar y proveer de todo lo necesario al marqués y a toda su gente, determinó con parecer del dicho marqués de dar alcance y perseguir al traidor de Quisquis porque estaba en gran manera enojado contra él por el amor y afición que había cobrado a los españoles. Y vista por el marqués la determinación con que mi padre se determinaba a hacer aquel viaje, se ofreció él también a la jornada, diciendo que no era cosa justa quedarse él en el pueblo yendo mi padre a la guerra, que más harían dos que uno. Mi padre Mango Inga, viendo el tan buen propósito del marqués, dijo que no se moviese por entonces sino que descansase y que holgase hasta que volviese, que presto daría la vuelta, que si quería que fuese con él alguna gente suya que él holgaría de llevar consigo de los que él le diese, mas que su persona no consentiría que por entonces [] saliese del pueblo.

El marqués don Francisco Pizarro, viendo que mi padre no le dejaba salir del pueblo para llevarlo consigo, tomó parecer con sus capitanes sobre el caso, a los cuales pareció que era justo lo que mi padre decía; y así ellos entre sí con el gobernador nombraron al capitán Antonio de Soto para que se fuese con mi padre, el cual llevó consigo cincuenta españoles soldados, y nombrado para el efecto [e]l dicho capitán Antonio de Soto, se fueron ambos el marqués y él a casa de mi padre, que ya estaba de partida, y le dieron cuenta de lo que tenían concertado; y mi padre como lo supo hubo de ello mucho contento y dijo que le parecía muy bien aquel concierto, que se aparejasen los soldados que ya él quería ir.

Este mismo día se salió mi padre del Cuzco con toda su gente llevando consigo al Capitán Antonio de Soto con su compañía, los cuales yendo por sus jornadas en breve tiempo dieron sobre el traidor de Quisquis; al cual hallaron en un pueblo llamado Capi,[12] quince leguas del Cuzco, []donde hubieron con él una cruda batalla en la cual le mataron gran suma de gente y le desbarataron. El cual se salió huyendo de entre los suyos sin saberlo ellos y se escapó. Y mi padre y el capitán Soto, desde que acabaron de desbaratar a Quisquis y a toda su gente, se volvieron al Cuzco, enviando mucha gente en pos del Quisquis para que se los trajesen vivo de dondequiera que lo hallasen.

Y llegados que fueron al Cuzco mi padre y el capitán Antonio de Soto del desbarate de Quisquis, fueron muy bien recibidos [por] el marqués don Francisco Pizarro y toda su gente y de los que en el pueblo había, esto con mucho regocijo y alegría por la victoria que habían habido de Quisquis y toda su gente. Y acabado todo aquello y el recibimiento, mi padre se recogió a su casa y los españoles a la suya. Y otro día por la mañana, juntándose toda la gente que mi padre había traído de la batalla de Quisquis y la que en el pueblo estaba, a casa de mi padre, comió con ellos el dicho mi padre y desde que hubo comido, mandó que so pena de la vida nadie se osase descomedir contra ninguna persona de las de aquella gente que nuevamente habían aportado a su tierra, mas que todos les respetasen y honrasen como a cosa del Viracochan, que quiere decir dios, y mandó más, que les diesen servicio, indios y gente para su casa, y aun el mismo mi padre dio de sus mismos criados que le servían servicio al marqués para que le sirviesen. Y hecho todo lo susodicho tornó otra vez a apercibir de nuevo [a] gente para ir en seguimiento del traidor de Quisquis, diciendo que, aunque fuese hasta en cabo del mundo, le había de seguir y matar, por la gran traición que había hecho así a él como a los viracochas.

Reformado que se hubo el dicho mi padre de las cosas necesarias para su viaje y dado orden en el gobierno del pueblo, dejando en su lugar a Paullu, su hermano, y Ticoc y otros capitanes, y despidiéndose del marqués, con homenaje que no había de volver hasta que matase aquel traidor de Quisquis, se salió otro día del Cuzco llevando consigo el dicho capitán Antonio de Soto con su compañía arriba dicha, los cuales se fueron poco a poco por sus jornadas hasta un pueblo llamado Vinchu, cincuenta leguas del Cuzco, adonde le encontraron los mensajeros que de la batalla de Cupi habían enviado en su seguimiento de Quisquis, los cuales dijeron que venían de buscar aquel traidor, y que ni rastro ni nueva habían hallado de él en toda la tierra, salvo que sus capitanes daban muchos saltos y que de él no había nueva.

Y mi padre, como oyó lo que los mensajeros decían, recibió de ello gran pena y quis[o] pasar adelante, sino que recibió allí cartas del marqués en que le significaba la gran soledad que padecía por su ausencia; que le rogaba mucho que se volviese, a lo cual mi padre por el amor que al marqués tenía, se volvió enviando desde allí mensajeros por toda la tierra por donde aquel traidor hubiese de pasar, para que todos, dondequiera que aportase, le diesen guerra y se lo matasen. Hecho esto y enviados los mensajeros para que por todas partes hasta Quito, cuatrocientas leguas de allí, donde el desventurado —como abajo se dirá— murió, no parasen. Se torna[ro]n al Cuzco adonde el dicho mi padre supo que después de muchas guazábaras que con aquel traidor hubieron en muchas y diversas partes, [] dieron matándole y robando mucha gente, hasta tanto que su misma gente, viendo que se había apocado en tanta manera que ya casi no había nadie, con gran despecho, afeándole sus bellaquerías y traición contra su rey, le cortaron la cabeza.

Desde que mi padre estuvo en el Cuzco, ya algún tanto sosegado y contento con la muerte de aquel traidor de Quisquis, hizo llamamiento a toda su gente, para que todos por cabeza diesen tributo a los españoles para su sustentación y el dicho mi padre, en tanto que se juntaba el tributo, para suplir su necesidad les dio gran suma de tesoro que de sus antepasados tenía, y el gobernador y sus compañeros lo recibieron con gran contento, dándole por ello las gracias.

Cómo los españoles prendieron a Mango Inga

Los españoles, como se vieron con tanta riqueza, quisieron entonces volverse a su tierra, pero mi padre, viendo que eran aún muy nuevos en la tierra, no les dejó ir por entonces, mas antes dijo que se quería holgar con ellos y tenerlos en su tierra, que avisasen ellos a la suya por extenso el suceso que había tenido en su viaje, y ellos lo tuvieron por bien e hicieron sus mensajeros enviando mucha parte del tesoro al emperador don Carlos, y de esta manera se estuvieron en el Cuzco muchos días holgando a su placer en compañía de mi padre. Y pasados algunos años, como la codicia de los hombres es tan grande, reinó en ellos, de tal suerte que, engañados por el demonio, amigo de toda maldad y enemigo de la virtud, [] se vinieron entre sí a concertar y tratar los unos con los otros la manera y el cómo molestarían a mi padre y sacarían de él más plata y oro de la sacada. Y concertados así, un día, estando mi padre en su casa quieto y sosegado, fueron a ella y otros más de cien españoles con traición so color que le iban a ver y llegados que fueron al dicho mi padre, como los vio, pensando que le iban a ver como otras veces solían, los *recibió con mucha alegría y contento, y ellos, como llevaban la traición armada, echaron mano de él, diciendo:*

Sabido tenemos,[13] Mango Inga, que te quieres levantar contra nosotros y matarnos como lo hizo tu hermano Ataguallpa; por tanto, sábete que manda el gobernador que te prendamos y echemos prisiones como a tu hermano Ataguallpa, porque no seas parte para hacernos mal.

Mi padre, como los vio de aquella manera determinados, se alteró en gran manera, diciendo:

¿Qué os he hecho yo? ¿Por qué me queréis tratar de esta manera y atarme como a perro? ¿De esa manera me pagáis la buena obra que os he hecho en meteros en mi tierra y daros de lo que en ella tenía con tanta voluntad y amor? Mal lo hacéis, ¿vosotros sois los que decís que sois wiraquchas y que os envía el Tecsi Viracochan? No es posible que vosotros seáis[14] sus hijos pues pretendéis hacer mal a quien os hace y ha hecho tanto bien. Por ventura, ¿no os envié a Cajamarca gran suma de oro y plata? ¿No tomasteis[15] a mi hermano Ataguallpa todo el tesoro que allí yo tenía de mis antepasados? ¿No os he dado en este pueblo todo lo que habéis querido, que uno y otro no tienen[16] suma porque son más de seis millones? ¿No os he dado servicio para vosotros y vuestros criados y he mandado a toda mi tierra [que] os tributen? ¿Qué queréis más que haga? Juzgadlo vosotros y veréis si tengo razón de quejarme.

A esto los españoles, como ciegos de aquella malvada codicia, tornaron a replicar sobre lo dicho, diciendo:

¡Ea, Sapay Inga! No curéis de dar ahora excusas, que certificados estamos que te quieres alzar con la tierra. ¡Oíd mozos, dad acá unos grillos!

Los cuales trajeron luego que sin más respecto ni más miramiento de quién era y del bien que les había hecho se los echaron a sus pies; y echados, mi padre, como se vio de aquella manera, con mucha tristeza dijo:

Verdaderamente digo que vosotros sois demonios y no viracochas, pues sin culpa me tratáis de esta manera. ¿Qué queréis?

Respondieron los españoles:

No queremos ahora nada sino que te estés preso.

Y dejándole así preso y con guardas, se volvieron a sus casas a dar parte de lo que habían hecho al gobernador, el cual no estaba muy inocente del negocio. Y después, como mi padre se sintió preso de aquella manera, estaba con gran congoja y con ella no sabía qué se hacer, porque no había quién le consolase si no era la gente de su tierra. Y al fin de ahí a no sé cuántos días, volvieron Hernando Pizarro y Juan Pizarro y Gonzalo Pizarro con otros muchos y dijeron a mi padre:

Señor Mango Inga, ¿queréis os todavía levantar con la tierra?

Dijo mi padre:

¿Con [qué]¹⁷ tierra me tengo de levantar yo? La tierra no es mía, pues ¿qué me decís de levantar?

A esto respondieron los españoles y dijeron:

Nos han dicho que nos queréis matar y por eso te hemos preso; por tanto, si no es así que no te quieres levantar, bueno será que redimas tu vejación y nos des algún oro y plata, que eso es lo que venimos a buscar, porque dándola te soltaremos.

Dijo entonces también Hernando Pizarro:

Aunque le soltéis vosotros y dé más oro y plata que cabe en cuatro bohíos, no se soltará de mi parte si no me da primero a la señora Coya, su hermana, llamada Cura Ocllo, por mi mujer.

Y esto decía él porque la había visto y se enamoró de ella porque era muy hermosa. Y mi padre, viéndolos tan determinados en su mal propósito, dijo:

¿Pues eso manda el Viracochan, que toméis por fuerza la hacienda y mujeres de nadie? No se usa tal entre nosotros y bien digo yo que vosotros no sois hijos de Viracochan sino del Supay —*que es nombre del demonio en nuestra lengua*— anda, que yo procuraré de buscar alguna cosa que os dar.

Y ellos replicaron:

No pienses que ha de ser como quiera[s], que tanto nos has de dar como nos diste cuando aquí llegamos y más, que era tesoro que no cabía en un galpón de indios por grande que fuese.

Y mi padre viéndolos tan importunos y tan determinados, por no gastar más palabras les dijo:

Anda y yo haré lo que pudiere y os enviaré la respuesta.

Y ellos, aunque con algún recelo si será así o no, se fueron. Y otro día el dicho mi padre mandó hacer llamamiento por toda su tierra y que se junte toda la gente ahí, para juntar aquella cantidad de tesoro que los españoles con tanto ahínco le pedían, y desde que los tuvo juntos les hizo el parlamento siguiente:

Parlamento que Mango Inga Yupangui hizo a sus capitanes sobre la junta del tesoro que dio a los españoles cuando le prendieron [por] la primera vez

Hermanos e hijos míos, los días pasados os hice juntar otra vez de esta manera para que vierais un género de nueva gente que había aportado a nuestra tierra, que son estos barbudos que están aquí en este pueblo. Y también porque me decían que eran viracochas y lo parecía[n] en el traje, os mandé que todos vosotros servídseles y acátaseles como a mi persona misma y déseles tributo de lo que en vuestras tierras teníais, pensando que era gente grata y enviada de aquel que ellos decían que era Tecsi

Viracochan —*que quiere decir Dios*— y paréceme que me ha salido al revés de lo que yo pensaba, porque sabed hermanos que éstos, según me han dado las muestras después que entraron en mi tierra, no son hijos del Viracochan sino del demonio, porque me hacen y han hecho, después que en ella estaban, obras de tales como podéis ver por vuestros ojos, que me parece que no podeos dejar si me amáis verdaderamente, de recibir gran pena y congoja en ver a mí, vuestro rey, aprisionado con prisiones y tratado de esta manera sin merecerlo, y esto por haber metido yo en mi tierra semejante gente que ésta, que yo mismo me he degollado. Por vida vuestra, que si me deseáis dar contento, que lo más presto que pudiereis busquéis entre vosotros alguna cosa en razonable cantidad de oro y plata, pues estos tanto se mueren por ella, para que pueda redimir mi vejación y salir de esta prisión que por vuestros ojos me veis estar tan apasionado y congojado.

Respuesta que los indios hicieron a Mango Inga sobre la junta del tesoro cuando estaba preso

Como toda la gente de la tierra juntada de las cuatro partes de ella, en las cuales está repartida toda ella más de mil y doscientas leguas de largo y otras casi trescientas de ancho, repartida en esta manera a la discreción del mundo, conviene a saber: en oriente y poniente y norte y sur, en nuestro uso llamamos Andesuyu, Chinchaysuyu, Condesuyu, Collasuyu, rodeando de esta manera: Andesuyu al oriente, Chinchaysuyu al norte, Condesuyu al poniente, Collasuyu al sur. Esto hacíamos puestos en el Cuzco, que es el centro y cabeza de toda la tierra, y por esto y por estar en el medio se nombraban mis antepasados puestos allí por ser su cepa, señores de Tahuantinsuyu,[18] que quiere decir señores de las cuatro partidas del mundo, porque pensaban de cierto que no había más mundo que éste, y a esta causa enviaban siempre desde aquí mensajeros a todas partes para que concurriese toda la gente a la cabeza, como hizo mi padre ahora en esta junta que arriba se dijo, porque por la mucha [gente][19] que había, que a quererla numerar sería imposible, decían todo esto a tanto que con haberse consumido en Cajamarca y en lo de Quisquis arriba dicho, sin número de gente y en otras muchas guazábaras y refriegas, que por evitar prolijidad callo, se juntaron a esta junta de solo los principales más de diez mil, y desde que así estuvieron juntos y puestos ante mi padre, como le vieron estar de aquella suerte, movidos con gran llanto dijeron:

Sapay Inga, ¿qué corazón hay en el mundo que viéndote a ti nuestro rey, que de esa suerte estás tan afligido y congojado con dolor no se haga pedazos y de lástima no se derrita? Por cierto, Sapay Inga, tú lo erraste mucho en meter en tu tierra semejante gente, mas pues que ya ello está hecho y no se puede remediar por otra suerte, aparejados estamos estos tus vasallos a hacer de muy entera voluntad todo lo que por ti nos fuere mandado. Y no decimos nosotros tan solamente eso que tú nos mandas que juntemos, que en comparación de lo que te debemos y somos obligados no es nada; y si no bastase eso que tú dices y fuese necesario que para redimir tu vejación, nos venderíamos a nosotros mismos y nuestras mujeres e hijos, lo haríamos de muy entera voluntad por tu servicio. Mira, señor, cuando mandas que se junte esto, que al punto y hora que mandares será justo y cumplido tu mandado sin faltar en ello un punto, aunque sepamos arañarlos con nuestras propias manos debajo de la tierra.

Mi padre Mango Inga Yupangui[20] *viendo la gran voluntad con que sus vasallos se le ofrecían a hacer lo que les rogaba, se lo agradeció mucho y dijo:*

Por cierto,[21] apoes —*que quiere decir señores*— en gran obligación me habéis echado por la gran voluntad que me mostráis de querer redimir la vejación en que estoy puesto, y para ello ofrecer vuestras personas y haciendas, y os doy mi palabra, como quien soy, que no perdáis nada en el negocio, que si yo no muero yo os lo pagaré, que pues yo me lo tomé por mis manos metiendo tan mala gente en mi tierra, yo me lo llevaré. Gran placer me haréis en daros la mayor prisa que pudiéreis en la junta de esto que os digo porque recibo grandísima pena en verme así preso y maltratado y porque no me molesten más éstos os será necesario que le hincháis aquel bohío que está allí —*el cual era una casa grande*— de oro y plata, que quizá viendo eso cesarán de molestarme.

Los capitanes y gente respondieron a una voz:

Señor Sapay Inga, para lo que te debemos no es nada eso. Luego se hará como tú lo mandas.

Y así se despidieron todos a buscar lo que mi padre les había mandado, los cuales volvieron en breve tiempo con lo que les había mandado que juntasen, y junto y puesto de la manera que mi padre había ordenado. Otro día el dicho mi padre envió a llamar a los españoles, los cuales vinieron luego a su llamado.

De cómo llegaron los españoles en casa de Mango Inga cuando estaba preso y lo que allí aconteció con su llegada

Llegado que fueron los españoles a donde mi padre estaba preso y aherrojado con grillos a sus pies, le saludaron según otras veces solían. Y mi padre como los vio venir y llegar a su casa les hizo el acatamiento acostumbrado, a los cuales comenzó a hablar en esta manera preguntándoles lo primero por el Machu Capito que no estaba allí a la sazón. El cual dijo así a Hernando Pizarro:

Apo, [¿]dónde está el Macho Capito?

Y Hernando Pizarro respondió diciendo que quedaba en casa, algo mal dispuesto, y mi padre, como le deseaba ver, dijo:

Pues, ¿no le enviaremos a llamar?

Y Gonzalo Pizarro y los demás dijeron:

En hora buena Mango Inga, váyanle a llamar y bueno sería que le fuesen a llamar de tu parte.

Y así mi padre envió algunos de sus capitanes a llamarle, y el gobernador respondió a los capitanes diciendo que se hallaba mal dispuesto por entonces, que en estando algo mejor, él iría a ver lo que mi padre mandaba, y mi padre, como vio que no venía, dijo a los españoles estas palabras:

Parlamento del Inga a los españoles estando en la prisión, cuando les dio el tesoro por la primera vez

Señores, muchos días ha que me hacéis gran desaguisado en tratarme de la manera que me tratáis, no os habiendo yo dado ocasión para ello; en especial habiéndolo hecho tan bien con vosotros en dejaros entrar en mi tierra y traeros con tanta honra y aparato a mi pueblo y casa y daros con tanta voluntad de lo que en mi tierra y casa tenía,[22] lo cual si vosotros queréis juzgarlo, no fue tan poco que no fueron más de dos millones de oro y plata que yo sé que vuestro rey no los tiene juntos. Y bien sabéis cómo estuvo en mi mano el entrar vosotros en la tierra o no, porque no queriéndolo yo, que bastantes erais vosotros ni otros diez tantos más a poder entrar en ella. No sabéis cuánto poderío de gente yo tengo en toda mi tierra y cuántas fortalezas y fuerzas con ella hay. Acordaros deberíais con cuánta voluntad yo os envié a llamar sin vosotros me lo hacer saber y cómo en señal de amistad, por lo que me dijeron que erais viracochas y enviados por el Tecsi Viracochan, os envié al camino lo que pude. Acordaros deberíais también cómo llegados que fuiste[is] a este pueblo, os hice proveer de servicio y mandé juntar la gente de toda mi tierra para que os tributasen, y en pago de todo esto y de hacerlo yo con tanta afición y voluntad me habéis preso y puesto ahora de la manera que estoy so color de que me quería alzar contra vosotros y mataros, no teniendo yo de ello tal pensamiento. Bien entiendo que la codicia os ha cegado para hacer tan gran desatino y mediante ella me habéis tratado de esta suerte. Nunca yo pensaba que gente que tan buenas muestras daba al principio, que se jactaba de hijos del Viracochan, había de hacer tal cosa. Por vida vuestra que me soltéis y entendáis que yo no os deseo dar pena, sino antes todo placer para hartar vuestra codicia que tanta hambre tenéis por plata, ahí os darán lo que pedís, y mirad que os doy esto con aditamento que a mí ni a gente ninguna de mi tierra habéis de molestar ni maltratar perpetuamente. Y no penséis que os doy esto de miedo que tenga de vosotros sino de mi voluntad mera, porque ¿qué miedo había yo de haber de vosotros estando toda la tierra debajo de mi poderío y mando? Y si yo quisiese en muy breve tiempo os podrían desbaratar a todos y estas prisiones que me habéis echado, no penséis que las tengo en nada, que si yo hubiera querido muy fácilmente me hubiera soltado de ellas, pero no lo he hecho porque entendáis que antes mi negocio emana de amor que de temor, y mediante éste os he hecho y hago el tratamiento que os he relatado. De aquí adelante todos tengamos paz y vivamos de amor y compañía, y si no la hubiere, bien sabéis que daréis pena al Viracochan —*que quiere decir Dios*— y a vuestro rey y yo no recibiré mucho contento.

Y como mi padre acabase el parlamento ya dicho, todos los españoles que vinieron con Hernando Pizarro y Gonzalo Pizarro y Juan Pizarro le agradecieron mucho lo que les había dicho y más lo que les daba, así del tesoro como de las demás joyas, y todos juntamente le rindieron las gracias, de esta manera:

Modo y manera como rindieron los españoles las gracias a Mango Inga del tesoro y joyas que les dio cuando le soltaron

Señor Mango Inga, entendido tenemos todos los que aquí estamos y el señor gobernador don Francisco Pizarro tiene lo mismo, que mediante ser Vuestra Merced quien es el hijo de tal padre como fue Guaina Capac, tenemos nosotros la tierra que hoy poseemos y estamos de la manera que estamos, con tanto contento y regocijo en estar en ella, que a no ser Vuestra Merced quien es de sangre real, ni tuviéramos la tierra que tenemos ni poseeríamos las riquezas que de su tan franca mano habemos recibido y poseemos. Pleg[a a] nuestro señor, Dios todopoderoso, a quien Vuestra Merced llama Viracochan, nuestro padre, que por quien su Divina Majestad es tan buena voluntad, como es la que Vuestra Merced nos ha mostrado y obras que nos ha hecho, le pague trayéndole a conocimiento de quién su Sacratísima Majestad es, para que conociéndole le ame y amándole le posea y poseyéndole se goce con él en su reino para siempre, así como nosotros nos gozamos poseyendo la merced que Vuestra Merced nos hace.

Hernando Pizarro, dando la palabra por todos, dijo así:

Todos estos caballeros y yo hemos recibido sumo contento con la merced que Vuestra Merced nos ha hecho en todo, quedamos en obligación de lo servir toda nuestra vida y protestamos de que ahora ni en ningún tiempo no habiendo demasiada ocasión, estos caballeros ni yo le daremos ninguna pena.

Acabado este razonamiento y hacimiento de gracias de los españoles a mi padre, el dicho mi padre les mandó entregar el tesoro que les tenía aparejado, los cuales lo recibieron en sí y no llegaron a ello hasta dar parte de lo que les había sucedido al gobernador. Y así sin hacer más, algunos de ellos le fueron luego a llamar para que lo uno, diese las gracias de semejante tesoro a mi padre y lo otro, se hallase presente al recibir y partir, porque según después pareció, por ruegos del gobernador habían los españoles ido a soltar a mi padre de la cárcel donde estaba, por que ellos no fueran, si ellos de él no fueran mandados. Y así para que viese cómo estaba ya suelto mi padre le fueron a llamar algunos de ellos, el cual entendiendo lo que pasaba y que mi padre estaba ya suelto luego vino, y llegado que fue saludó a mi padre en esta manera:

Llegada del Gobernador a la casa de Mango Inga

Dios guarde a Vuestra Merced, señor Mango Inga. Por haber estado algo mal dispuesto, no vine juntamente con estos caballeros a besar las manos a Vuestra Merced, de que he estado con alguna pena por no haber hecho lo que yo tanto deseaba, que era verme con Vuestra Merced,[23] pero ya que hasta aquí ha habido falta que ha sido como dicho tengo por mi indisposición, de aquí adelante no la habrá. Gran pena he recibido de la congoja que me dicen Vuestra Merced ha recibido en su prisión, en especial si fue sin culpa, lo cual si ha sido es de recibir mayor; que bien creo que según Vuestra Merced es de bueno, es así. Y teniendo esto entendido, como siempre lo tuve de su bondad, rogué a estos caballeros que no molestasen tanto a Vuestra Merced, porque entendido tenía yo que quien con tanta voluntad nos trajo a su tierra y tan de pleno nos la entregó con los tesoros que en ella había, no se había de mover tan fácilmente por ninguna cosa, a hacer cosa que no debiese. Suplico a Vuestra Merced, por me hacer merced, no tenga pena, que estos caballeros y yo de aquí adelante procuraremos de no se la dar más, antes tener el respeto que a semejante persona como Vuestra Merced conviene.

Paréceme que todavía hace Vuestra Merced con estos caballeros y conmigo lo que suele hacer, como parece por la merced de tan gran riqueza y tesoro como hoy les ha dado. Por la parte que a mí me toca de ser su gobernador y por la que de su Majestad del quinto le ha de caber, beso las manos a Vuestra Merced, que yo sé que ha de recibir tanto contento como con los demás que hasta aquí dado por Vuestra Merced le he enviado. Quedo por esta merced en tanta obligación, que por palabra no la sabré significar.

Respuesta de Mango Inga al Gobernador

Apo —*que quiere decir Señor*— vienes en hora buena. Muchos días ha que te he deseado ver y no sé qué ha sido la causa por que no me has querido dar este contento, pues tanto yo lo he deseado y te he enviado a llamar, no sé cuántas veces, para quejarme a ti de estos tus soldados. Y por les aplacar a ellos no me has querido dar a mí contento, pues por cierto que te lo he deseado yo dar y aún procurado. Mal me pagáis vosotros mi tan buen deseo y obras. Estos tus soldados me han molestado y fatigado sin yo merecerlo, teniéndome aquí aherrojado con hierros como si yo fuera su llama —*que quiere decir carnero*— más me parece esta molestia codiciosa que hazaña poderosa. Porque a la clara se ve que me han tenido antes preso por su hambrienta codicia, que por poderío que sobre mí pudiesen tener. Y como tú has visto y de todo eres testigo, no me vencisteis vosotros a mí por fuerza de armas sino por hermosas palabras, que si no me dijerais que erais hijos del Viracochan y que él os enviaba y yo por vuestras insignias de tantos enlabiamientos como conmigo usasteis no lo pensara, no sé yo cómo lo hubierais en la entrada de mi tierra. Y por haberlo yo hecho con vosotros de la manera que lo he hecho me tratáis de esta manera. Gentil pago me dais por tan buena obra como yo os he hecho. Aquí he dado a estos tus soldados no sé qué oro y plata por sus importunaciones. Hazlo repartir allá como a ti te pareciere y mira que, pues eres tan buen apo, que mandes que de aquí adelante no me den más enojo pues yo no se lo deseo dar a ellos, que te hago saber de cierto que si ellos me lo dan que yo procuraré de dárselo de tal suerte que quizá les pese.

El gobernador, oída la respuesta que mi padre le dio, holgase mucho con ella y mandó recibir aquel tesoro a los españoles, diciendo:

Recíbase eso que con tanta buena voluntad nos hace merced el señor Mango Inga Yupangui, él cual no lo ha de ahora el hacernos semejantes mercedes sino de muy otras. Y miren vuestras mercedes, señores los que aquí están presentes, que tenemos ya mucho recibido del Señor Mango Inga después que estamos en su tierra y que se lo pagamos muy mal según la voluntad con que nos lo da. De aquí en adelante por su vida que le respeten y tengan en mucho, pues lo merece.

Todos los soldados, con el contento que recibieron con el don del tesoro que mi padre les había dado, respondieron con gran gozo al gobernador estas palabras:

Respuesta de Hernando Pizarro y Gonzalo Pizarro y Juan Pizarro y de los demás soldados al Gobernador

Por cierto Vuestra Señoría tiene muy gran razón en reprehendernos y afearnos semejante cosa que esa, porque si hubiera miramiento en nosotros no lo habíamos de haber hecho de esta suerte sino agradecer el bien a quien nos lo hace. De aquí adelante se hará como Vuestra Señoría lo manda.

Acabadas todas estas razones de una parte y de otra, todos los españoles repartieron aquel tesoro por cabezas, dando a cada uno según su calidad, lo cual repartió Hernando Pizarro como principal autor en aquel caso porque él había sido el que había preso a mi padre, el cual tesoro repartieron a costales, porque según era la cantidad se tardaron mucho en repartirlo por peso. Y desde que hubieron ya repartido el tesoro entre sí, mi padre en señal de agradecimiento al gobernador, le dijo estas palabras.

Apo, paréceme que tú has sido parte para que estos tus soldados me hayan soltado de la prisión en que estaba, la cual pareció ser sin culpa. Ruégote que no te vayas tan presto sino que en señal de la confederación de nuestra amistad hagamos juntos colación, que yo espero que de mi parte no ha de quebrar lo por mí prometido.

Y el gobernador, por le dar contento a mi padre y porque la demanda era justa y no dañosa la hubo por bien y sentándose todos en la sala donde mi padre estaba, recibieron colación con gran regocijo y chacota. Recibida la colación y confederados mi padre y los españoles se fueron a sus casas cada uno con la ración que le cupo de la empresa del tesoro; de creer es que irían acompañados al gobernador y que allá se regocijarían entre sí cada uno con lo que llevaban, el cual regocijo, según adelante se verá, no les duró mucho porque como el demonio sea tan malo como es, y amigo de disensiones y diferencias, nunca para.

Revuelta de Gonzalo Pizarro contra el Inga

No pasaron, según mi padre me dijo, tres meses cuando la envidia, que es enemiga de toda bondad, reinó en Gonzalo Pizarro, lo uno por ver que a su hermano le habían dado tanta cantidad de oro y plata por no más de que había preso a mi padre con codicia cuando era corregidor, y lo otro porque como se vio con vara y mando por la ausencia del marqués don Francisco Pizarro, que a la sazón se había partido para Lima despidiéndose de mi padre con gran amor y amistad estando siempre conformes, quiso mostrar fausto y autoridad con la vara a costa de mi padre, achacándole que se quería alzar, diciendo que una noche había de dar sobre ellos estando durmiendo. Y con este achaque falso el dicho Gonzalo Pizarro se procuró de armar y tomar consigo a su hermano Juan Pizarro y a otros para ir a prender a mi padre, los cuales todos se fueron a la casa donde mi padre estaba holgándose con toda su gente en una fiesta que a la sazón hacía, y llegados que fueron, mi padre no sospechando la traición que tenía armada, lo recibió con gran benevolencia y afabilidad y ellos, como llevaban la traición dañada, aguardaron a que se saliese a alguna cosa a su casa y luego fueron tras de él y en ella al tiempo que quiso salir le prendieron, diciendo él, Gonzalo Pizarro, estas palabras:

Segunda Prisión de Mango Inga por Gonzalo Pizarro

Señor Mango Inga, el otro día quedaste[is] con mi hermano Hernando Pizarro de no urdir ni tratar más negocios y paréceme que no habéis guardado lo que prometisteis, que informados estamos cómo tenéis concertado de dar sobre nosotros esta noche y para eso tenéis junta tanta gente. Por tanto, sed preso por el rey y no penséis que ha de ser ahora como el otro día que dijisteis que no teníais en nada todas nuestras prisiones, ahora lo experimentaréis si se quiebran o no.

Y luego de manos a boca, mandó traer Gonzalo Pizarro unos grillos y una cadena con que aherrojasen a su sabor a mi padre, los cuales grillos y cadenas mandó que luego se le echasen, y mi padre viendo que con tanto vituperio le querían parar de aquella suerte, se quiso defender, diciendo:

Respuesta de Mango Inga

¿En que andáis aquí conmigo cada triquite haciéndome befas? ¿Vosotros no sabéis que yo soy hijo del sol e hijo del Viracochan como vosotros os jactáis? ¿Soy quiera quiera [sic] o algún indio de baja suerte? ¿Queréis escandalizar toda la tierra y que os hagan pedazos a todos? No me maltratéis que no os he hecho ¿por qué pensáis que se me da nada por vuestras prisiones? ¿No las tengo en lo que huello?

Gonzalo Pizarro y sus alféreces, como vieron a mi padre con tanta furia, [ar]remetieron todos contra él para le echar la cadena al pescuezo, diciendo:

No os defendáis, Mango Inga, mira que os ataremos pies y manos de arte que no sea bastante cuantos hay en el mundo a desataros porque si os prendemos es en nombre y voz del emperador (y no de nuestra autoridad y que lo fuera). Nos habéis de dar ahora mucho más oro y plata que el otro día y más me habéis de dar a la señora Coya Cura Ocllo, vuestra hermana, para mi mujer.

Y luego incontinente todos de mancomún como allí estaban le echaron la cadena al pescuezo y los grillos a los pies.

Parlamento de Mango Inga [] estando en prisión [por la segunda vez]

Mi padre, como se vio así atado y preso de aquella manera con tanta igno-
minia y deshonra, dijo con mucha lástima estas palabras:

¿Por ventura soy yo perro o carnero o algún oyua vuestro que porque no me huya me atáis de esta manera? ¿Soy ladrón o he hecho alguna traición al Viracochan, a vuestro rey? Sí que no, pues si no soy perro ni ninguna cosa de las que dicho tengo, ¿qué es la causa porque de tal manera me tratáis? Verdaderamente ahora digo y me afirmo en ello, que vosotros sois antes hijos de supay que criados de Viracochan, cuanto y más hijos porque si como arriba dicho tengo vosotros fuereis, no digo yo hijos verdaderos, sino criados del Viracochan, lo uno, no me tratarais de la manera que me tratáis, mas antes mirarais a quién yo soy y cúyo hijo y el poderío que he tenido y tengo, el cual por vuestro respeto he dejado, y lo otro, miraréis que no ha habido en toda mi tierra después que entrasteis en ella cosa ninguna alta y baja, pequeña ni grande, de que se os haya negado. Mas antes si riquezas yo tenía, vosotros las poseéis, si gente a vosotros sirven —así hombre como mujeres, chicos y grandes y menores— si tierras las mejores que en mi tierra hay, debajo de vuestro poderío están, pues, ¿qué cosa hay en el mundo de que hayáis tenido necesidad que yo no la haya proveído a vosotros ingratos? Cierto sois indignos de toda contrición.

Gonzalo Pizarro y Juan Pizarro y los demás que con ellos vinieron, no
haciendo caso de lo que mi padre les decía, con un género de desdén dijeron:

Sosiegue, sosiegue, señor Sapay Inga, y repose un poco que está ahora con mucha cólera. Mañana hablaremos largo, en todo procure dar orden cómo se junta mucha plata y oro y acuerde de darnos la Coya que la deseo mucho haber.

Dijo Gonzalo Pizarro. Acabadas de decir estas buenas razones los españoles
a mi padre, se fueron a sus casas a comer porque este prendimiento había sido
a la mañana. Idos que fueron los españoles a sus posadas y dejando buenas
guardas que guardasen a mi padre, luego toda la gente que estaba en una plaza,
llamada Pumacurco, de donde mi padre se levantó aquella mañana de comer
con todos ellos para ir a su casa, a algo que le convenía, cuando le prendieron
los españoles, vino con gran sobresalto a la casa donde mi padre estaba a ver por
qué causa no había venido a la pampa en tanta distancia de tiempo y como lle-
garon a la puerta hallaron todos los criados de mi padre alborotados y como llo-
rando por ver a su amo preso de aquella suerte. Los capitanes y gente que así
venían a saber lo que pasaba, todos enmudecieron haciendo entre sí grandes
exclamaciones y unos a otros como maravillándose se preguntaban:

¿qué es esto? ¿qué es esto?

Y estando así alborotados, entraron adentro los capitanes más principales de toda la tierra a certificarse de veras cómo pasaba el caso y a ver qué hacía mi padre, y estando más adentro, que les fue dado para ellos licencia, sin la cual nadie podía entrar, llegaron a donde mi padre estaba preso y de la manera arriba dicho y viéndolo todos de aquella manera hicieron un gran llanto que fue cierto cosa de ver, adonde llama[n]do todos a alta voz uno de ellos llamado Vila Oma, persona que gobernaba la tierra como mi padre, como general de toda ella, dijo como conquistándose e increpando a mi padre de esta manera:

Sapay Inga, ¿qué es esto en que andan estos viracochas? Hoy te prenden, mañana te sueltan, parece que andan contigo jugando a juego de niños. Pero no me maravillo que te traten de esta suerte, pues tú te lo quisiste, metiendo en tu tierra de tu voluntad, sin nuestro parecer, gente tan mala. Yo te digo que si tú me [hubieses] deja[do] a mí cuando ellos llegaron a Cajamarca, que nunca ellos llegar[í]an donde tú estás ahora porque yo y Challco Chima, aunque ellos no quisieran, con la gente de nuestro bando les estorbáramos la entrada y no creo yo que nos hubiera ido tan mal como nos ha ido por ser tú tan bueno. Porque si tú nos dijeras que eran viracochas y enviados por el Hatun Viracochan[24] —*que quiere decir gran dios*— y [nos] mandaras que les obedeciésemos y respetáramos por tal, es porque así lo hacías tú; poca necesidad teníamos nosotros ser vejados y molestados de la suerte que ahora estamos desposeídos de nuestras haciendas, de nuestras chacaras y vernos vasallos de quien no conocemos, tan opresos, tan fatigados que hasta con nuestras capas nos hacen limpiar la suciedad de los caballos. Mira señor, hasta cuánta bajeza nos has hecho venir por quererlo tú. Y pues tú has querido, no te maravilles que te traten de esa manera, bien sabes que aún cuando tú saliste a Vilcacunga a recibirlos [yo] [s]e los estorbaba. Yo te fui a la mano muchas veces sobre que no les metieses en tu tierra y aún si se te acuerda, te dije cuando tuvimos nueva que habían llegado a la tierra, que yo iría por la posta con diez o doce mil indios y los haría pedazos a todos y tú nunca me dejaste, sino antes, "calla, calla que son viracochas o sus hijos", como si no barruntáramos nosotros que gente de esta manera, que venía de tan lejos tierra, que antes venía a mandar que a obedecer. Yo y toda tu gente tenemos de lo pasado gran pena y de verte de la manera que estás, gran compasión; y te parece porque entiendas que soy el que ser solía, dame licencia que yo te soltaré y a estos barbudos los acabaré bien breve, porque gente tienes tú en tu tierra que me ayudará, que bien sabes tú que en toda la tierra arriba y abajo ni al través, después de ti no hay a quien más respetan que a mí, pues sobre todas soy general.

Acabado que hubo de relatar a mi padre lo arriba dicho, este capitán Vila Oma juntamente con otro llamado Ticoc, su compañero, se volvieron a los españoles, que a la sazón allí estaban presentes, y con rostros alterados y severos dijeron estas palabras:

Increpación hecha por los capitanes del Inga a los españoles, sobre el mal tratamiento que hacían a su rey y su señor

¿Qué andáis vosotros aquí con nuestro Inga de acá por allá cada día, hoy prendiéndolo, mañana molestándole y ese otro día haciéndole befas, qué os ha hecho este hombre? ¿Así le pagáis la buena obra que os hizo en meternos a su tierra contra nuestra voluntad? ¿Qué queréis de él? ¿Qué más os puede hacer de lo que ha hecho? ¿No os dejó entrar en su tierra con toda paz y sosiego y con mucha honra no os envió a llamar a Cajamarca? ¿A los mensajeros que le enviasteis, no os los envió muy honrados con mucha plata y oro y con mucha gente no fueron y vinieron en hamacas trayéndoles su gente a cuestas en Cajamarca? ¿No tomasteis dos casas grandes de oro y plata que le pertenecían y más lo que os dio Ataguallpa que todo era de mi Inga y lo que él os envió de aquí a Cajamarca que fue gran cantidad de oro y plata? De Cajamarca a este pueblo en ciento y treinta leguas que hay de camino de allá acá, ¿no os hicieron todo buen tratamiento dándoos muchos refrescos y gente que os trajesen? ¿Él mismo no os salió a recibir al camino seis leguas de aquí? En Jaquijahuana, por vuestro respeto, ¿no quemó la persona más principal que tenía en toda su tierra que fue Challco Chima?, llegados que fuiste[is] aquí ¿no os dio casas y asientos y criados y mujeres y sementeras?, ¿no mandó llamar a toda su gente para que os tributasen?, ¿no os han tributado sí que sí? El otro día, cuando le prendisteis, por redimir su vejación ¿no os dio una casa llena de oro y plata? A nosotros los principales y a toda la gente ¿no habéis quitado las mujeres nuestras e hijos e hijas y a todo callarnos porque él lo quiere por bien y por no darle pena?, nuestra gente ¿no os sirve hasta limpiar con sus capas la suciedad de los caballos y de vuestras casas, ¿qué más queréis?, todas cuantas veces habéis dicho de acá oro, de acá plata, de acá oro, de acá plata, junta esto, junta esto otro, ¿no lo ha hecho siempre hasta daros sus mismos criados que os sirvan? ¿Qué más pedís a este hombre? Vosotros ¿no le engañasteis diciendo que veníais por el viento por mandado del Viracochan, que erais sus hijos? Y decíais que veníais a servir al Inga, a quererle mucho, a tratarle como a vuestras personas mismas a él y a toda su gente. Bien sabéis vosotros y lo veis si lo queréis mirar atentamente, que en todo habéis faltado y que en lugar de tratarle como publicasteis al principio le habéis molestado y molestáis cada credo sin merecerlo ni haberos dado la menor ocasión del mundo. ¿De dónde pensáis que ha de sacar tanto oro y plata como vosotros le pedís? Pues os ha dado hasta quitarnos a nosotros nuestras joyas, todo cuanto en su tierra tenía. ¿Qué pensáis que os ha de dar ahora por la prisión en que le tenéis preso? ¿De dónde ha de sacar esto que le pedís ni aun nada si no lo tiene ni tiene qué daros? Toda la gente de esta tierra está muy escandalizada y amedrentada de tal manera de ver vuestras cosas que no saben ya qué decir ni a dónde se pueden ir, porque lo uno, se ven desposeídos de su rey, lo otro, de sus mujeres, de sus hijos, de sus casas, de sus haciendas, de sus tierras, finalmente de todo cuanto poseían, que cierto están en tanta tribulación que no les resta sino ahorcarse o dar al través con todo y aun me lo han dicho a mí muchas veces. Por tanto, señores, lo más acertado que a mí me parece sería que dejaseis ya descansar a mi Sapay Inga, pues por vuestra causa está con tanta necesidad y trabajo y le soltaréis de la prisión en que está por que estos sus indios no estén con tanta congoja.

Respuesta de los españoles a Vila Oma

¿Quién te manda a ti hablar con tanta autoridad al corregidor del rey? ¿Sabes tú qué gente somos nosotros los españoles? Calla, sino por vida de su Majestad que si te arrebato que os haga un juego a ti y a tus compañeros que se os acuerde para toda vuestra vida. Juro a tal si no callas que te abrase vivo y te haga pedazos. Mira quién le manda a él parlar con tanta autoridad delante de mí.

Esto dijo Gonzalo Pizarro por meter miedo, así a Vila Oma como a los demás que estaban presentes.

El cual tornó luego a replicar sobre lo dicho, diciendo:

Acabaos prisa a juntar esa plata y oro que os he mandado sino yo os juro a tal que de la prisión no me salga vuestro rey hasta que se junte aunque sea de aquí a un año, por eso no me repliquéis más ni me representéis hazañas: de acá fue de acullá vino.

Acabadas todas estas cosas entre los españoles y aquel capitán Vila Oma, los españoles le dijeron yéndose a sus casas y él se vino a mi padre a decirle por extensión todo lo que les había dicho y la respuesta que ellos le dieron también, y mi padre, como los vio de aquella manera y que con tanta lástima se condolían de su trabajo, les dijo de la manera siguiente:

Hijos y hermanos míos, bien entiendo que yo me tengo mi merecido por haber consentido a esta gente entrar en esta tierra y también veo la razón que de quejaros de mí tenéis, más pues ya no hay otro remedio, por vida vuestra que con la más brevedad que podáis juntar algo con que esta tan agraviada vejación redima y doleos de ver a vuestro rey atado, como a perro, con cadena al pescuezo, y como esclavo y cosa fugitiva, grillos a los pies.

Los capitanes y gente, con la gran compasión que les dio de ver a mi padre de aquella manera tan mal tratado, no tuvieron qué responder sino con todo silencio y amortiguamiento de ojos, unos en pos de otros se salieron a buscar cuál más podría lo que mi padre les mandaba por si pudiesen con mucha brevedad soltarle, pero no pudieron tan presto que no pasaron más de dos meses primero que pudiesen juntar lo que juntaron. Lo cual fue quitándose los unos a los otros sus dijes y trajes que traían en sus personas, de los cuales según que fue la cantidad de la gente que lo juntó, hinchieron de todo ello un bohío muy grande, habiendo entre ello algunas vajillas que a mi padre le habían quedado en su casa para servicio de su persona. Y ya junto todo, por el acosamiento tan grande que aquellos hombres le acosaban cada vez, diciendo:

No se junta. Si [no] se junta esta plata no acabáis. ¿Hasta cuándo nos habéis de hacer esperar? Acabad ya.

Con estas y otras palabras que fatigaban a mi padre de continuo, les envió a llamar diciendo que para que acabasen aquellos ya de molestarle les llamasen porque les quería dar aquello que tenía junto. Y así los fueron a llamar, los cuales vinieron luego y llegados que fueron a donde mi padre estaba preso le saludaron diciendo:

Dios os guarde, señor Sapay Inga ¿qué es lo que nos mandáis y por qué nos habéis enviado a llamar?

Mi padre, como los vio así venir, porque entendía que ya se llegaba la hora en que le habían de soltar de las prisiones en que estaba, dijo a los españoles estas palabras:

Parlamento del Inga a los españoles

Apocona —*que quiere decir señores*— los días pasados cuando me prendisteis la otra vez os dije que no era posible que fueseis hijos del Viracochan pues tan mal tratabais a quien tanto bien os ha deseado hacer y ha hecho y hace y os di las razones bien equivalentes para ello: y ahora que esta segunda vez tan pesadamente y tan sin piedad habéis agraviado mi molestia, doblándome las prisiones y tiempo, pues ha, ay, más de dos meses que estoy preso y aherrojado como perro, no dejaré de deciros que lo habéis hecho no como cristianos e hijos que decís que sois del Viracochan sino como siervos del Supay, cuyas pisadas vosotros seguís, haciendo mal a quien os hace bien. Y aun peores sois vosotros, que él cual no busca plata ni oro porque no la ha menester y vosotros buscáosla y queréosla sacar por fuerza de donde no la hay. Peores sois que los yungas, los cuales por un poquillo de plata matarían a su madre y a su padre y negarían a todo lo del mundo. Y así vosotros, no se os acordando de tanto bien que de mí habéis recibido, amándoos yo con tanta voluntad y deseando vuestra amistad, me habéis negado por un poco de plata, y tratándome por causa de ella peor que tratáis a vuestros perros, por donde parece que tenéis en más un poco de plata que la amistad de todos los hombres del mundo, pues por amor de ella habéis perdido la mía y la de todos de mi tierra. Pues por vuestra importunación y demasiada codicia yo y ellos nos habemos desposeído de nuestras joyas y riquezas, las cuales vosotros nos habéis tomado a puras fuerzas y molestias y agras importunaciones. Yo os digo que, a lo que yo entiendo, no os ha de lucir mucho esto: que a mí y a mi gente nos tomáis tan sin justicia y razón; hayan juntado esos pobres indios con harto trabajo no sé qué. Mandadlo recibir y acaba ya de quitarme de esta prisión.

Todo esto decía mi padre con mucha lástima y aun con lágrimas de sus ojos por verse tratado de aquella suerte.

La manera de cómo los españoles quisieron soltar a Mango Inga de la segunda prisión y de cómo les dio la Coya

Pues como los españoles oyeron lo que mi padre les dijo, con alguna alegría y placer por la plata que estaba junta, dijeron que se holgaban mucho de ello, y haciendo algún ademán de quererlo ir a soltar, lo cual todo era fingido; salió muy de presto Gonzalo Pizarro y dijo:

¿Qué es? ¡Voto a tal, no suelte! que primero nos ha de dar a la señora Coya, su hermana, que el otro día vimos, ¿qué prisa tenéis vosotros de quererlo soltar sin que se lo manden? ¡Ea, señor Mango Inga, venga la señora Coya! que lo de la plata bueno está, que eso es lo que principalmente deseábamos.

La manera del dar de la Coya

Mi padre, como los vio que con tanta importunidad le pedían la Coya y que no se podía evadir de ellos de otra suerte, mandó sacar una india muy hermosa, peinada y muy bien aderezada para dársela en lugar de la Coya que ellos pedían y ellos como la vieron, desconociendo la Coya dijeron que no les parecía a ellos que era aquella la Coya que ellos pedían sino otra india por ahí, que les diese la Coya y acabase de negocios. Y mi padre por tentarlos hizo sacar otras más de veinte casi de aquella suerte unas buenas y otras mejores y ninguna les contentaba. Ya que le pareció a mi padre que era tiempo, mandó que saliese una —la más principal mujer que en su casa tenía— compañera de su hermana la Coya, la cual le parecía casi en todo, en especial si se vestía como ella, la cual se llamaba Inguill —que quiere decir flor— y que aquella les diesen, la cual salió ahí en presencia de todos vestida y aderezada ni más ni menos que Coya —que quiere decir reina— y como los españoles la viesen salir de aquella suerte, tan bien aderezada y tan hermosa dijeron con mucho regocijo y contento:

Esta sí, ésta sí. Pese tal es la señora Coya, que no las otras.

Gonzalo Pizarro, como era el que más deseaba de todos, pues particularmente la había pretendido, dijo a mi padre estas palabras:

Señor Mango Inga, si ella es para mí, dáseme luego porque ya no lo puedo sufrir.

Y mi padre como la tenía bien catequizada dijo:

Mucho de enhorabuena hace lo que quisiereis.

Y él así delante de todos, sin más mirar a cosa, se fue para ella a la besar y abrazar como si fuera su mujer legítima, de lo cual se rió mucho mi padre y los demás puso en admiración, y la Inguill en espanto y pavor, como se vio abrazar de gente que no conocía daba gritos como una loca diciendo que no quería arrostrar a semejante gente, mas antes se huía y ni por pensamiento los quería ver. Y mi padre como la vio tan zahareña y que tanto rehusaba la ida con los españoles, por ver que en aquella estaba el ser él suelto o no, la mandó con mucha furia que se fuese con ellos. Y ella, viendo a mi padre tan enojado, más de miedo que de otra cosa hizo lo que le mandaba y fuese con ellos.

Cómo Gonzalo Pizarro recibió el tesoro y la Coya de mano de Mango Inga y de cómo en señal de amistad se fue a comer con él

Él, Gonzalo Pizarro, la recibió en sí y mandó que quitasen a mi padre las prisiones y suelto recibieron el tesoro y lo repartieron entre sí. El cual repartido, rogó Gonzalo Pizarro a mi padre diciendo que pues les había dado tantas cosas así de oro como de plata y sobre todo a la señora Coya para sí tanto deseada, que le rogaba mucho para señal de que la amistad había de durar mucho entre los dos por causa del cuñadazgo, les hiciese merced de irse con él y con aquellos caballeros a su casa a recibir servicio en ella, la cual se ofrecía desde entonces por suya. Y mi padre, lo uno por el deseo que tenía ya de salir fuera y ver el campo, y lo otro por darle aquel contento, pensando que por aquella vía había de durar mucho tiempo la amistad con los españoles, hizo lo que Gonzalo Pizarro le rogó y se fue con él y con sus compañeros a comer aquel día en su casa, adonde hubo gran fiesta y gran regocijo. Y desde que hubieron comido los unos con los otros, el dicho mi padre dijo que se quería volver a su casa porque era ya tarde y los españoles le acompañaron hasta allá, en la cual dejándole con mucho contento ellos se volvieron a las suyas. Entienda el que esto leyere que cuando estos negocios pasaron del dar de la

Coya y la prisión de las cadenas y grillos, el marqués don Francisco Pizarro ya era ido a Lima y a la sazón no estaba en el Cuzco y por eso no piense nadie que en todo se halló.

Pasadas todas aquellas cosas de la prisión segunda y el dar de la Inguill en lugar de la Coya a Gonzalo Pizarro, no pasaron muchos días que Gonzalo Pizarro, digo que mi padre Mango Inga, hizo una fiesta muy principal en la cual se horadaba las orejas y en esta fiesta nosotros los Ingas solemos hacer la mayor fiesta que hacemos en todo el año porque entonces nos dan mucho nombre y nuevo nombre del que teníamos antes. Que tira casi esta ceremonia a lo que los cristianos hacen cuando se confirman. En la cual fiesta mi padre salió con toda la autoridad real conforme a nuestro uso, llevando delante sus cetros reales y el uno de ellos como más principal era de oro macizo y con sus borlas de lo mismo; llevando todos los demás que con él iban juntamente cada uno el suyo, los cuales eran la mitad de plata y la mitad de cobre, que serían más de mil todos unos y otros los que iban a rebautizar, que en nuestro uso llamamos vacaroc. Y estando que estuvieron todos nuestros indios y los españoles que estaban en un llano de un cerro que se llama Anahuarque, adonde se hacía la ceremonia, acabada de hacer —el cómo se hace se dirá adelante— al tiempo que se iban a lavar los que así habían sido rebautizados en el bautismo [que] es trasquilar y horadar las orejas, los españoles, no sé si por codicia de la plata que iba en los cetros o de algún recelo que de ver tanta gente les debió de caer, se pusieron en arma y comenzaron a alborotar a toda la gente echando mano a sus espadas con este apellido, los cuales decían:

¡O, bellacos! Vosotros levantaros queréis, pues no ha de ser así. ¡Esperad, esperad!

Y así de esta manera arremetieron a los cetros para los quitar a los cuales llevaban con deseo de llegar a quitar el de mi padre y como tenía tanta guarda al derredor de sí por sus mangas no pudieron llegar sino quitaron de los otros los que pudieron que fueron muchos. Mi padre, que así oyó tanto ruido y murmullo entre la gente, atendió a ver lo que pasaba y desde que supo que los españoles se habían desvergonzado de aquella manera, alzó la voz diciendo:

¿Qué es esto?

Y los indios todos como llorando se le quejaron de esta suerte, los cuales dijeron:

Sapay Inga, qué gente es ésta que tenéis en tu tierra que no se contentan con tanto oro y plata como les has dado y por fuerza nos han quitado nuestros yauris de plata —que quiere decir cetros— nos han quitado con amenazas, de lo cual recibimos gran pena. Diles que nos los vuelvan y que les baste ya la plata y oro que les habemos dado.

Y mi padre, viendo que con tanta ansia se le quejaban aquellos indios, recibió de ello pena y, hablando hacia los españoles, dijo así:

Razonamiento del Inga a los españoles cuando la tercera vez hicieron además a prenderle

Señores, paréceme que todavía estáis en darme pena a mí y a mi gente, no queriendo yo dárosla ni teniendo tal pensamiento. El otro día ¿no me prometisteis a mí y a mi gente diciendo que no daríais más pena? No tenéis razón porque yo no os he hecho por donde me la hayáis de dar, ¿no estáis hartos de plata que me venís a quitar aun una migaja que traigo en mis fiestas? Si lo hacéis por incitarme para que me levante contra vosotros yo o la gente de mi tierra, decídmelo porque andaré apercibido y lo mismo mi gente. No andaré tan descuidado como ahora venía y si no, pues nos dimos unos y otros más palabras el otro día en casa del Apo y en la mía de conservarnos en paz y amor los unos con los otros, guardémonosla y así ni vosotros tenéis recelo ni nosotros temor.

Y los españoles, oyendo lo que mi padre les decía, dijeron:

Señor Mango Inga, no deseamos dar aquí pena a Vuestra Merced. Algunos soldados por pasar tiempo harían por ahí algún aspaviento; no reciba Vuestra Merced pena que no es nada.

Y mi padre viendo la gente ya quieta y sosegada calló y acabó de hacer sus fiestas, yéndose los españoles a sus casas porque ya era tarde y hora de recogerse a dormir.

Muerte de Pascac, hermano del Inga

Acabadas todas las fiestas y lo que arriba se ha dicho, estando un día mi padre quieto y sosegado en su casa, le aconteció una brava hazaña y fue que un hermano suyo que allí tenía llamado Pascac, algo orgulloso; no se sabe por inducción de quién, le vino pensamiento de matar a mi padre diciendo que muerto él sería alzado por rey. Y no sé si por la persona o personas que allí le insistieron o no sé por quién le fue dado un puñal, con el cual yendo que fue a ver a mi padre, debajo de que le iba a mochar como a señor, le diese de puñaladas con aquel puñal y que luego muerto que fuese sería alzado por rey y podría dar mucha plata a los españoles, que así le dieron aquel puñal para aquel efecto. Y como ninguna cosa hay secreta que no sea tarde o temprano manifiesta, un cierto español cuyo nombre no se sabe, el cual era criado de mi padre y estaba siempre en su casa, le avisó:

Sábete, Señor Mango Inga, que tu hermano Pascac te anda por matar y trae para tal efecto debajo de la manta escondido un puñal, el cual te ha de matar cuando te venga a hacer la mocha. Por eso cuando le vieres venir está sobre aviso, que si tú me mandares que yo le mate a él, yo le mataré.

Y mi padre, como fue avisado de esta manera por aquel su criado español, agradeciéndoselo mucho y tuvo cuenta para cuando viese venir a su hermano como otras veces solía hacerle la mocha. Y cuando le vio le dejó hacer la mocha y con un puñal que para el efecto tenía le dio de puñaladas y el español que así había dado el aviso le acabó de matar. Visto todo esto por los circunstantes que allí estaban presentes, les cayó a todos gran admiración de ver un hecho tan extraño y tan súbito y no hubo nadie que osase a hablar palabra.

Pasadas todas estas cosas y otras muchas más que a haberlos de contar por extenso era alargarnos mucho, por lo cual y por evitar prolijidad pasaré con mi intento que es dar a entender qué fue de mi padre y en qué pararon los españoles después de todo esto. Para lo cual sabrán que como Gonzalo Pizarro, siendo corregidor del Cuzco en nombre del gobernador don Francisco Pizarro, estuviese en él con Hernando Pizarro y Juan Pizarro y otros muchos, acaeció que Juan Pizarro, hermano de Hernando Pizarro y Gonzalo Pizarro, como viese que a sus hermanos entrambos a dos mi padre les había dado tanta cantidad de moneda, cobró de ello gran envidia diciendo:

¿Pues a mis hermanos solamente han de dar plata y a mí no? Voto a tal que no ha de pasar de esta manera, si no que me han de dar a mí también oro y plata como a ellos y sino, que les tengo de hacer un juego que se les acuerde.

Y con estos fieros andaba moviendo toda la gente y decía:

Prendamos, prendamos a Mango Inga.

Y mi padre, como oyó que en el pueblo se trataba la traición que estaba armada contra él, mandó juntar a todos los principales de la tierra, que mucha parte de ellos estaban en el Cuzco haciéndole cuerpo de guardia, y desde que los tuvo juntos les hizo el parlamento avisado por el capitán general Vila Oma arriba dicho.

Parlamento del Inga a sus capitanes sobre lo del Cerco del Cuzco

Muy amados hijos y hermanos míos, nunca pensé que me fuera necesario haberos de hacer lo que ahora pienso, porque pensé y tuve siempre por muy cierto que esta gente barbuda que vosotros llamáis viracochas, por habérselo yo dicho antiguamente por pensar que era así que venían del Viracochan, me habían de ser aviesos ni darme pena en ninguna cosa, pero ahora que veo como he hallado siempre por experiencia y vosotros también habéis visto cuán mal me han tratado y cuán mal me han agradecido lo que por ellos he hecho, haciéndome mil befas y prendiéndome y atándome como a perro los pies y el pescuezo, y que sobre todo después de me haber dado su palabra que ellos conmigo y yo con ellos habernos confederado en amor y amistad, diciendo que perpetuamente habríamos de lo pasado, andan ahora otra vez urdiendo cómo me podrían prender y matar. No dejaré de rogaros como a hijos que miréis cuántas veces vosotros me habéis importunado a que yo haga esto que ahora quiero hacer diciendo que me levante contra éstos y que para qué los consiento en mi tierra y yo no he querido por pensar que no sucediera lo que ahora veo. Y pues así es y ellos no quieren sino porfiar en darme enojo, forzado me será dárselo yo también y no consentir más negocios por vida vuestra, que pues siempre me habéis mostrado tanto amor y deseado darme contento, en este me lo deis, y sea que todos juntos así como estáis os concertéis en uno y enviéis vuestros mensajeros a toda la tierra para que de aquí a veinte días estén todos en este pueblo sin que de ello entiendan nada estos barbudos. Y yo enviaré a Lima a Queso Yupangui,[25] mi capitán que gobierna a aquella tierra, a avisarle que para el día que aquí diéremos sobre los españoles, dé él allá con su gente sobre los que allá hubiere. Y haciéndonos a una, él allá y nosotros acá, luego los acabaremos sin que quede ninguno y quitaremos esta pesadilla de sobre nosotros y holgarnos hemos.

Acabado este razonamiento que mi padre hizo a sus capitanes para lo que habían de hacer en el apercibimiento de esa gente para la batalla que con los españoles se esperaba, todos en uno y a una voz respondieron que recibían de aquello mucho contento y estaban prestos y aparejados de hacer lo que por mi padre les era mandado. Y así sin ninguna dilación luego lo pusieron por la obra y enviaron por sus parcialidades cada uno como le cabía: la vez de los Chinchaysuyo envió Vila Oma, a Coyllas y a Ozca y a Cori Atao y a Taipi; que trajesen la gente de aquella parcialidad de los Collasuyo fue Lliclli y otros muchos capitanes para que trajesen la gente de aquella parcialidad; a Condesuyo, Suranvaman, Quicana y Suri Vallpa y otros muchos capitanes; y los de Andesuyo Ronpa Yupangui y otros muchos capitanes, para que todos éstos cada suyo por sí juntasen la gente necesaria para el efecto. Nota que estos cuatro suyos que aquí son nombrados, conviene a saber como arriba tengo dicho, son las cuatro partes en que toda esta tierra está divisa y repartida, como más por extenso arriba está declarado. Después que se hubieron enviado a las partes arriba dichas, andando como andaba el dicho Juan Pizarro de mala manera y con malos intentos, un indio lengua de los españoles llamado Antonio llegó donde estaba mi padre y le dio aviso diciendo que Juan Pizarro y los demás le querían prender otro día y aún matarle si no les daba mucho oro y plata. Y mi padre, como oyó lo que el indio le decía, le creyó y fingió luego que quería ir a Calca a cazar. Y los españoles, no cayendo en lo que mi padre pensaba hacer lo tuvieron por bien pensado que a la vuelta, porque creían sería breve, habría efecto su mal propósito.

Desde que mi padre estuvo en Calca algunos días, en tanto que se juntaba alguna gente de la que habían enviado a llamar, despachó desde allí por la posta a Queso Yupangui que estaba en Lima para que estuviese avisado del día y la hora en que él acá había de dar sobre los españoles, que juntamente él diese y fuese todo a una el Queso Yupangui en Lima y el dicho mi padre en Cuzco. Y al tiempo que esto hizo mi padre, los españoles le enviaron muchas cartas diciendo que se diese prisa a volverse a su casa que no se hallaban un punto sin él. El cual dicho mi padre les tornó a responder diciendo que aún no había acabado de cazar, que volvería lo más presto que pudiera. Y los españoles, viendo que de cuantas veces le enviaban a llamar no quería venir ninguna, mas antes de día en día se alargaba más y les enviaba peores respuestas, determinaron de ir sobre él para o traerle por fuerza o matarle. Los cuales hicieron su campo un capitán de ellos con su gente se fue la vía de Calca con su gente para el efecto dicho, quedando los demás en el Cuzco a punto de guerra para ir en su seguimiento si fuese menester. Los cuales llegaron hasta el puente del río de Calca, en el cual sobre el pasaje recibieron cierta refriega con las guardas de ella. Las cuales les defendieron el paso y allí se desafiaron los españoles a la gente de mi padre y hecho el desafío se volvieron al Cuzco, viniendo en seguimiento, dando muchos alaridos y gran grita mucha gente de la que estaba con mi padre. Llegados que fueron al Cuzco los españoles, algo escandalizados de la guazábara pasada y de la gente que venía en su seguimiento desde Carmenca, que es parte donde se señorea el Cuzco, dieron voces a sus compañeros pidiendo socorro y los compañeros que no estaban descuidados acudieron con su favor a los que con necesidad estaban y allí en la dicha Carmenca hubieron otra gran refriega con la gente que le seguía y en mucha otra que al apellido acudió. Y acabada la refriega los acorralaron al Cuzco sin matar ninguno y esa misma noche los tuvieron muy acosados con gran gritería, cercados de todas partes, y no dieron sobre ellos porque esperaban la gente[] que otro día llegó y también porque mi padre les había dicho que no diesen sobre ellos, lo uno hasta que llegase la gente porque les pudiesen tomar a manos, y lo otro porque decía que él se quería ver con ellos.

Cerco del Cuzco

Otro día ha, después que fueron de esta manera retraídos al Cuzco, habiéndoles puesto la misma noche muchas guardas y bien apercibidas por todos los pasos, esa tarde llegó a vista del Cuzco el tumulto de la gente, los cuales no entraron entonces porque les parecía que era muy [de] noche y no se podría aprovechar, siendo noche, de sus enemigos por la oscuridad grande que hacía. Y a esta causa hicieron alto por todos los visos y cerros de donde pudiese señorearse el pueblo, poniendo grandes guardas y centinelas a sus campos.

Otro día de mañana, a hora de las nueve, estando todos los españoles en escuadrón en la plaza del Cuzco bien apercibidos, cuyo número no se sabe, salvo que dicen que era mucha gente y que tenían muchos negros consigo, asomaron por todas las vistas del Cuzco a la redonda de él en el cerco gran suma de gente con muchos chiflos y bocinas y trompetas y gran gritería de voces que asombraban a todo el mundo, que en número serían más de cuatrocientos mil indios, los cuales entraron repartidos en esta manera.

Entrada de la gente al Cerco

Por la parte de Carmenca, que es hacia Chinchaysuyo, entraron Cori Atao[26] y Coyllas[27] y Taipi y otros muchos que cerraron aquel postigo con la gente que traían, por la parte del Condesuyo, que es hacia Caocachi, entraron Vamani, Quicana[28] y Curi Guallpa[29] y otros muchos que cerraron una gran milla de más de media legua de voz, todos muy bien aderezados en orden de guerra. Por la parte de Collasuyo, entraron Lliclli[30] y otros muchos capitanes con grandísima suma de gente, la mayor cantidad que se halló en este cerco, por la parte de Andesuyo, entraron Anta Allca y Ranpa Yupangui y otros muchos, los cuales acabaron de cercar el cerco que a los españoles pusieron este día. Y después de puesto este cerco, el cual estaba tan cerrado que era cosa de ver, luego quisieron dar sobre los españoles, pero no osaron hasta que por mi padre les fuese mandado lo que habían de hacer; el cual, como arriba dije, había mandado que so pena de la vida nadie se mudase del lugar adonde estaba. Y Vila Oma, capitán general de aquella gente, viéndola ya toda apercibida y a punto, le hizo luego saber a mi padre, el cual estaba a la sazón en Calca, diciendo que ya los tenía cercados y en gran aprieto, que si los matarían o qué harían de ellos. Y mi padre le envió a decir que los dejase estar así en aquel aprieto con aquella congoja que ellos también le habían a él acongojado, que padeciesen también lo que había él padecido, que él llegaría otro día y los acabaría. La cual respuesta vino a Vila Oma y el dicho Vila Oma, como vio lo que mi padre le enviaba a mandar, recibió gran pena porque quisiera él luego acabarlos así como estaban, que tenía harto aparejo para ello, mas no osó por lo que mi padre le envió a mandar. El cual mandó luego a pregonar por todo el ejército que so pena de la vida nadie se menease del lugar donde estaba hasta que él se lo mandase y mandó también soltar todas las acequias de agua que había en el pueblo para que anegasen todos los campos y caminos que a la redonda y dentro de él estaba; esto porque si acaso los españoles se quisiesen huir, que hallasen toda la tierra anegada y así atollando los caballos pudiesen ser señores de sus enemigos a pie y en el lodazal, porque gente vestida amañase mal en el lodo, lo cual todo fue cumplido ni más ni menos que el general Vila Oma lo mandó. Los españoles, como se vieron muy cercados en tanto aprieto y que tanta gente les cercaba, sospechando entre sí que allí sería[n] los postrimeros días de sus vidas, no viendo de ninguna parte ningún remedio, no sabían qué hacer porque de una parte se veían cercados de aquella manera, por otra parte veían los escarnios y las befas que los indios les hacían tirándoles muchas piedras a los toldos y alcanzándoles la perneta por el poco caso que de ellos hacían, les comenzaban a quemar las casas. Acometieron a ponerles fuego a la iglesia sino que los negros que encima de ellos estaban se lo estorbaban aunque con hartos flechazos que los indios satis y andes les tiraron, a los cuales no hizo daño ninguno por guardarles Dios y ellos escudarse, pues como estuviesen de esta manera desconfiados de remedio, tuvieron por principal socorro en acudir[] a Dios, los cuales estuvieron toda aquella noche en la iglesia llamando a Dios que les ayudase, puestos de rodillas y las manos junto a la boca, que lo vieron muchos indios y aun los que estaban en la plaza en la vela hacían lo mismo y muchos indios de los que eran de su banda, los cuales habían venido con ellos desde Cajamarca.

Batalla de los españoles contra los indios en la Fortaleza

Otro día de mañana bien de mañana todos salieron de la iglesia y se pusieron encima de sus caballos a guisa de pelear y comenzaron a mirar a una parte y a otra y así pusieron piernas a sus caballos y a más correr, a pesar de sus enemigos, rompieron aquel puertillo que como muro estaba cerrado y echaron a huir por la cuesta arriba a mata caballo. Los indios que en el cerro del Cuzco estaban, como los vieron así huir, comenzaron a gritar diciendo:

¡A que se van a Castilla! ¡A que se van a Castilla! ¡Atajadlos!

Y así todo el cerco que estaba hecho se deshizo, los unos en su seguimiento, los otros a atajarlos. Algunos a dar aviso a las guardas de los puentes por que no se pudiese escapar ninguno por ninguna parte. Y los españoles, como vieron que les seguía tanta gente, volvieron la rienda a sus caballos e hicieron una vuelta por un cerro llamado Quencalla y llegaron a tomarles las espaldas de la parte por donde estaba Vila Oma, el que se había subido con toda su gente a hacerse fuerte en la fortaleza del Cuzco llamada Sacsahuaman. Y allí pelearon fuertemente y les cogieron las cuatro puertas de la fortaleza, desde los muros de la cual que son muy fuertes, arrojaban muchas galgas, tiraban muchas flechas, muchos dardos, muchas lanzas que fatigaban gravemente a los españoles, con las cuales galgas mataron a Juan Pizarro y a dos negros y muchos indios de los que les ayudaban. Como a los de Vila Oma se les acabase la munición de galgas y de lo demás mediante el favor divino tuvieron lugar los españoles de entrar en la fortaleza y tomarla por fuerza matando y destrozando muchos indios de los que dentro estaban. Otros se arrojaban de los muros abajo y, como son altos, todos los que primero cayeron murieron y los que después, como ya había gran rimero de gente muerta, caían sobre ellos [y] se escapaban algunos. Fue esta batalla de una parte y de otra muy ensangrentada por la mucha gente de indios que favorecían a los españoles, entre los cuales estaban los dos hermanos de mi padre, llamados el uno Inguill y el otro Vaypar, con mucha gente de su bando y chachapoyas y cañaris.

Duró esta batalla de una parte y de otra tres días después de la toma de esta fortaleza, porque otro día después se retornaron a reformar los indios para ver si podrían tornar a recobrar el fuerte que habían perdido y con gran ánimo acometieron a los españoles que estaban en el fuerte. Mas no pudieron hacerles ninguna cosa por las muchas guardas que de todas partes tenían, así de cañaris que les ayudaban como de los mismos españoles, y lo otro, porque dicen estos indios que un caballo blanco que allí andaba, el cual fue el primero que entró en la fortaleza al tiempo que se tomó, les hacía mucho daño, y duró todo el día este rebate. Y ya que la noche les sobrevenía por la mucha oscuridad que en ella hacía, no se pudiendo aprovechar de sus enemigos, se retrajeron a sus sitios y los españoles, por no dejar el fuerte que tenían y desampararlo, los dejaron ir. Y otro día de mañana tornaron a la batalla comenzada, la cual riñeron muy fuertemente los unos con los otros; y al fin viniendo con gran ánimo los indios contra los españoles con gran esfuerzo arremetiéndose, los indios se retrajeron hacia donde mi padre estaba, que era en Calca, y fueron tras de ellos matando y desbaratando gran parte de la gente hasta el río de Yucay, en el cual los indios dieron lado a los españoles, los cuales españoles pasaron adelante derecho a Calca adonde mi padre estaba, al cual no le hallaron allí porque estaba haciendo una fiesta en el pueblo llamado Sacsasiray; y como no le hallasen allí dieron la vuelta hacia el Cuzco por otro camino con harta pérdida de fardaje que los indios cogieron en la retaguardia saliendo del lado que les habían dado, con el cual despojo se fueron derecho a donde mi padre estaba haciendo la fiesta.

Hecha mi padre esta fiesta en aquel pueblo Sacsasiray, se salió de allí para el pueblo de Tambo pasando de camino por Yucay, adormitó sólo una noche; y llegado que fue a Tambo mandó que se juntase allí toda la tierra porque quería hacer una fortaleza muy fuerte para en ella defenderse de todos los españoles que le quisiesen acometer, la cual gente fue junta muy breve y desde que la tuvo junta les hizo el parlamento siguiente.

Parlamento que hizo el Inga a todos sus capitanes y gente en el pueblo de Tambo. Luego cómo se recogió a Él después del desbarate del Cuzco

Muy amados hijos y hermanos míos, en las pláticas pasadas que os he hecho antes de ahora, habréis entendido cómo yo siempre os estorbé que no hiciereis mal a aquella gente tan mala que debajo de engaño y por decir que eran hijos del Viracochan y enviados por su mandado habían entrado en mi tierra, a lo cual yo les di consentimiento. Y por esto y por otras muchas y muy buenas obras que les hice dándoles lo que yo tenía en ella: plata y oro, ropas y maíz, ganados, vasallos, mujeres, criados y otras muchas cosas sin número, me prendieron, ultrajaron y maltrataron sin yo merecérselo y después me trataron la muerte, la cual entendí por aviso de Antonico, su lengua, el cual está aquí presente, que se huyó de los españoles [por no los] poder sufrir. Y como entendisteis por el parlamento que sobre el cerco del Cuzco os hice, para la junta de él me recogí yo a Calca para que desde allí sin entenderlo ellos les diésemos en la cabeza, lo cual me parece que así se hizo como yo lo mandé, aunque no me hallé presente como pensaba, de lo cual recibisteis detrimento en la toma de Sacsahuaman que por descuido os tomaron y después os desbarataron siguiéndoos hasta Yucay sin poderles hacer nada. Pena me habéis dado de que siendo tanta gente vosotros y ellos tan pocos se os saliesen de las manos, quizá el Viracochan les ayudó por lo que me habéis dicho de que estuvieron de rodillas toda la noche mochándole, porque si no les ayudara ¿cómo se podrían escapar de vuestras manos siendo vosotros sin número? Ya está hecho, por vuestra vida que de aquí adelante miréis cómo habéis con ellos, porque sabed que son nuestros enemigos capitales y nosotros lo habemos de ser suyos perpetuamente pues ellos lo han querido. Yo me quiero hacer fuerte en este pueblo y hacer aquí una fortaleza para que nadie me pueda entrar en él, por vida vuestra que me hagáis este placer que algún día podrá ser que nos aproveche.

Respuesta que los capitanes hicieron al Inga

Sapay Inga, estos tus pobres criados te besamos las manos y con muy gran confusión y vergüenza venimos ante ti por habérsenos escapado de entre las manos tan gran empresa como era la de aquella gente maligna, habiéndote hecho tantos y tan malos tratamientos y habiéndote sido tan ingratos a lo mucho que por ellos hicisteis. Nos ha caído tanta confusión que no te osamos mirar a la cara, pero en alguna manera nos da algún alivio el poderte echar a ti alguna culpa y es porque te enviamos a preguntar qué haríamos de ellos cuando los teníamos cercados y sin ninguna esperanza de remedio y nos enviaste decir que los dejásemos padecer como ellos habían hecho a ti, que tú vendrías y los acabarías. Y nosotros, por no ir contra lo que tú mandabas, dejémoslos un día y una noche aguardándote, y cuando pensamos que estábamos seguros y que más ciertos los teníamos en las manos se nos escabulleron sin ser señores de hacerles nada. No sabemos qué fue la causa ni qué te digamos de éstos sino que fue nuestra desdicha en no acudir con tiempo y la tuya en no nos dar licencia para ello. Aparejados estamos para recibir el castigo que por esta culpa nos quisieres dar. Y lo que dices que te hagamos aquí, fuerte en este pueblo para poderte defender de aquella gente y de todos los que te quisieren acometer, decimos que lo haremos de muy entera voluntad, que más que esto te debemos.

Y así lo hicieron una de las más fuertes que hay en el Perú, en año y medio que estuvo en Tambo.

En este medio tiempo, ya que había hablado a los indios y dándoles a entender la desgracia que les había acontecido, llegaron al dicho pueblo de Tambo los mensajeros del desbarate que había habido en Lima y Cullcomayo, que es en Jauja, donde hubieron una refriega los españoles con los indios, en que los indios hubieron la victoria y trajeron a mi padre muchas cabezas de los españoles y dos españoles vivos y un negro y cuatro caballos; los cuales llegaron con gran regocijo de la victoria habida y mi padre los recibió muy honradamente y animó a todos los demás a pelear de aquella suerte. Y allí mismo llegó al dicho pueblo de Tambo el capitán Diego Ordóñez con una cuadrilla de soldados a pelear con mi padre y sabido por él le salieron al encuentro muchos indios antes que llegasen al fuerte de Tambo, ya pasado el río, y en un llano llamado Pascapampa y Pachar hubieron gran refriega los unos con los otros y al fin no se conoció de ninguna parte la victoria porque los mismos españoles, por causa de unas espinas que allí estaban, se desbarataron y aún murió el uno de ellos en la revuelta y tres negros. Y los indios cogieron otro allá en su fuerte porque se quiso aventurar. Y ya que la noche los despartió, se recogieron todos cada uno a su fuerte y los españoles asentaron su toldo a prima noche e hicieron sus lumbradas a la madrugada a guisa de [que] querían pelear y antes que amaneciese volvieron las espaldas hacia el Cuzco. Y cuando los indios pensaron que estaban allí a la mañana, no hallaron ninguno que les dio muy gran risa diciendo que se habían huido de miedo. Después que pasó todo esto y los españoles se fueron a sus casas, quedase mi padre en Tambo dando prisa a su fortaleza. Y estando así en el mismo Tambo dos españoles presos rendido[s] que allí tenía consigo, a los cuales hacía muy buen tratamiento dándolos de comer junto a sí, se le huyeron por avisos que del Cuzco les vino y no se sabiendo dar maña los tornaron desde un pueblo llamado Maras, dos leguas del dicho pueblo de Tambo, a los cuales como mi padre preguntase la causa por qué se huían, no supieron dar razón de sí. Y visto por mi padre que aún estos le pagaban tan mal el bien que les hacía y aún al uno de ellos que era Antonico arriba dicho, que había avisado a mi padre en el Cuzco de lo que los españoles trataban contra él, no sabiendo conocer el tratamiento que mi padre le había hecho y hacía trayéndole en hamaca y haciéndole el tratamiento de hijo, le aconteció lo que a los demás, que fue que los mandó entregar a unos indios moyos moyos y antis para que despedazados los comiesen.

Acabado todo esto y acabada también la fortaleza, determinó mi padre de quererse entrar a los Andes y dejar aquella tierra de ella fuera porque le daban mucha pena los españoles y los andes le importunaban mucho a que se fuese a su tierra que ellos le guardarían allá y le servirían como a su señor y su rey. Y ya determinado que estuvo en la dicha entrada, hizo juntar a su gente para les dar a entender la manera que habían de tener en la vivienda con los españoles. El cual les dijo así:

Documento que Mango Inga dio a los indios, cuando se quiso recoger a los andes. La manera que habían de tener con los españoles

Muy amados hijos y hermanos míos, los que aquí estáis presentes y me habéis seguido en todos mis trabajos y tribulaciones, bien creo no sabéis la causa por qué en uno os he mandado juntar ahora ante mí. Yo os la diré en breve. Por vida vuestra que no os alteréis de lo que os dijere porque bien sabéis que la necesidad muchas veces compela a los hombres a hacer aquello que no querrían y por eso, por serme forzado dar contento a estos andes que tanto tiempo ha que me importunan que los vaya a ver, habré de darles este contento por algunos días. Ruégoos mucho que de ello no recibáis pena porque yo no os la deseo dar pues os amo como a hijos, por lo que aquí os rogaré me daréis mucho contento haciéndolo.

Bien sabéis cómo muchas veces sin ésta os lo he dicho la manera cómo aquella gente barbuda entró en mi tierra so color que decían que eran viracochas. Lo cual por sus trajes y divisas tan diferentes de las nuestras, vosotros y aún yo lo pensamos, por el cual pensamiento y certificación de los tallanas yungas que de cosas que les vieron hacer en su tierra me hicieron, como habéis visto, los trajese a mi tierra y pueblo y les hice el tratamiento ya notorio a toda la tierra y les di las cosas que sabéis, por la cual y por ellas me trataron de la manera que habéis visto. Y no solamente ellos sino mis hermanos Pascac e Inguill y Vaypar me desposeyeron de mi tierra y aun me trataron la muerte, de la cual yo me libré por el aviso que os dije de Antonico, como el otro día aquí os dije, al cual comieron los andes por no se saber valer. Y viendo todas aquellas cosas y otras muchas que por prolijidad dejo, os mandé juntar al Cuzco para que les diésemos algún tartago de los muchos que nos habían dado y paréceme que, o porque su dios les ayudó o porque no me hallé yo presente, no salisteis con vuestro intento, de lo cual yo he recibido gran pena. Pero como a los hombres no les suceden todas las cosas como desean siempre, no nos hemos de maravillar ni congojarnos demasiado, por lo cual os ruego que vosotros no tengáis congoja, que en fin no nos ha ido tan mal que no les hayamos cogido, porque como sabéis en Lima y en Chullcomayo y Jauja les cogimos algunas cosas que no dejan de dar algún alivio, aunque no equivalente a la pena que ellos nos han dado.

Ya me parece se va haciendo tiempo de partirme a la tierra de los andes como arriba os dije y que me será forzado detenerme allá algunos días. Mirad que os mando que no se os olvide lo que os he dicho. Pienso decir ahora que es que miréis cuánto tiempo ha que mis abuelos y bisabuelos y yo hemos sustentado y guardado, favorecido y gobernado todas vuestras casas, proveyéndolas de la manera que habéis habido menester, por lo cual tenéis todos obligación de no nos olvidar en toda vuestra vida vosotros y vuestros descendientes, así a mí como a mis abuelos y bisabuelos, y tener mucho respeto y hacer mucho caso de mi hijo y hermano Titu Cusi Yupangui y de todos los demás mis hijos que de él descendieren. Pues en ello me daréis a mí mucho contento y ellos os lo agradecerán como yo se lo dejo mandado, por tanto bastaos esto acerca de lo dicho.

Respuesta de los indios al Inga

Sapay Inga, ¿con qué corazón quieres dejar a estos tus hijos solos que con tanta voluntad te han deseado y desean siempre servir y que si necesario fuese pondrían mil veces la vida por ti si fuese menester? ¿A qué rey, a qué señor, a quién los dejas encomendados?, ¿qué deservicios, qué traiciones, qué maldades te hemos hecho para que nos quier[a]s dejar así desamparados y sin señor ni rey a quién respetar?, pues jamás hemos conocido otro señor ni padre sino a ti y a Guaina Capac, tu padre y sus antepasados. No nos dejes señor de esa manera desamparados, mas antes d[a]nos este contento si fueres servido de llevarnos contigo a dondequiera que fueres, que chicos y grandes y viejos y viejas aparejados estamos para no dejar de seguirte aunque tú no nos dejes.

Y luego el dicho mi padre, viendo que con tanta ansia le deseaban servir toda su gente, les volvió a decir lo que aquí parecerá:

Yo os agradezco, hijos, la buena voluntad y deseo que mostráis de quererme seguir dondequiera que vaya. No perderéis la paga de mí que yo os lo agradeceré y pagaré antes que vosotros pensáis. Y ahora, por vida vuestra que os reportéis y no tengáis tanta pena, que muy breve os volveré a ver. Y de aquí a que vuelva, o hasta que os envíe mis mensajeros para lo que hayáis de hacer, tendréis este modo en vuestra vivienda: lo primero que haréis será que a estos barbudos, que tantas befas a mí me han hecho por fiarme yo de ellos, en tanto no les creáis cosa que dijeren porque mienten mucho como a mí en todo lo que conmigo han tratado me han mentido y así harán a vosotros. Lo que podréis hacer será dar muestras por de fuera de que consintáis a los que os mandan y dar algún camarico y lo que pudieres que en vuestras tierras hubiere, porque como esta gente es tan brava y de diferente condición, de la nuestra podría ser que no se lo dando vosotros os lo tomasen por fuerza o vos maltratasen. Por ello y por evitar esto os será buen remedio hacer lo que os digo. Lo otro, que estéis siempre con aviso para cuando os enviare a llamar o avisar de lo que con esta gente habéis de hacer y si acaso ellos os acometieren o quisieren tomar vuestras tierras no dejéis de defenderos y sobre ello perder la vida si fuera menester. Y si también se os ofreciere necesidad extrema de que hayáis necesidad de mi persona, dadme aviso por la posta a dondequiera que yo estuviere, y mira[d] que éstos engañan por buenas palabras y después no cumplen lo que dicen que así como habéis visto hicieron a mí, que me dijeron que eran hijos del Viracochan y me mostraron al principio gran afabilidad y mucho amor y después hicieron conmigo lo que visteis; si ellos fueran hijos del Viracochan como se jactaban, no hubieran hecho lo que han hecho, por que el Viracha puede allanar los cerros, sacar las aguas, hacer cerros donde no los hay. No hace mal a nadie, y éstos no vemos que han hecho esto, mas antes en lugar de hacer bien nos han hecho mal tomándonos nuestras haciendas, nuestras mujeres, nuestros hijos, nuestras hijas, nuestras chacaras, nuestras comidas y otras muchas cosas que en nuestra tierra teníamos por fuerza y con engaños y contra nuestra voluntad y a gente que esto hace no les podemos llamar hijos del Viracochan sino, como otras veces os he dicho, del Supay y peores porque en sus obras le han imitado, pues han hecho obras de tal, que por ser tan vergonzosas no las quiero decir.

Lo que más habéis de hacer es que por ventura éstos os dirán que adoréis a lo que ellos adoran, que son unos paños pintados, los cuales dicen que es Viracochan, y que le adoréis como a guaca, el cual no es sino paño, no lo hagáis sino lo que nosotros tenemos eso tened, porque como veis las villcas hablan con nosotros y al sol y a la luna vémoslos por nuestros ojos y lo que esos dicen no lo vemos bien. Creo que alguna vez por fuerza o con engaño os han de hacer adorar lo que ellos adoran, cuando más no pudiereis, hacedlo delante de ellos y por otra parte no olvidéis nuestras ceremonias. Y si os dijeren que quebrantéis nuestras guacas y eso por fuerza, mostradles lo que no pudiereis hacer menos y lo demás guardadlo, que en ello me daréis a mí mucho contento.

Acabadas todas estas cosas arriba dichas y otras muchas, se despidió mi padre de los indios, trayéndome a mí allí delante para les decir cómo yo era su hijo y cómo después de sus días me habían de tener en su lugar por señor de todos ellos, el cual lo hizo y se levantó en pie para partirse de su gente, la cual cuando lo vio en pie comenzaron a dar gritos, que parecería que se horadaban los cerros, y la gente con la ansia que tenía todavía le quería seguir, pero nunca mi padre les dejó si no fue a cual que no tenían impedimento que les estorbasen, porque decía a aquellos que con tanta ansia le querían seguir, que ¿cómo habían de dejar sus sementeras, sus casas, sus mujeres y sus hijos, sus oyvas o crías para seguirle?, que se reportasen y que muy breve volvería a verlos o les enviaría a decir lo que habían de hacer, y así se partió de todos ellos para el pueblo de Vitcos.

Llegada del Inga a Vitcos

Llegados que fuimos a Vitcos, que es pueblo [a] treinta leguas del Cuzco, con la gente que a mi padre seguía, asentamos nuestro pueblo y asiento con intención de vivir allí algunos días y descansar. Hizo hacer mi padre una casa para dormir porque las que antiguamente había eran de mis abuelos Pachacuti Inga, Topa Inga Yupangui y Guaina Capac y los demás cuyos cuerpos pusimos allí porque no los osamos dejar en el Cuzco ni en Tambo. Y después de esto, ya que mi padre estuvo quieto y sosegado, descuidado[ ] de que nadie había de entrar en esta tierra, quiso hacer una fiesta muy solemne convidado por los andes y gente de esta tierra. Y al mejor tiempo que estaban en ella desacordados de lo que les sucedió, se hallaron cercados de españoles. Y como estaban pesados los indios por lo mucho que habían bebido y tenían las armas en sus casas y no tuvieron lugar de poderse defender porque los tomaron de sobresalto don Diego de Almagro y el capitán Diego Ordóñez y Gonzalo Pizarro y otros muchos que nombrarlos sería muy largo, los cuales llevaron por delante todos cuantos indios e indias pudieron antecoger y los cuerpos de mis antepasados, los cuales se llamaban Vainacauri, Viracochan Inga, Pachacuti Inga, Topa Inga Yupangui y Guaina Capac y otros muchos cuerpos de mujeres con muchas joyas y riquezas que habían en la fiesta, más de cincuenta mil cabezas de ganado y estos escogidos los mejores que acá había que fue de mis antepasados y de mi padre y llevaron a mí y a otras muchas Coyas y mi padre escabullese lo mejor que pudo con algunos. Y los españoles se tornaron al Cuzco con la presa que llevaban y conmigo, muy contentos. Y aportados que fuimos al Cuzco, un fulano Oñate me recogió a mí en su casa y me hizo mucho regalo y buen tratamiento. Y sabido por mi padre, le envió a llamar y se lo agradeció y me encomendó de nuevo a él, a mí y a otras hermanas suyas, diciendo que mirase por mí y por ellas, que él se lo pagaría. Después de pasadas todas estas cosas, estando yo en el Cuzco en casa de aquel Oñate que dije, mi padre se salió de Vitcos porque le dijeron unos capitanes chachapoyas que le llevaron a su pueblo llamado Rabantu y que allí estaba en un buen fuerte donde se podían defender de todos sus enemigos. Y tomando su parecer les siguió. Y en el camino, viendo que iban a aquel Rabantu, en un pueblo llamado Oroncoy, descansó algunos días porque le hicieron fiesta los del pueblo. Y acabadas las fiestas, estando un poco de asiento, envió sus corredores a los caminos a saber si había españoles o gente alguna que le estorbase el pasaje. Y desde que los hubo enviado, esa misma noche a la madrugada llegaron al dicho pueblo de Oroncoy diciendo que más de doscientos españoles armados de todas armas y en sus caballos en busca de mi padre, los cuales tomaron las guardas de las puentes que allí estaban y les dieron trato de cuerda para saber dónde estaba el dicho mi padre, los cuales les dijeron que estaba allí arriba en el pueblo de Oroncoy. Y dejadas las guardas, se fueron uno en pos de otro a más correr por la cuesta arriba, pensando [] coger a mi padre durmiendo. Y acaso saliéndose a proveer mi tía Cura Ocllo, hermana de mi padre, vio la gente que venía desde lejos y hubo el tropel de los caballos y vino corriendo donde mi padre estaba en la cama y le dijo con gran alboroto que venían enemigos, que se levantase y fuese a ellos. Mi padre, como la vio tan despavorida, sin hacer caso de nada se levantó con gran prisa para ir a reconocer si era así lo que su hermana le decía y desde que se asomó al viso vio ser así lo que le había dicho y volvió a casa con gran prisa y mandó que le echasen el freno al caballo para de presto, así como estaba, poner cobro en su gente por que no le tomasen los enemigos de sobresalto, sino estar apercibido. Y ya que lo tuvo puesto a punto de guerra, mandó que le echasen la silla al caballo porque estaban ya cerca los enemigos, a la vista de los cuales puso en un cerro muchas mujeres en rengleras, todas con lanzas en las manos para que pensasen que eran hombres. Y hecho esto, con gran ligereza encima de su caballo, con su lanza en la mano, cercaba él solo toda la gente por que no pudiese ser empecida de sus enemigos hasta en tanto que llegasen los corredores que habían ido a correr al campo, los cuales que así llegaron a una con los españoles al viso a tiempo que mi padre solo lo traía a mal andar. Y como llegaron y vieron a su amo que andaba de aquella suerte, tan fatigados aunque cansados de la cuesta arriba, cobraron nuevo esfuerzo para pelear contra sus enemigos que de la parte de abajo estaban, con el cual refuerzo dieron de tropel sobre ellos con sus lanzas y adargas de tal arte que les hicieron retirarlos cuesta abajo más que de paso. Y desde que les dieron esta refriega descansaron un poco para tomar aliento. Y desde que los españoles vieron que estaban sentados bebiendo, pensaron que ya no podían más y con grande ánimo volvieron la cuesta arriba hacia los que no estaban descuidados, mas antes más fortalecidos, y con más gente que les había sobrevenido de una parte y de otra, los cuales como vieron venir a sus enemigos tan determinados, volvieron sobre ellos de tal suerte que de un envión, cual encima, cual en bajo, los desbarataron y desbarrancaron por unas barrancas y peñas abajo, sin poder ser señores de sí, más antes ellos mismos se desbarataron a sí mismos por no ser señores de sí en cuesta tan áspera por la mucha fatiga que las armas les daban y el gran calor que los ahogaban, que todo junto les causó la muerte a todos ellos, sin escapar caballo ni hombre vivo sino fueron dos, los cuales el uno pasó el río a nado y el otro se salvó por una crisneja del puente.

Y así la gente de mi padre, alcanzada aquella victoria, recogieron el despojo de los españoles y desnudándolos a todos los que pudieron haber, les quitaron los vestidos y armas que tenían y junto todo lo llevaron arriba al pueblo de Oroncoy, y mi padre y ellos, por la victoria que habían alcanzado se regocijaron mucho e hicieron fiestas y bailes cinco días por honra de aquel despojo y victoria.

Acabadas estas fiestas y hecho lo arriba dicho, se partió mi padre con toda la gente caminando por sus jornadas derecho al pueblo de Rabantu, que es hacia Quito, y en el camino, en el valle de Jauja, en un pueblo que llaman Llactapallanga, supo cómo los guancas naturales de aquella tierra se habían aunado con los españoles y recibió de ello mucho enojo y determinó de hacerles un castigo, el cual fuese sonado por toda aquella tierra, diciendo que les había de quemar a ellos y a sus casas sin dejar a ninguno con vida y esto porque habían dado la obediencia a los españoles y sujetándose a ellos y sus mujeres e hijos a su servicio, con una guaca principal que en el valle tenían llamada Guari Villca,[31] que es cinco leguas de Llactapallanga.

Sabido todo esto por los guancas y que mi padre se había enojado de tal manera con ellos que decía que les había de quemar a ellos y a Guari Villca, su ídolo, por la confederación que con los españoles habían hecho siendo él su señor natural, determinaron de defenderle la entrada dando parte a los españoles, debajo de cuyo amparo se habían puesto, para que les viniesen a ayudar en el aprieto en que estaban. Y sabido por los españoles la determinación de mi padre contra los guancas, vinieron con gran prisa (dicen que cien españoles) a los socorrer y llegados que fueron tuvo de ello aviso mi padre

*y enderezó su derrota para allá, habiendo en el camino muchas refriegas con
los guancas de una parte y de otras del camino, matando y destrozando en
ellos en gran manera, diciéndoles,*

[Que] os ayuden vuestros amos.

*Y de esta manera llegó por sus jornadas a Jauja la Grande, que así es lla-
mada, adonde tuvo una gran refriega con los españoles arriba dichos y con los
guancas, la cual refriega duró dos días, y al fin por la mucha gente que mi
padre llevaba y por darse buena maña los venció y mataron cincuenta
españoles y los demás se escaparon a uña de caballo. Y algunos de los nuestros
siguieron el alcance algún rato y como vieron que se daban tanta prisa, se
volvieron adonde mi padre estaba encima de su caballo blandeando su lanza,
sobre el cual había peleado fuertemente con los españoles. Y ya que se hubo
acabado esta batalla, mi padre, que algo cansado quedaba del pelear, se apeó
de su caballo y se fue a descansar con los suyos, que muy cansados y heridos
algunos de ellos habían quedado de la refriega pasada.*

*Otro día después, ya algo refaccionada la gente, se tiró de allí por las jor-
nadas que había ido, a un pueblo llamado Vayocoche, que es la parte donde
estaba el ídolo llamado Guari Villca, y en un día que allí descansó lo mandó
sacar del lugar donde estaba enterrado hasta los hombros y cavada la
redondez de ella mandó sacar todo el tesoro que le tenían ofrecido. Y los yana-
conas y criados que estaban diputados para el servicio de aquella guaca, en la
cual la gente de aquella tierra tenía mucha confianza, les mandó matar a
todos para que entendiesen que él era el señor. Y al ídolo, echándolo una soga
al pescuezo, lo trajeron arrastrando por todo el camino con gran denuesto por
cerros y piedras y ciénegas y todas las veinte leguas de[l] camino, diciendo:*

Veis aquí la confianza que tenían aquellos guancas de este ídolo al que
tenían por Viracochan, mira en qué han parado ellas y ellos y sus amos los
españoles.

*Y viniendo así por su camino llegaron a un pueblo llamado Acostambo y
allí descansaron un año, donde hicieron sus casas y heredades que ahora
poseen los españoles, lo cual llaman Vinaca porque se da allí mucho vino de
Castilla. La guaca o ídolo llamado Guari Villca, la mandó mi padre echar a
un gran río.*

*Después de esto, por importunaciones de unos capitanes andes que le
importunaron, se fue a la tierra y pueblo llamado Pilcosuni, adonde tuvo otra
refriega con ciertos españoles que le vinieron a buscar y los venció y desbarató.
Él, como sería muy largo, salvo se sepa que trajo de allí mucha artillería,
arcabuces, lanzas, ballestas y otras armas. Y después que en Icñupay hubo
aquella refriega con los españoles y descansó allí un año y así se volvió por sus
jornadas y pueblos, que por la brevedad no cuento, al pueblo de Vitcos y desde*

ahí hasta Vilcabamba, adonde estuvo algunos días sosega[n]do y descansando, haciendo sus casas y aposentos para hacer en este asiento porque es buen temple el asiento principal de su persona.

Después de haber descansado algunos días y que ya pensaba que le querían dejar los españoles, oyó decir por los espías que tenía puestos en los caminos, cómo venían sobre él Gonzalo Pizarro y el capitán Diego Maldonado y Ordóñez y otros muchos y que venían con ellos tres hermanos suyos, conviene a saber, don Pablo e Inguill y Vaypar, a los cuales traían antepuesto porque decían que querían hacer con mi padre contra los españoles. Y mi padre los salió a recibir tres leguas de aquí a una fortaleza que allí tenía para en ella defenderse de ellos y no dejar aquella fuerza. Llegado que fue allí, se encontró con no sé cuántos españoles, que por ser montes espesos no se podían contar, adonde peleó fuertemente con ellos a la orilla de un río, unos de una parte y otros de otra, que en diez días no se acabó la pelea porque peleaban a remuda los españoles con la gente de mi padre y con mi padre y siempre les iba mal por el fuerte que nosotros teníamos. Y vinieron a tanto, que viniendo allí un hermano carnal de mi tía Cura Ocllo, llamado Vaypar, y mi padre se enojó tanto con él porque le venía a buscar, que le vino a costar la vida el negocio, y queriéndole matar mi padre con el enojo que tenía, la Cura Ocllo se lo quiso estorbar porque le quería mucho, y mi padre no queriendo consentir a sus ruegos, les cortó las cabezas a él y a otro su hermano llamado Inguill, diciendo estas palabras:

Más justo es que corte yo sus cabezas que no que lleven ellos la mía.

Y mi tía, por el enojo que recibió de la muerte de sus hermanos, nunca jamás se quiso mudar del lugar donde estaban muertos.

Y en estos medios, ya que esto fue acabado por la parte adonde mi padre estaba, vinieron ciertos españoles y como los vio venir, viendo que no se podía escapar, tomó por remedio echarse al agua y pasar el río a nado. Y desde que se vio de la otra parte comenzó a dar voces diciendo:

Yo soy Mango Inga, yo soy Mango Inga.

Los españoles, como vieron que no se podían aprovechar de él, determinaron de volverse al Cuzco y llevaron por delante a mi tía Cura Ocllo y a Cusi Rimache, hermano también de mi padre que consigo tenía, y otras cosas, los cuales llegaron con mi tía al pueblo de Pampa Conac, adonde intentaron a querer forzar a mi tía y ella no queriendo se defendía fuertemente en tanto que vino a ponerse en su cuerpo cosas hediondas y de desprecio por que los que quisiesen llegar a ella tuviesen asco. Y así se defendió muchas veces en todo el camino hasta el pueblo de Tambo donde los españoles, de muy enojados con ella, lo uno porque no quiso consentir a lo que ellos querían y lo otro porque era hermana de mi padre, la enterraron viva, sufriéndolo ella por la castidad, la cual dijo estas palabras cuando la asaetearon:

En una mujer vengáis vuestros enojos, que más hiciera otra mujer como yo, daos prisa a acabarme porque se cumpla vuestro apetito en todo.

Y así la acabaron de presto, teniendo con un paño tapados sus ojos ella misma.

Vila Oma, capitán general que fue de mi padre, y Tisoc y Taipi y Yanqui Guallpa[32] *y Orco Varanca y Atoc Suyru y otros muchos capitanes que fueron de mi padre, como vieron que habían llevado los españoles y la Coya y que la habían tratado de aquella manera, mostraron recibir pena de ello y los españoles, como lo sintieron, los prendieron diciendo:*

Vosotros tornaros, deberéis de querer al Inga y hacerlos con él, pues no ha de ser así sino que habéis de acabar la vida juntamente con vuestra ama.

Y ellos defendiéndose decían que no pensaban tal sino ser siempre con los españoles y servirles, mas los españoles no creyendo de ellos, sino pensando que lo que decían era fingido, los mandaron quemar a todos. Y quemados éstos y muerta la Coya, se fueron a Yucay donde quemaron a Ozcollo y a Cori Atao y a otros muchos por que no se tornasen a hacer con mi padre y por tener las espaldas seguras. Pasadas todas estas cosas arriba dichas y otras muchas que por abreviar he dejado, el dicho mi padre se tornó a Vilcabamba, cabeza de toda esta provincia, adonde estuvo con algún sosiego algunos días y desde este pueblo porque no se hallaba sin mí, me envió a llamar al Cuzco, adonde yo estuve desde que me llevaron a Vitcos, en casa de Oñate arriba dicho, los cuales mensajeros me hurtaron del Cuzco a mí y a mi padre me trajeron escondidamente hasta el pueblo de Vitcos, al cual ya mi padre se había salido a tomar fresco porque es tierra fría. Y allí estuvimos mi padre y yo muchos días, adonde aportaron siete españoles en diferentes tiempos, diciendo que se venían huyendo de allá fuera por delitos que habían hecho y que protestaban de servir a mi padre con todas sus fuerzas toda su vida, que le rogaban mucho que les dejase estar en su tierra y acabar en ella sus días. Y mi padre, viendo que venían de buena boya, aunque estaría resentido de los españoles, mandó a sus capitanes que no les hiciesen daño porque él los quería tener en su tierra como a criados, que les hiciesen casas en que morasen. Y así los capitanes de mi padre, aunque quisieran luego acabarlos, hicieron lo que mi padre les mandó. Y el dicho mi padre los tuvo muchos días y años consigo, haciéndoles muy buen tratamiento y dándoles lo que habían menester hasta mandar que sus mismas mujeres del dicho mi padre les hiciesen la comida y la bebida y aun él mismo los traía consigo y les daba de comer junto a sí como a su persona misma y se holgaba con ellos como si fueran sus hermanos propios.

Después ya de algunos días y años, estos españoles arriba dichos estuvieron en compañía de mi padre en el dicho pueblo de Vitcos, en la misma casa de mi padre. Estaban un día con mucho regocijo jugando al herrón, solos mi padre y ellos y yo —quien entonces era muchacho— sin pensar mi padre cosa ninguna ni haber dado crédito a una india de uno de ellos, llamada Buba, que le había dicho muchos días antes, que aquellos españoles le querían matar. Sin ninguna sospecha de esto, ni de otra cosa, se holgaba con ellos como antes, y en este juego como dicho tengo. Yendo el dicho padre a levantar el herrón para haber de jugar, cargaron todos sobre él, con puñales y cuchillos y algunas espadas. Y mi padre, como se sintió herido, con la rabia de la muerte procuraba defenderse de una parte y de otra, mas como era solo y ellos eran siete y mi padre no tenía arma ninguna, al fin le derrocaron al suelo con muchas heridas, le dejaron por muerto. Y como yo era pequeño y vi a mi padre tratar de aquella manera, quise ir allá a guarecerle y se volvieron contra mí muy enojados, arrojándome un bote de lanza con la misma lanza de mi padre, que a la sazón allí estaba, que erraron poco que no me mataron a mí también. Y yo, de miedo, como espantado de aquello, me huí por unos montes abajo porque aunque me buscasen no me pudiesen hallar. Y ellos, como dejaron a mi padre ya para esperar, salieron por la puerta con mucho regocijo, diciendo:

Ya hemos muerto al Inga, no hayáis miedo.

Y unos andes que a la sazón llegaron y el Capitán Rimache Yupangui les pararon luego de tal suerte que, antes que pudiesen huir mucho trecho avance, tornaron del camino mal de su grado, derrocándolos de sus caballos abajo y trayéndolos por fuerza para hacer de ellos sacrificio. A todos los cuales dieron muy crudas muertes y aun algunos quemaron. Y después de todo esto vivió el dicho mi padre tres días, él cual antes que muriese mandó llamar a todos sus capitanes a mí para nos hablar antes que se muriese. El dijo estas palabras a los capitanes:

Parlamento que hizo Mango Inga a sus capitanes cuando estaba a la muerte, el cual dijo

Hijos, ya me veis de la manera que estoy por haberme fiado tanto de esta gente española, en especial de estos siete que aquí vosotros habéis visto, que me han guardado tanto tiempo ha y que les he tratado como a hijos, por el cual tratamiento me han puesto de esta suerte. Bien creo que no escaparé de ésta. Por esta vida que se os acuerde de lo que tantas veces os he dicho y amonestado en el Cuzco y en Tambo y en todas las demás partes adonde os habéis juntado a mi llamamiento y por las partes adonde habéis andado conmigo. Lo cual, porque sé que lo tenéis todo en la memoria, no me quiero más alargar, lo uno porque mi dolor excesivo no me da más lugar, y lo otro porque no hay para qué más os molestar. Encomendaos mucho a mi hijo Titu Cusi Yupangui para que miréis por él, pues sabéis que es la lumbrera de mis ojos y que yo le tenía a ese muchacho no solamente por hijo mas por hermano, por el mucho entendimiento que tiene, y así le he encomendado yo [que] mire y tenga cuenta con todos vosotros y con todos mis hijos como yo pudiera tener y os ruego que así como lo habéis hecho conmigo lo hagáis con él, que yo tengo de él tal concepto que os lo agradecerá y pagará muy bien: por tanto llamádmele acá para que le dé mi bendición y diga lo que ha de hacer.

Parlamento que Mango Inga hizo a su hijo al punto de la muerte

Hijo mío muy amado: bien me ves cuál estoy y por eso no tengo que significarte por palabras más mi dolor de lo que las obras dan testimonio. No llores, que si alguien había de llorar habría de ser yo si de la suerte en que estoy, fiándome tanto de semejante gente que ésta y haciéndoles tanto regalo como les he hecho, no lo mereciendo ellos, que como tú sabes vinieron aquí huyendo de sus compañeros por delitos que allá habían de haber hecho, a los cuales recogí, favorecí con entrañas de padre. Mira que te mando que perpetuamente nunca tengas ley perfecta con semejante gente que ésta por que no te acontezca a ti otro tanto como a mí. No consientas que entren en tu tierra aunque más te conviden con palabras, porque sus palabras melosas me engañaron a mí y así harán a ti si los crees.

Te encomiendo a tus hermanos y hermanas y a tu madre para que mires por ellos y los remedies y favorezcas como yo hiciera a ti y mira que no des pena a mis huesos tratando mal a tus hermanos y madre porque bien sabes vosotros que la recibirán grande.

Te encomiendo también a estos pobres indios que mires por ellos como es razón y mira cómo me han seguido y guardado y amparado en todas mis necesidades, dejando sus tierras y naturaleza por amor a mí. No les trabajes demasiado, no les acoses, no les riñ[a]s ni castigues sin culpa, porque en ello darás mucho enojo al Viracochan. Yo les he mandado a ellos que te respeten y acaten por señor en mi lugar, pues eres mi primer hijo y heredero de mi reino y ésta es mi postrimera voluntad. Yo confío de su bondad de todos ellos que te acatarán y respetarán por tal y que no harán más de lo que yo les he mandado y tú les dijeres.

El cual luego finó y me dejó a mí en el pueblo de Vitcos y de allí me vine a este Vilcabamba, donde estuve más de veinte años hasta que me desosegaron unos indios de Huamachuco por mandado de la justicia del Cuzco puesta por Gonzalo Pizarro, que a la sazón andaba alterado contra el rey.

Aquí comienza la manera y modo por la vía que yo, don Diego de Castro Titu Cusi Yupanqui, vine a tener paz con los españoles, de la cual paz, por la bondad de Dios, a quien nosotros antiguamente llamamos Viracochan, vine a ser cristiano. La cual es ésta que se sigue:

En lo sobredicho arriba por mí declarado, di a entender llana y sucintamente la manera como mi padre Mango Inga Yupangui fue señor natural de estos reinos del Perú y el modo y la manera de la entrada de los españoles en su tierra y cómo y a qué efecto se les reveló, que fue por sus muchos malos tratamientos y el discurso y fin de vida. En ésta quiero declarar el cómo yo me he habido después de sus días y la manera por donde me he venido a tornar cristiano y tener paz con los españoles, que fue mediante Dios, por ser su Señoría del señor gobernador el licenciado Lope García de Castro, quien regía y gobernaba los reinos del Perú, la cual manera pasa así:

En el tiempo que fue virrey de los reinos del Perú, el marqués de Cañete me envió a esta tierra donde estoy un padre de la orden de[l] señor Santo Domingo para que tratase conmigo de sacarme allá fuera al Cuzco, diciendo que el señor virrey traía mandado del emperador Don Carlos para que saliendo yo allá fuera y queriendo ser cristiano me darían de comer conforme a mi calidad. Y yo, acordándome del tratamiento que los españoles habían hecho a mi padre estando en el Cuzco en su compañía y por lo que el dicho mi padre me dejó mandado al fin de sus días, pensando que por ventura me aconteciera a mí lo que a mi padre, no quise entonces dar consentimiento a lo que padre fray Melchor de los Reyes, que fue el que vino con la embajada y un Juan Sierra, su compañero, por mandado del señor virrey me dijeron. Antes, para certificarme de lo que el padre y su compañero me decían si era así o no, envié con el dicho padre ciertos capitanes míos al marqués para que ellos me trajesen la certinidad del negocio y que si era así como me decían enviaría un hermano mío allá fuera en mi lugar. Esto para que experimentase la vivienda de los españoles y me diese aviso de cómo hacían con él y que si lo hiciesen bien, entonces yo saldría.

Después de pasado un año volvió el dicho padre con los dichos mis capitanes con la certinidad de todo y yo, visto que una persona como aquella me lo rogaba tanto y que me daba tan cierta certificación de que me darían de comer, envié al dicho mi hermano llamado Sayre Tupa al cual di industria de cómo se había de haber. Y dada, se fue con el dicho padre al virrey, el cual le recibió muy bien y le dio de comer en el valle de Yucay y otros repartimientos, donde murió cristiano. Y yo, desde que supe su muerte, recibí gran pena, pensando que los españoles le habían muerto como mataron a mi padre, con la cual pena estuve algunos días hasta que del Cuzco me envió el licenciado Polo con Martín de Pando, mi notario que hasta hoy día me guarda, con Juan de Betanzos la certinidad de cómo mi hermano don Diego Sayre Topa había muerto su muerte natural. Y por mí visto, detuve en mi tierra al dicho Martín de Pando para certificarme de él de cosas que me convenían y dejé ir a Juan de Betanzos con la respuesta. Y así estuve algunos días hasta que por parte del conde Nieva, virrey sucesor al marqués de Cañete, me vinieron otros mensajeros con cosas tocantes a la paz que de mí pretendían con los españoles, el cual me enviaba a decir lo mismo que el marqués. Y yo respondí que, como me gratificasen algo de lo mucho que el rey poseía de las tierras de mi padre, aparejado estaba para tener paz, los cuales mensajeros se fueron con esta respuesta.

Todas estas paces entiendo yo que procuraban los españoles por una de tres vías: o por entender que yo andaba dando saltos en sus tierras atrayéndoles mucha gente de los naturales, o porque el rey se lo mandaba por lo que le dictaba la conciencia acerca de lo que de mi padre posee, o por ventura sería por quererme tener allá consigo en su tierra para certificarse que no les haría más mal como estuviese allá, porque como yo no estaba industriado en las cosas de la fe, no sospechaba que fuese la principal causa como ahora sospecho el quererme hacer cristiano. Pero ahora, después que los padres me lo dicen, alcanzo que fuera una de las causas dichas y más principal aquella.

Después de idos los mensajeros arriba dichos que vinieron por parte del conde de Nieva, volvió otra vez con el mismo mensaje el tesorero García de Melo a rogarme que por que tuviesen sosiego los españoles, me quietase yo a mí mismo y que no anduviese de acá para allá, que el rey me daba su palabra de me lo gratificar como yo consintiese que entrasen en mi tierra sacerdotes a predicar la palabra de Dios. Al cual yo respondí que a lo que decía de quietarme yo y no hacer mal a los indios ni inquietar a los españoles, que yo le daba mi palabra de que, no me dando ellos ocasión que yo me quedaría muy a gusto como lo vería por las obras. Y a lo que decía de que consintiese que entrasen sacerdotes en mi tierra, que yo no sabía nada de aquel menester, que se efectuase una vez la paz y después se haría lo que fuese justo, con la cual respuesta se fue el tesorero Melo la primera vez.

En estos medios de idas y venidas del Cuzco a mi tierra y de mi tierra al Cuzco, estando por corregidor en él el doctor Cuenca, oidor de su Majestad, acaeció que unos indios encomendados en Nuño de Mendoza que residían lindes de esta mi tierra, en un río llamado Acobamba, por ciertos malos tratamientos que recibieron de un español que los tenía a cargo, se huyeron de él y se pasaron a esta mi tierra a reconocerme por señor. Lo cual, sabido por el doctor Cuenca, pensando que yo los había traído por fuerza, me escribió una carta muy descomedida, en la cual me decía que volviese los indios a su dueño y sino que me había de dar la más cruda guerra que se había dado a hombre. La cual carta, como yo la vi, recibí mucha pena con ella y respondí que no era así lo que me importunaban y, que si guerra quería, aparejado estaba para cada y cuando que viniesen. Y con este enojo apercibí mi gente para el efecto y mandé poner espías por no sé qué partes por que no me cogiesen descuidado los que me quisiesen hacer mal. El cual doctor Cuenca nunca más me respondió cosa ninguna, mas antes yo fui al camino por donde había de pasar para ver si todavía me quería dar la guerra dicha y de esta salida traje para casa más de quinientos indios de diversas partes. Y me volví a quietar a mi casa, en la cual recibí una carta del dicho doctor Cuenca, escrita en Lima, que no sé por dónde se me pasó, en la cual se me ofreció mucho y me rogaba que lo pasado fuese pasado.

Después de esto tornó otra vez a venir el tesorero García de Melo con el despacho de Vuestra Señoría. El cual me aconsejó por lo que yo le advertí que casásemos a mi hijo don Felipe Quispe Tito con su prima Doña Beatriz y así lo concertamos como se hiciesen las paces, que después hicimos en Acobamba por mandado de Vuestra Señoría él y yo, trayendo para ello los testigos que Vuestra Señoría señaló, a lo cual se halló presente Diego Rodríguez como corregidor y Martín de Pando como secretario. El cual concierto y capitulación cómo y de la manera que pasó, porque Vuestra Señoría lo tiene allá más por extenso y lo podrá enseñar a su Majestad. No lo pongo aquí ni ninguna cosa pondré especificada pues de todo es Vuestra Señoría el autor si no fuere lo de Chuquichaca de la venida de Hernando Matienzo y mi conversión y bautismo, lo cual quiero que su Majestad entienda de mí que fue Vuestra Señoría la principal causa de todo.

Como Vuestra Señoría sabe, cuando me envió a Diego Rodríguez que fuese corregidor de esta mi tierra, yo lo recibí por mandarlos Vuestra Señoría y por ver que yo había dado mi palabra de tener con el rey nuestro señor y con sus vasallos, la cual ratifiqué en todo, lo uno con el recibimiento que hice al oidor licenciado Matienzo en el puente de Chuquichaca, dándole a entender algunas cosas que en mi tierra me pasaban, y lo otro en recibir sacerdotes en mi tierra para que industriasen a mí y a mi gente en las cosas de Dios, como fue al padre Vera que Vuestra Señoría me envió, él cual bautizó a mi hijo don Felipe Quispe Tito, y estuvo en la tierra casi año y medio, el cual salió por la venida de los frailes agustinos que vinieron a bautizarme.

Da también testimonio de esta paz y confírmalo en todo la renunciación que yo a Vuestra Señoría hice en nombre de su Majestad de todos mis reinos y señoríos ni más ni menos que mi padre los poseía, lo cual todo concluyó el tesorero Melo en Acobamba, pues dejadas todas cosas aparte, siendo como es

Vuestra Señoría de todo como principal actor, es esta la manera que yo tuve y he tenido en mi cristianismo hasta ahora.

Por escribirme Vuestra Señoría muchas cartas rogándome que me volviese cristiano, diciendo que convenía para seguridad de la paz, procuré de inquirir de Diego Rodríguez y de Martín de Pando quién era en el Cuzco la persona más principal de los religiosos que en ella había y cuál religión la más apropiada y de más tomo. Y me dijeron que la religión de más tomo y de más autoridad y que más florecía, en toda la tierra, aunque de menos frailes, era la de señor San Agustín y el prior de ella, digo de los frailes que residen en el Cuzco, era la persona más principal de todos lo que en el Cuzco había. Y oído y entendido ser esto así, me aficioné en gran manera a aquella orden y religión más que a otra ninguna y determiné de escribir al dicho prior muchas cartas rogándole que me viniese a bautizar él en persona, porque me daba gusto ser bautizado por su mano, por ser persona tan principal antes que por otro. Y así, siendo como es tan honrado religioso, me hizo merced de tomar el trabajo y llegarse a esta mi tierra a bautizarme, trayendo consigo a otro reli-gioso y a Gonzalo Pérez de Vivero y Tilano de Anaya, los cuales llegaron a Rayangalla, a doce días del mes de agosto del año de mil y quinientos y sesenta y ocho, adonde yo salí de este Vilcabamba a recibir el bautismo como entendí que me lo venían a dar. Y allí, en el dicho pueblo de Rayangalla estuvo el dicho prior llamado fray Juan de Vivero con sus compañeros y los demás catorce días industriándome en las cosas de la fe, a cabo de los cuales, día del glorioso doctor San Agustín, me bautizó el dicho prior, siendo mi padrino Gonzalo Pérez de Vivero y madrina doña Angelina Sisa Ocllo.[33] Y desde que me hubo bautizado estuvo otros ocho días el dicho prior rectificándome de todo en todo en las cosas de nuestra santa fe católica y enseñándome las cosas y misterios de ella. Acabado todo uno y otro, se fue el dicho prior con Gonzalo Pérez de Vivero y me dejó en la tierra al compañero llamado fray Marcos García para que me fuese poco a poco advirtiendo de las cosas que el dicho prior me había enseñado por que no se me olvidasen y para que enseñase y predicase a la gente de mi tierra la palabra de Dios. Y yo, antes que se fuese, les di a entender a mis indios la causa por que me había bautizado y traído aquella gente a mi tierra y el efecto que de bautizarse los hombres sacaban y para qué quedaba este padre dicho en la tierra. Todos me respondieron que se holgaban de mi bautismo y de que quedase el padre en la tierra, que ellos procurarían de hacer otro tanto en breve pues el padre queda-ba para el efecto en la dicha tierra.

Pasados dos meses que este dicho padre estuvo en Rayangalla después que se fue el prior, enseñando e industriando en las cosas de la fe y bautizando algunas criaturas por consentimiento de sus padres, acordé de ir con Martín de Pando a visitar la tierra que está de la otra parte de los puertos hacia Huamanga, en la cual estuve cuatro meses haciendo el mismo oficio y poniendo cruces y haciendo iglesias en los pueblos adonde llegué, que fueron ocho los pueblos y tres las iglesias y en los demás cruces, bautizó en todos ellos noventa criaturas. Lo cual hecho todo y dejando muchachos para que dijesen la doctrina, se volvió al dicho pueblo de Rayangalla, adonde estuvo sólo siete meses bautizando y enseñando a los indios de toda la comarca. Y por el mes de septiembre, le vino otro padre compañero y ambos juntos se estuvieron en aquella tierra hasta que yo les traje a este Vilcabamba donde ahora estamos. No han bautizado aquí ninguno porque aún es muy nueva la gente de esta tierra en las cosas que han de saber y entender tocantes a la ley y mandamientos de Dios. Yo procuraré que poco a poco lo sepan. Por tanto, porque entienda Vuestra Señoría y me haga mercedes de lo de dar a entender a su Majestad, he procurado por la vía arriba dicha declarar sumariamente sin especificarlo más la manera y vivienda de mi padre y el suceso y el fin de mis negocios hasta el fin y punto en que ahora estoy, si acaso fuere menester que vaya uno y otro declarado más por extenso cómo y de la manera que fue y ha sido hasta ahora, cuando Vuestra Señoría lo mandare. Por ahora paréceme que basta esto, aunque había otras muchas cosas que avisar y que decir, en especial de nuestro origen y principio y trajes y manera de nuestras costumbres conforme a nuestro uso. Todo lo dejo por evitar prolijidad y porque no hacen a nuestro propósito acerca de lo que vamos tratando. Sólo suplicaré a Vuestra Señoría, pues en todo me ha hecho merced, en dar muy de veras y con todo calor a entender esto que aquí va escrito a su Majestad me haga merced muy grande, pues tengo entendido que siempre me ha de favorecer como mi señor. Y porque me parece que me ha alargado mucho ceso con esto.

Fue hecho y ordenado todo lo arriba escrito dando aviso de todo el Ilustre señor don Diego de Castro Titu Cusi Yupangui, hijo de Mango Inga Yupangui, señor natural que fue de los reinos del Perú, por el muy reverendo padre fray Marcos García, fraile presbítero de la orden del señor San Agustín, que reside en esta provincia de Vilcabamba, teniendo como tiene a cargo la administración de las ánimas que en toda ella residen, a honra y gloria de Dios todo poderoso, padre e hijo y espíritu santo, tres personas y un solo Dios verdadero y de la gloriosa reina de los ángeles, madre de Dios, Santa María, nuestra señora, ahora y para siempre jamás. Amén.

Yo, Martín de Pando, escribano de comisión por el Ilustre señor el Licenciado Lope García de Castro, gobernador que fue de estos reinos, doy fe que todo lo arriba escrito lo relató y ordenó el dicho padre a insistencia del dicho don Diego de Castro, lo cual yo escribí por mis manos propias de la manera que el dicho padre me lo relataba. Siendo testigos a lo ver, escribir y

relatar el Reverendo padre de la dicha orden que juntamente reside en com-
pañía del autor de esto, y tres capitanes del dicho don Diego de Castro, llama-
dos el uno Suta Yupangui y Rimache Yupangui y Sullca Varac. Y porque hago
fe todo lo susodicho, lo firmé de mi nombre. Hecho en el pueblo de San
Salvador de Vilcabamba, a seis de febrero del año de mil y quinientos y
setenta años, lo cual para que haga más fe lo firmaron de sus nombres el dicho
padre fray Marcos García y fray Diego Ortiz y yo el dicho Martín de Pando.
Fray Marcos García. Digo que lo vi escribir por testigo fray Diego Ortiz. En
testimonio de verdad Martín de Pando, escribano.

Yo, don Diego de Castro Titu Cusi Yupangui, hijo que soy de Mango Inga
Yupangui señor natural que fue de estos reinos del Perú, digo que por cuanto
me es necesario hacer relación al Rey don Felipe, nuestro señor, de cosas con-
venientes a mí y a mis sucesores y no sé las frases y la manera que los españoles
tienen en semejantes avisos, rogué al muy reverendo padre fray Marcos
García y a Martín de Pando, que, conforme al uso de su natural, me orde-
nasen y compusiesen esta relación arriba dicha, para enviarla a los reinos de
España al muy Ilustre señor el Licenciado Lope García de Castro, para que
por mí y en mi nombre, llevando como lleva mi poder, me haga merced de la
enseñar y relatar a su Majestad del Rey don Felipe nuestro señor, para que,
vista la razón que yo tengo de ser gratificado, me haga mercedes para mí y
para mis hijos y descendientes, como quien su Majestad es. Y porque es ver-
dad lo sobredicho de ésta, firmada de mi nombre, que es hecho día mes y año
susodicho. Don Diego de Castro Titu Cusi Yupangui.

Poder para el señor Gobernador el Licenciado Lope García de Castro

Sepan cuantos esta carta de poder vieren como yo, el Sapay Inga don Diego
de Castro Titu Cusi Yupangui, hijo mayorazgo que soy de Mango Inga
Yupangui y nieto de Guaina Capac, señores naturales que fueron de estos
reinos y provincias del Perú, digo que por cuanto yo tengo necesidad de
tratar en los reinos de España, muchas cosas y negocios con el Rey don
Felipe nuestro señor y con otras justicias, de cualquier estado y condición
que sean, así seculares como eclesiásticos, y juntamente con algunas otras
personas que de estos reinos hayan ido a los de España, que allá puedan
residir o residan, y no podría hallar persona que con más calor ni solicitud
pudiese solicitar mis negocios, como es el señor gobernador el licenciado
Castro, que a los reinos de España ahora va, ni quien con más amor los haga
ni pueda hacer, como ha tenido y tiene de costumbre de hacerme merced,
que por ésta, con la confianza que de su persona tengo, le doy todo mi
poder bastante libre y suficiente, cual de derecho más puede valer, así como

yo lo he y tengo, y de derecho en tal caso se requiere para que por mí y en mi nombre y como mi persona misma, pueda parecer ante su Majestad y presentar a su real nombre cualesquier petición y peticiones, y decir y declarar todo lo que le fuere preguntado tocante a mis negocios, de la misma manera que si yo lo dijese y declarase y pueda parecer ante cualesquier consejos, audiencias, alcaldes y regimiento y ante otras cualesquier justicias de su Majestad, así eclesiásticas como seculares, y pedir y demandar, amparar y defender, todas y cualesquier cosas que vea que me puedan y deban pertenecer, las cuales pueda poseer, regir y adjudicar como si yo mismo las poseyese, rigiese y adjudicase, con mi propia persona, y para lo que así hubiere de pesos de oro y plata, haciendas, rentas, ganados y otras cualesquier cosas que hubiere, me las pueda enviar a estos reinos a mi costa y misión, y para que por mí y en mi nombre, y si le pareciere de cualesquier pesos de oro que me pertenezcan, me pueda hacer comprar y compre cualesquier haciendas, rentas y mercaderías que le parezca que me convengan, así muebles como raíces. Así mismo, para que pueda hacer cualesquier pedimentos, requerimientos, juramentos de calumnia y decisorio, decir verdad, responder a lo hecho de contrario, concluir, presentar testigos, probanzas, escrituras, provisiones, cédulas reales y otro género de prueba y lo sacar, contradecir lo de en contrario, poner cualesquier recusaciones, sospechas, objetos, jurarlas, apartarse de ellas; tomar y aprehender en mi nombre cualesquier posesiones de cualesquier mis bienes y haciendas que me convengan, y sobre la aprehensión, hacer lo que fuere justo y convenga a los dichos bienes; oír sentencias a favor, consentir lo de en contrario, apelar y suplicar adonde y con derecho deba, seguir la causa hasta la final conclusión; pedir costas y jurarlas en efecto; hacer todo aquello que yo podría, aunque aquí no vaya declarado ni expresado y sean cosas de calidad que requieran mi presencia, que cuan y cumplido poder como tengo y de derecho se requiere dar y otorgar, otro tal y ése mismo lo doy y otorgo, con todas sus incidencias y dependencias, anexidades y conexidades y con libre y general administración y para que este dicho poder lo pueda sustituir en una o más personas como le pareciere y los revocar, a los cuales y a él relevo. En formal para firmeza de ello, obligo los bienes, tributos, rentas, haciendas que así me convengan, muebles, raíces habidos y por haber; y para testimonio de lo susodicho, lo firmé de mi nombre, que es hecho a seis días del mes de febrero de mil y quinientos y setenta años. Testigos que fueron presentes a lo ver sacar, los muy reverendos padres fray Marcos García y fray Diego Ortiz y don Pablo Guallpa Yupangui y don Martín Cusi Guaman[34] y don Gaspar Sulca Yanac. Yo, Martín de Pando, escribano de comisión, por el muy Ilustre señor el licenciado Castro, doy fe de cómo es verdad todo lo susodicho y que el dicho Inga don Diego de Castro dio este poder al dicho señor licenciado Castro, gobernador que fue de estos reinos, como y de la manera en que derecho se requiere, en testimonio de lo cual puse en su nombre, don Diego de Castro y su firma, como abajo aparecerá en el original. Don Diego de Castro Titu Cusi Yupangui, por testigo fray Marcos García, por testigo fray Diego Ortiz. Y en testimonio de verdad, hice aquí este mi signo. Martín de Pando, escribano de comisión.

Endnotes

1. En el texto original se encuentra escrito junto o <Guainacapac>. Para que su correspondencia a la refonologización al Quechua moderno hecha en la traducción al inglés, he optado por escribirlo <Guaina Capac>.

2. En el manuscrito se escribe <Topa Inga Yupangui>. Sin embargo, en el texto, la mayoría de veces se escribe <Ynga>. He optado por normalizar la ortografía con el primer uso.

3. <atauallpa> es otra ortografía alternativa que se encuentra en el texto.

4. O también <Uascar Ynga>

5. <tomes>

6. <Çapay Ynga>

7. <Biracochan>

8. Se repite "lo que les decía" (Ver Edición 1985: 5; Edición 1992: 12)

9. <Challcochima>, ver nota 1.

10. Únicamente en la edición de Millones se encuentra este "diciendo" (Edición 1985: 6); en las otras ediciones no se da esta interrupción al discurso de Francisco Pizarro (Edición 1916: 28; Edición 1992: 13).

11. Hernando de Soto.

12. Cupi.

13. "Hemos" en las ediciones de 1916 y 1992 (29; 16). "Tenemos" en la edición de 1985 (8).

14. "Sois" (Edición 1916: 30; Edición 1985: 8; Edición 1992: 17).

15. "Tomastes" (Edición 1916: 30; Edición 1985: 8; Edición 1992: 17).

16. "Tiene" ver notas 14 y 15.

17. Sugerencia de Millones (Edición 1985: 8).

18. <Tauantinsuyu>

19. No se encuentra en la edición de Millones (Edición 1985: 9) pero sí se encuentra en las ediciones de Urteaga y Regalado (Edicion 1916: 34; Edición 1992: 19).

20. <Yupanqui>

21. Regalado en su edición incluye "por cierto" como parte de la narración (ver Edición 1992: 20). Urteaga, Carrillo y Millones la incluyen como parte del discurso de Manku Inqa lo cual cobra más sentido (Edición 1916: 34; Edición Carrillo: 41; Edición 1985: 10).

22. La edición de Regalado es la única que ofrece esta versión: "y traeros con tanta honra y aparato a my pueblo y cassa tenia, lo cual si vosotros quereis juzgarlo [. . .]" (Edición 1992: 22).

23. Solamente Regalado en su edición omite esta sección de manera que se lee así: "no bine juntamente con estos cavalleros a besar las manos a vuestra merced, pero ya que hasta aquí a avido [. . .]" (Edición 1992: 24).

24. <atunbiracochan>, ver notas 1 y 7.

25. Alternativamente <Quisu Yupangui>. He refonologizado a partir de <Queso>.

26. ~<Coriatao>, ver nota 1.

27. ~<Cuyllas>

28. ~<Quicaña>

29. ~<Curiguallpa>

30. ~<Lliclis>

31. <Guarivillca>

32. <Yanquiguallpa>

33. <Angelina Çiça Ocllo>. Como en la modernización del castellano, para las voces en lengua andina cuya ortografía en el manuscrito original tuviere <ç>, las he reemplazado con el grafema que le corresponde a las sibilantes en las lenguas andinas modernas, o sea <s>. De la misma manera, <ç> ha sido reemplazada en las voces y nombres castellanos con <c> o <s> de acuerdo con las normas modernas.

34. <Cusiguaman>, ver nota 1.

Instruction of the Inqa Don Diego de Castro Titu Kusi Yupanki for His Most Illustrious Lord Licentiate Lope García de Castro (1570)

(First Full English Translation and Annotated Edition)

Instruction of the Inqa[1] Don Diego de Castro Titu Kusi Yupanki[2] for His Most Illustrious Lord Licentiate Lope Garcia de Castro—who governed these Kingdoms of Peru—with reference to this business with His Majesty, and in whose Name and Representation he is to engage in the following:

As I, Don Diego de Castro Titu Kusi Yupanki am the grandson of Wayna Qhapaq[3] and son of Manku Inqa Yupanki, who were the native rulers of these kingdoms and provinces of Peru, have been much graced and favored by the most Illustrious Lord Licentiate Lope García de Castro, who governed these kingdoms for His Majesty King Felipe our Lord, and since your lordship is leaving these kingdoms for Spain and is a most valiant and Christian person, I could find no other of better title or will to favor me in all of my business before his Majesty which you are to present and negotiate, in all things necessary to myself and to my children and their descendants. To this purpose—because of the great esteem in which I hold you—I will not forget to leave everything in your hands as you have already been so generous with me, on past occasions, and I trust that in this important business you will perform as best befits your Illustrious Person.

And because the memory of men is weak and thin and if we do not turn to the written word to benefit from it in our hour of need, it would be impossible for us to remember at length all of the important events that present themselves and for this reason, trying to be as brief as possible, I must necessarily recollect some things essential for your Lordship, so that in my representation you may favor me before his Majesty in all things, as these will be declared and narrated below. The recollection of these things is the following:

Firstly, his Lordship, upon a safe arrival in the kingdoms of Spain, would serve me well by explaining to his Majesty the King Don Felipe our

Lord, under whose protection I have placed myself, who I am and my wants caused by his Majesty's possession, of the lands that belonged to my ancestors for which I suffer in these forests.[4] And your lordship could begin this account, being served by this source, by beginning first with who I am and whose son I am, so that his Majesty can further account for the reason, which I have stated above, to gratify me.

I believe that there are many who have already written of the native rulers of old and whence and how they came forth and for this reason I will not detain myself in their narrative.[5] Your lordship need only indulge me by telling his Majesty how I am the legitimate son, I say, the first heir that my father Manku Inqa Yupanki left among many others, amongst whom he left me in charge, with orders to look after them as if they were my own person, which I have done from the day he died till the present and as I will do for as long as I live, so help me God, for it is fair for sons to do what their fathers order, especially on their dying days.

Also, let his Majesty know that my father Manku Inqa Yupanki, is the son of Wayna Qhapaq and grandson of Inqa Thupaq Yupanki, by the direct lineage of his forefathers the most powerful lord of all the kingdoms of Peru, anointed as such by his father Wayna Qhapaq and held and obeyed as such in all the land for the rest of his days as I have been, am and will be in this land, after my father's death.

And also explain to his Majesty the reason for which I find myself here, in such need, among these forests where my father left me whence he reigned and governed Peru and all the land, at the time that the Spaniards ruined and killed him.

And let his Majesty know as well, which is to be declared below, how and whence the Spaniards entered Peru and their treatment of my father for the rest of his days until they killed him here, in these lands now under my possession. The account is the following:

Account of how the Spaniards entered Peru and the events experienced by Manku Inqa among them.

At the time that the Spaniards landed in Peru in the town of Cajamarca,[6] approximately one hundred ninety leagues[7] from here, my father Manku Inqa was in the city of Cuzco, at that time with all the power and might with which his father Wayna Qhapaq had left him whence he received the news from certain messengers hailing from Cajamarca that an elder brother of his (though a bastard) called Ataw Wallpa and some Yungas Tallanes Indians— who live at the shores of the Southern Sea, fifteen or twenty leagues from the aforesaid Cajamarca—said that they had seen certain persons very different to ourselves arrive and that they seemed like Wiraquchas[8]—which is the name that we gave in ancient times to the creator of all things—saying Tiqsin Wiraquchan,[9] which means the beginning and maker of all things. And they named, in this way, these people whom they had seen, because they were very different in clothing and appearance, and because they rode some very large animals, silver footed, and they said this because of the shining of their horse-shoes. And they also called them Wiraquchas because they had seen them speak to themselves in some painted clothes as one person speaks to another and this they said for the reading of books and letters. And they called them Wiraquchas because of their excellent appearance and the great differences among them: because some had black beards and others none; and because they saw them eat on silver plates; and because they had Illapas[10]—name that we give to thunder—and this they said for the muskets they fired because they thought they were lightning bolts from the sky.

Among these Wiraquchas two were brought by some Yungas[11] before my uncle Ataw Wallpa (who happened to be in Cajamarca) who cordially received them and gave them each to drink, a drink that we drink, from a golden cup. The Spaniard, upon receiving the drink in his hand, spilled it which greatly angered my uncle. And after that, the two Spaniards showed my uncle a letter, or book, or something, saying that this was the qillqa[12] of God and the King and my uncle, as he felt offended by the spilling of the chicha,[13] took the letter (or whatever it was) and knocked it to the ground, saying:

I don't know what you have given me. Go on, leave.

And the Spaniards returned to their cohorts, who surely told them of what they had seen and what had came to pass with my uncle Ataw Wallpa.[14]

Many days later, with my uncle Ataw Wallpa at war with his brother Waskar Inqa, over who would be the true king of this land, neither of whom were the legitimate heir as they both had usurped my father of his kingdom (he being quite young at the time) for each of their many uncles and aunts had asked themselves, "why should a boy be king?" Even though his father on his deathbed had named him so, the elder sons and not the younger were kings. Surely this was not reason but passion, greed and ambition for, though they were sons of Wayna Qhapaq, their mothers were of base and soiled blood and my father was the legitimate son of royal blood as Pachakutiq Inqa had been, the grandfather of Wayna Qhapaq.[15] And being in these disputes as I have said, one against the other though they were brothers on different thrones, there arrived in Cajamarca, the aforesaid town, about forty or fifty Spaniards, it is said, on well-saddled horses. When these events were known by my uncle Ataw Wallpa, who was nearby in a town called Huamachuco hosting the fes-tivities there,[16] he left with his guards not with arms to attack nor harness to *defend but with tumis and lassos, as we call our knives with which we hunt this type of new llamas, as we call our livestock, and they said so because of the horses which had appeared again and they took tumis[17] and knives to skin and quarter the animals, thinking little of the small number of men.*

And when my uncle arrived in Cajamarca with his people, the Spaniards received them in the baths of Conoc,[18] a league and a half from Cajamarca, and so they went with him to Cajamarca. And having arrived, he asked them why they had come and they replied under the mandate of Wiraqucha to tell them how they were to know Him. And my uncle, as he heard what they told them he started and was silent and offered them drink in the aforesaid manner to see whether they would spill the drink in the same way the others had, and so they did, because they didn't drink or listen. And my uncle seeing that they respected little said:

Since you don't respect me I won't respect you either.

And angry, he stood and shouted for the death of the Spaniards and the Spaniards, who were on guard, seized the four entrances to the plaza so that the Indians were surrounded on all sides.

Since the plaza was surrounded and the many Indians inside were like sheep, unable to move and unarmed because they had left their weapons behind, thinking little of the small number of men because they had thought little of the Spaniards; they were carrying only lassos and tumis, as I said before. The Spaniards, infuriated, attacked the center of the plaza where the Inqa's throne stood, as tall as a fortress—what we call an usnu[19]—which they took over and stopped my uncle from mounting. At the foot of the throne they threw him down from his litter and overturning and seizing its contents and the fringe and diadem—which among us is the crown—and having seized everything they attacked him. And as the Indians screamed, with swords they were killed by the horsemen, with muskets, as one who kills sheep, with no resistance given by ten thousand, two hundred who could not escape. And when all were slaughtered, they took my uncle to a prison in the night, where he was held naked, the entire night, with a chain about his neck. The next morning they gave him his clothes and his diadem saying:

Are you the king of this land?

And he replied:

Yes.

And they said:

There is none other besides you? Because we know there is another named Manku Inqa. Where is he?

And my uncle replied:

In Cuzco.

And they replied:
Well, where is Cuzco?
And my uncle responded:
Cuzco is two hundred leagues from here.[20]
And the Spaniards replied:
Since he is in Cuzco (as we have had news that it is the head[21] and capital of this land) he must therefore be king.
And my uncle said:
My father ordered it so, but as he is so young I govern in his place.
And the Spaniards said:
Though he is young it is fair that he be made aware of our arrival and of our mandate from Wiraquchan. Tell him.
And my uncle said:
Who do you wish me to send when you have killed all of my people and I am in this way?

(And he said this because he was not on good terms with my father and feared that if he told my father of the arrival of the Wiraquchas they would do him in because he thought them powerful and, at the time, still believed that they were Wiraquchas.)

The Spaniards, when they saw that my uncle Ataw Wallpa was reluctant to announce their arrival to my father, decided to send him messengers on their own. And during this interlude when the Spaniards sent messages, the Tallanes Yungas, confused and fearing my father for they knew him to be king, decided to go to Cuzco without telling either my uncle or the Spaniards. And upon their arrival they said these words to my father:

Sapay Inqa[22]—*which means your only lordship*—we have come to tell you how this kind of people have arrived in your land, who without a doubt are Wiraquchas—*how they say gods*—never seen nor heard before among our nations, have arrived in Cajamarca where your brother is. And he has told them and asserted that he is the lord and king of this land, for which we, as your vassals, have received much grief and because of this, incapable of suffering such injury to our ears, have come to tell you what has come to pass for we would not have you think of us as rebels or slipshod in your service.

And my father, having heard their delegation, was distraught, saying,
But, how could such people dare to enter my land without my mandate or consent? What are these people?
And the messengers replied,
Lord, these people without a doubt must be Wiraquchas because they say they come by the wind and they are bearded and very beautiful and

very white: they eat on plates of silver and even the sheep they mount, which are large, wear silver shoes that drop illapas like the sky. Look, such people who govern and order themselves in this way must be Wiraquchas. And by our own eyes we have seen them alone speaking to some white clothes and naming us by our names, without our telling them, only by looking at the cloth before them;[23] and they are people like no other for only their face and hands appear as their clothing is better than ours, made of silver and gold; people such as these can be none other than Wiraquchas.[24]

And to this my father, as a man who surely wished to verify what they were, threatened the messengers in this way,

Look well that you have not lied to me in what you have said for you already know and understand what my ancestors and I do to liars.

And they replied, aghast and terrified,

Sapay Inqa, if we had not seen them with our own eyes and if we did not fear you as your vassals, we would not have dared to come and see you with such news! And if you do not wish to believe us send whomever you deem fit to Cajamarca and there you will see the people of whom we speak. They are awaiting your reply to our message.

And my father seeing that they verily certified what they said and giving them some credit for their news, said,

Since you have troubled yourselves to verify the arrival of these people, go and bring me some of them here so that I may look upon them and believe with knowing eyes.

And the messengers did what my father ordered and returned to Cajamarca with I don't know how many Indians that my father sent to certify what had been said and to beg the Spaniards to visit him where he was because he wished to see the good people for whom the Yungas Tallanes had gone through such trouble (to assure him of what they were). And finally one and all of the messengers left Cuzco, by my father's mandate, for Cajamarca to see these Wiraquchas.

And upon their arrival, the Marquis Don Francisco Pizarro[25] received them well and was pleased to hear from my father and the little things he had sent, who, as I have already stated, had sent the messengers to beg the Spaniards to return with them. The latter received the news well and decided to send two Spaniards to kiss my father's hands, one Villegas and the other Antano (for the Indians did not know to call him otherwise).[26] And they left for Cajamarca by order of the Marquis and approval of the others and arrived in Cuzco without any fear or hindrance. My father, knowing of their arrival beforehand, sent them food and drinks along the way and even sent messengers from Cuzco to bear them in litters. And so it was. And when they arrived in Cuzco and were presented to my father, he received them honorably and sent them off to be lodged and provided for.

The next day he sent for them and made a great feast with many people and vessels, flasks, cups, and plates of gold and silver; and the Spaniards, seeing so much gold and silver, asked my father to give them some to show the Marquis and their cohorts evidence of his splendor and power. And my father thought well of it and gave them many flasks and cups of gold and other jewels and riches for themselves and their friends. And he sent them with many people to the governor, saying that since they had come to see him, by mandate of the Wiraquchan, they should all visit his lands in good time.

While these two Spaniards had gone to kiss the hands of my father in Cuzco, my uncle Ataw Wallpa, because he feared the Wiraquchas and also because he wanted to use them against Manku Inqa, my father, and Waskar Inqa, his brother, gave them a large sum of treasure in gold and silver which belonged to my father. And because he was still wary of my uncle Waskar Inqa, he sent certain messengers (from the place where he was) to plot with his own people to kill him and so keep that part of his back secure, believing himself secure with the Spaniards (as I have said) because of the treasure that he had given them, which was not his own but my father's. These messengers obeyed him so well that they killed Waskar Inqa in a battle in a town called Huánuco Pampa.[27] And learning of the death of Washar Inqa, his brother, Ataw Wallpa was pleased for he felt he no longer had anyone to fear, for all was secure, as he had destroyed his greatest enemy and he had bribed the Wiraquchas; he thought he no longer had anyone to fear. And the opposite was true for when the two Spaniards arrived and gave the Marquis—whom we call Machu Kapitu[28]—my father's message (that my father Manku Inqa Yupanki was the true king in all the land, whom everyone respected, had and held as their overlord and that Ataw Wallpa, his older brother, was a tyrant in his kingdom) he was pleased to hear such news from my father, from such an important person, and happy to receive the presents he had sent with such good will. He was very pleased and aggrieved to see how his brother had unjustly tried to vex and torment him, by usurping his kingdom unjustly, and who was later punished as he well deserved.

Upon their arrival, as I have said above, the Spanish messengers who had seen my father on his throne and the other Indians whom my father had sent with his presents of gold and silver, more than the aforesaid two million, each gave their messages to the governor as my father Manku Inqa Yupanki had ordered saying that my father had been greatly pleased by the arrival of such good people to his land and that he was begging them to come to Cuzco, where

*he was, and that he would receive them honorably and gave them his word to
do everything that they asked because they had come by Wiraquchan's mandate and he also had them know that in those parts there was a brother of his,
Ataw Wallpa, who called himself king of the land and they were to ignore
these claims because he was the king and native lord of the land, signaled as
such by his father Wayna Qhapaq, and that Ataw Wallpa had revolted
against his will.*

*Having learned this from one and many sources, the governor received my
father's messengers and aforesaid presents with much joy, ordering that they
be lodged and honored as befitted the messengers of such a lord. Several days
later, the Indian messengers of my father returned with his answer. The
Marquis remained in Cajamarca, keeping Ataw Wallpa imprisoned ever since
he and his cohorts had arrived in the land as he was suspicious of him, and
also because he wanted to certify my father's answer and for this reason he
kept him in prison for so long, until he received another order from my father.*

*And my uncle Ataw Wallpa, seeing the messengers and the large amounts
of gold and silver that had been sent to the Spaniards, was greatly grieved to
see how quickly they had united and how quickly the Spaniards had accepted
Manku Inqa as king and overlord for he suspected that he would be the one
to suffer most from this union. Moved by these suspicions and fears he determined to unite all of his captains and people in a circle to tell them the straits
he was in and when they were together he said these words:*

Apu[29]—*which means lords*—the people who have come to our lands
have confabulated and are at peace with my brother Manku Inqa. If you all
agree, let us strike at their head and kill them all for, though they are small
in number, yet they are brave and we must remain supreme in this land, as
we were before, for my brother Waskar Inqa is dead and if we do not kill
them now they will join my brother Manku Inqa. As they are so brave and
maybe even Wiraquchas, our endeavor may fail for my brother is angry
and has made captains of them and has called all of the earth to do battle
against us; let us strike first—they will not stop before killing us.

*The captains and people thought well of my uncle's reasoning and said as
one voice,*

Hu Hu[30] Sapay Inqa—*which means Lord, you have spoken well*—let us
kill these people. There aren't enough of them to make us a meal.

*And all of them decided the day and hour for the killing. When the
Marquis received news of their treachery, I know not how, and knowing of
their plans to kill them he dined upon them first for he ordered spies to follow
them and to be wary. Without hesitating, he ordered Ataw Wallpa, my uncle,
into the plaza and, on a stick, giving no resistance, the Marquis slit his*

throat.[31] *And after his execution, the Marquis broke camp to go see my father and he left so quickly that he was able to avoid the Indians who had descended like rain, for one of Ataw Wallpa's Indian general captains called Challku Chima and another called Kiskis,*[32] *his cohort, both brave and powerful, gathered a great number of people to pursue the Marquis. There were so many people in their pursuit that with much effort and many losses they made their way, receiving* guazábaras[33] *from their seekers.*

My father, learning of their predicament, called people to their aid and so he left Cuzco with one hundred thousand men for Vilcacunga where he found the Marquis and Challku Chima in chains and the Marquis, upon seeing him, was greatly pleased. And my father in his litter of crystal and of gold and wearing his royal diadem alighted and embraced the Marquis who had dismounted his horse and the Marquis, upon seeing him, was greatly pleased. And the Marquis and my father were united as one and sent for their people to join them and ordered for none to leave unless it were in pursuit of Kiskis, who was still roaming around with many people, because he refused to leave Challku Chima.

Having received each other as one, my father and the Marquis left for Vilcacunga and that night in Jaquijahuana[34] *where the Marquis handed my father Challku Chima saying,*

See here Lord Manku Inqa, I bring your chief enemy Challku Chima in chains.

Saying,

See what is to be done with him.

And my father had him burned for all to see so that Kiskis, his cohort, would receive the news and so that his punishment would be an example for all.

Having punished this dire Indian, dire as he was, they left for Cuzco together, although my father was anxious to see that scoundrel Kiskis. And upon their arrival in Cuzco my father ordered all of his people to respect and esteem the Marquis and his own and to provide for them in everything necessary until his return, saying that he wanted to kill and destroy that rogue Kiskis and his seed, for having humiliated him and the Spaniards whom he esteemed as at the time, the Marquis Don Francisco Pizarro had made a good impression on him.

The pursuit of Kiskis, Traitor to His Royal Person and King Manku Inqa by Manku Inqa and the Captain Antonio de Soto

After my father had lodged and provided for the Marquis and his people, he determined, with the Marquis's agreement to pursue Kiskis the Traitor because he was so enraged with him as a result of the great love and affection he felt toward the Spaniards. And the Marquis, seeing the determination with which my father had decided to make this expedition, offered to join him on this journey, saying it was not fair for him to stay in town while my father went to war, that two could do more than one. My father, Manku Inqa, seeing the good will of the Marquis, told him not to move for now but to rest and relax until he returned, for he would return soon, and if he wished he could send some of his men for he would be happy to receive them, but he would not have the Marquis leave town.

The Marquis Don Francisco Pizarro, seeing that my father would not allow him to leave town to join him, spoke with his captains about the situation and they agreed that my father's wishes were fair and so among themselves, with the governor, they named Captain Antonio de Soto[35] *to join my father with fifty other Spanish soldiers. And having been named for the mission, the aforesaid Antonio de Soto, he and the Marquis left for the house of my father who was about to leave and told him what had been decided. And my father, having learned of their decision, was greatly pleased and told them that the decision was good and that the soldiers should make ready because he wanted to leave soon.*

That same day my father left Cuzco with all his men, taking with him Captain Antonio de Soto and his company, and all left in their shared pursuit of Kiskis. Soon enough they came upon Kiskis the Traitor, whom they found in a town called Cupi,[36] *fifteen leagues from Cuzco, where they waged a raw battle in which a large number of men were killed and scattered, and among his own Kiskis escaped without their knowledge. And my father and Captain Soto, after they had scattered Kiskis and his men, returned to Cuzco sending many after Kiskis to bring him alive wherever he was.*

And upon their arrival in Cuzco my father and the Captain Antonio de Soto, after their battle with Kiskis, were well received by the Marquis Francisco Pizarro and all of his people and the townspeople, with much joy and delight for the victory they had had with Kiskis and his men. And having finished everything and their welcome, my father returned to his house and the Spaniards to theirs. And the next morning, calling all of the men from the Battle of Kiskis and the townspeople to my father's house, he ate with them and after having eaten he ordered that no one, under penalty of death, dare to disobey the new men he had brought to his land, and that they should respect and honor them as things of Wiraquchan, which means god. And he ordered Indians and people for their houses, to serve them and my father even gave his own servants to serve the Marquis. And having done all of the above he again chose men for the pursuit of Kiskis, saying that he would trail him to the end of the world to kill him for betraying him and the Wiraquchas.

Having gathered all of the things necessary for his trip and having given his orders to the government of the town, leaving Pawllu,[37] *his brother, and Tikuq and other captains in charge, he took leave from the Marquis by swearing that he would never return until he had killed Kiskis, the Traitor. He left the next day from Cuzco, taking the aforesaid Antonio de Soto with him in his aforesaid company. They left little by little, day by day, until they arrived in a town called Vinchu, fifty leagues from Cuzco, where they found the messengers that had been sent from the Battle of Cupi to trail Kiskis, and they said that they had been searching for that traitor and could find no trace of him in all the earth—only that his captains were apprehensive with the lack of news of him.*

And my father, when he heard what the messengers said, was aggrieved and wanted to push on, but he received letters from the Marquis in which he said he was suffering his absence in solitude and begged for his return. My father, because of the love he had for the Marquis, returned, leaving messengers in all of the earth where the traitor would have to pass, so that wherever he stepped they would wage war on him and kill him. Having done this and sent the messengers everywhere, even Quito, four hundred leagues from here, where the worthless man, as will be told below, died, they returned to Cuzco where my aforesaid father learned that after so many guazábaras *the traitor had robbed and killed so many people in so many places, even his own people, that he had left the land deserted. Seeing him so heartless, having left the land deserted, with great disgust—the betrayal of his king and his carnage rendering him ugly*[38]*—they cut off his head.*

When my father had been in Cuzco awhile, calm and content with the death of that Kiskis the Traitor, he called all of his people to him so that their chiefs would give tribute to the Spaniards for their nourishment and my aforesaid father, as he collected the tribute to fill their needs, gave them a large sum of treasure that belonged to his ancestors, and the governor and his cohorts received these with much joy and gave him thanks.

How the Spaniards Imprisoned Manku Inqa

The Spaniards, seeing themselves with such wealth, wanted to return to their homeland but my father, seeing that they had not stayed long in the land, did not allow them to leave asking them to rest with him instead and stay in the land and that they should inform their homeland of what had happened on their trip, and they thought well of this plan and had messengers take a large sum of the treasure to the Emperor Don Carlos and in this manner they remained in Cuzco for many days, at their pleasure, in my father's company. And several years later, for the greed of men is large, the devil—friend of all evil and the enemy of all virtue—won them over and they took to conspiring among themselves on how to torment my father and milk him for more gold and silver than what they already had received. And whence my father was in his house, still and quiet, they went there with another hundred Spaniards to betray him under the pretense that they had come to visit, as they were wont, and he received them with much joy and delight, and they, through their armed betrayal, seized him, saying:

We know, Manku Inqa that you wish to revolt against us as your brother Ataw Wallpa did. Know this: the governor demands that we seize you and imprison you like your brother Ataw Wallpa so that you cannot do us ill.

My father, seeing them so determined, was greatly offended and said:

What have I done to you? Why do you wish to treat me in this way and tie me up like a dog? Is this your repayment for the good will I have shown you in my land and her gifts I bestowed upon you with all my love and affection? You do wrongly. You call yourselves Wiraquchas sent by the Tiqsin Wiraquchan? You could not possibly be his sons as you wish to do ill to someone who has only done you good. Did I not send you a large sum of gold and silver to Cajamarca? Did you not take all of the treasure of my ancestors, which my brother Ataw Wallpa had in his keeping? Have I not given you everything you have wanted, which altogether must be much more than six million?[39] Have I not given you servants and ordered all the land to render you tributes? What more do you want from me? Judge for yourselves and you will see that I am right.

The Spaniards, as if they were blinded by that evil greed, responded, saying,

Sapay Inqa, do not give us excuses because we are sure that you will revolt against us with all the land. Young men, hand us those chains.

They brought these to them, who looked not on whom he was and the good he had done them or what they were binding to his feet. My father, seeing himself, was overcome with sadness and said:

Verily I say that you are demons and not Wiraquchas for you have bound me innocent. What do you want?

And the Spaniards replied,

We do not want anything, only your imprisonment.

And they left him in shackles and guarded and returned to their houses to let the governor, who was not innocent in this endeavor, know what they had done. And after my father felt his imprisonment, he was greatly grieved and knew not what to do because there were none to console him, not even the people of his land. And after I don't know how many days, Hernando Pizarro and Juan Pizarro and Gonzalo Pizarro and many others said to my father:

Lord Manku Inqa, do you still wish to revolt with all the earth?

And my father replied,

With what earth am I to revolt, for it is not mine, how am I then to revolt?

To this the Spaniards replied and said:

They have told us that you wish to kill us and for this reason we have imprisoned you, so if it's true that you do not wish to revolt you would do well to redeem yourself by giving us some gold and silver, which we have come to collect. Grant us this and you will be released.

Hernando Pizarro added,

Even if you release him and he gives us all of the gold and silver that fits in four *bohíos* I will not release him unless he gives me his wife Quya,[40] his sister, called Kura Uqllu, as my wife.

And he said this because he had seen her and fallen in love with her because she was very beautiful. And my father, seeing them so determined with this evil purpose, said:

Such is the mandate of Wiraquchan? That you take the lands and women of people by force? This is not our custom and I say that you are not the sons of Wiraquchan but are Supay[41]—*which means demon in our tongue.* Leave, and I will procure something to give you.

And they replied:

Do not think to do as you like, for you must give us as much as you gave us when we arrived and more: so much treasure that it could not fit in the largest *bohío* of an Indian.

And my father, seeing them so steadfast and determined, decided to waste no more words and said,

Go on. I will do what I can and will send you my answer.

And they left. And the next day my aforesaid father called all of the people in all the land to gather the treasure that the Spaniards so desperately required and when he received it he gave the following speech:

Speech that Manku Inqa Yupanki Gave to his Captains as to the Treasure Collection which he gave to the Spaniards when they Imprisoned him for the First Time.

My sons and brothers, these past few days I have made you gather once more so that you could see the type of new people that I have brought to this land: these bearded ones who are here in our town, because they told me that they were Wiraquchas and so it seemed because of their clothing. And I sent you all to serve them and obey them as you would my own person and give them tribute from your lands, believing them to be grateful people sent from the Tiqsin Wiraquchan—*which means god*—as they said they were and, it seems to me, the opposite of what I believed is true. Know this, brothers: these people have revealed themselves to be, after entering my land, not sons of Wiraquchan but of the devil himself through their own actions, as you can see with your own eyes. And it seems to me that you cannot but grieve, if you love me truly, at the sight of me, your king, shackled in manacles and treated in this way, without deserving it, for inviting such people into my land—for I would slit my own throat for your lives. If you wish to please me, find a reasonable amount of gold and silver as quickly as you can, because they would die for it, so that I can redeem myself and leave this prison in which you can see, with your own eyes, how distressed and disconcerted I am.

Response given to Manku Inqa by the Indians about the Treasure Hunt when he was in Prison

As all the people of the land searched its four corners, one thousand two hundred leagues long and almost three hundred leagues wide, which were distributed in this way throughout the world (it is convenient to know): in the east and west, north and south, what we call Antisuyu, Chinchaysuyu, Kuntisuyu, Qullasuyu; Antisuyu to the east, Kuntisuyu to the north and Chinchaysuyu to the west, and Qullasuyu to the south. This we said from Cuzco, which is the center and head of all the earth. And for this reason, because we were at the center, my ancestors, who had been placed there by their ancestors, were called Lords of the Tawantinsuyu, which means Lords of the Four Quadrants of the world for they thought there was no world beyond our own.[42] *They always sent messengers to the four quadrants so that all the people would unite at the head, as my father did then for the collection as I said above. Though there was a lot of treasure, to give numbers would be impossible, everyone said that with all of the deaths in Cajamarca and the aforementioned Kiskis affair, countless people in many* guazábaras *and battles, which I avoid for the sake of order, only ten thousand chiefs would arrive at the meeting. And when they were united before my father, as they saw his ill luck, they were moved to tears and said:*

Sapay Inqa, there is no heart in this world that, upon seeing our king so distressed and disconcerted with pain, would not shatter and melt with pity. Surely, Sapay Inqa, you were wrong to invite such people into your lands, but what is done is done and cannot be undone. As your vassals, we are ready to obey your will and mandate and to only speak your orders to collect what in comparison to what we owe you is nothing and if what you ask of us is not enough to redeem you from your lot we will even sell ourselves and our women and children, out of our own free will to serve you. Look, Lord, when you ask us to collect this, that your order will be completed fully even if we must scratch with our own hands beneath the surface of the earth.

My father, Manku Inqa seeing the great will with which his vassals offered to do what he begged of them, thanked them and said:

Certainly, Apu—*which means lords*—I am greatly obliged, for the great will you show to redeem my lot and for this I offer your people and lands, and I give you my word, as I am whom I am, that you will lose nothing in this business and if I should not die I will repay you, for I brought this upon myself by inviting these people into my land, and I alone will carry this burden. You would greatly please me by collecting this treasure with the greatest speed and I tell you this because I am aggrieved to see myself imprisoned and abused, and so that these people will torment me no longer I must ask you to fill that *bohío* over there, *which was a large house*, with gold and silver, because perhaps upon seeing this they will stop tormenting me.

The captains and people responded in one voice:

Lord Sapay Inqa, what you request of us is nothing compared to our debt to you. We will do as you wish.

And so they all parted to hunt for what my father required, and they soon returned with what he had ordered to collect, gather and order as my father commanded. Another day my aforesaid father called the Spaniards to him, and they drew near to his call.

How the Spaniards arrived in the House of Manku Inqa, where he was Imprisoned, and what happened upon their Arrival

Upon their arrival in the place where my father was imprisoned and manacled with shackles at his feet, they greeted him as they had on other occasions. And my father, seeing them enter his house, received them as he was wont, and spoke to them in this fashion; asking them firstly, "where is the Machu Kapitu?" who was not there, to Hernando Pizarro:

Hey, where is the Machu Kapitu?

Hernando Pizarro replied that he had stayed home, somewhat ill disposed, and my father, as he wished to see him, said:

Well, should we not call for him?

And Gonzalo Pizarro and the rest said:

In good time, Manku Inqa, we will call for him and it would be best if he were called at your behest.

So my father sent some of his captains to call for him and the governor replied to his captains that he was ill disposed for now, that when he felt better he would do as my father commanded and my father, seeing that he would not come, said these words to the Spaniards:

Speech of the Imprisoned Inqa to the Spaniards when he gave them the Treasure for the First Time

Lords, for many days now you have offended me with your abuse, when I have given you no reason to do so, especially after having treated you all so well: inviting you into my land with all the honor and pageantry that my house and lands could command. If you wish to judge for yourselves, it must have been more than two million in gold and silver,[43] which I know your king can't find among all of his possessions, and you all know full well that it was in my hands whether or not to let you into my lands, for had I not desired it so not even ten of you could have stepped foot inside my land. You do not know how many people I have at my command nor how many fortresses and forts I control. You would do well to remember my good will with which I sent for you whence your presence was unannounced and how as a sign of friendship (because you had told me that you were Wiraquchas sent by the Tiqsi Wiraquchan) I sent you everything I could as you approached. You should remember how, upon your arrival in this town, I had you served and how I commanded all the people of my land to give you tribute, and in repayment, having done this all with such affection and good will, you have imprisoned me under the pretense that I wished to revolt against you and kill you when I was free of any such thoughts. I understand that your greed has blinded you to do harm and to treat me to this lot. I never thought that people who showed me such good signs in the beginning, who boasted to be none other than the sons of Wiraquchan would do such a thing. For your own lives, please, release me and understand that I wish you no ill will. Instead, I will suffer your pleasure by satisfying your greed, that insatiable hunger you have for silver. There they will give you what you require and look well that you never abuse any of my people as I have speedily fulfilled your demands. And do not think that I have complied out of fear, for all this land is at my command and had I desired it so I could have annihilated you all in record time. And these shackles that you have bound me with, do not think that they constrained me, for I could have freed myself of them if I so chose, but I have not done so, so that you might understand that my actions begin with love and not fear and despite them I have and do care for you as I do. From now on let us live in peace and love and in one another's company for you know full well that you are giving grief to Wiraquchan—*which means God*—and to your king and I will be displeased.

And as my father finished his speech, all of the Spaniards that came with Hernando Pizarro and Gonzalo Pizarro and Juan Pizarro thanked him very much for what he had said (and more for what he had given them in treasure and jewels) and they all thanked him in the following manner:

How the Spaniards gave Manku Inqa Thanks for the Treasure and Jewels he gave upon his Release

Lord Manku Inqa, all of us here before you, and the lord governor Don Francisco Pizarro, know that because you are the son of your father Wayna Qhapaq, we possess the lands we do, and today are content and joyful. If it weren't for Your Majesty, who is of royal blood, we would not have the land we have or possess the wealth we do, received from such a liberal hand as your own. May our Lord the almighty God, whom your Majesty calls Wiraquchan, our father, by his Divine Majesty whose good will is like that demonstrated by Your Majesty's works, repay you with the revelation of his Sacred Majesty, so that knowing Him, you will love Him and possess Him, and by possessing Him enjoy with Him his Kingdom forever, as we enjoy the possession of the gifts Your Majesty has given us.

Hernando Pizarro, speaking for all, said,

All of these knights and I have been very pleased by Your Majesty's gifts. We will be obliged to you in everything for the rest of our lives and we swear that now and forever, these knights are never again to cause you grief, having no occasion to do so.

Having finished their speeches in gratitude to my father, my aforesaid father ordered the treasure that had been separated for them to be handed over, and the Spaniards received it but did not retrieve it until they had told the governor everything that had happened. And without further ado, some called on my father to give him thanks for such treasure, and to have him present at the receipt and distribution of the treasure, because as it was made apparent later, the governor's entreaties had forced the Spaniards to release my father from his prison, for they would not have gone if they had not been so ordered. So that he could see that my father had been released, they later called upon him, and he, knowing of my father's visit, came and upon his arrival greeted my father in this way:

Arrival of the Governor in the House of Manku Inqa

God save Your Majesty Lord Manku Inqa! My illness impeded me from joining these knights to kiss your majesty's hands; I was profoundly distressed by my inability to do what I so desired, to see your Majesty. Yet my failure was due to my illness and this will no longer occur. I was profoundly distressed by the grief they tell me your Majesty suffered in prison, especially if you were innocent—and if so, all the more reason for your affliction—and I do believe in your Majesty's innocence. And having known your innocence much as I have always known your Majesty's kindness, I begged these knights not to torment your Majesty so, as I know that it was you who invited us to your land with such good will and so wholeheartedly gave us this land's many treasures. You were confined so as not to do things that should not be done. I beg your Majesty to please me by no longer being distressed, for these knights and I will procure to give you grief no more, and respect such a person as Your Majesty above all else.

It seems to me that Your Majesty still treats these knights and myself as you wish, exemplified by the great bounty and wealth that you have given them. As for myself, I will correspondingly be your governor and can assure you that his Majesty, who receives a fifth part of the treasure[44] will be very pleased, as we all are, by what your Majesty has given us and what I have sent him up until now[45] and for this cover your Majesty's hands with kisses. We are all so obliged by your generosity that words have no meaning.

Manku Inqa's reply to the Governor

Apu—*which means lord*—you come in good time. For many days now I have wanted to see you, not knowing the reason why you would not fulfill my desire as I so wished. I had you called for, I don't know how many times, to give you my grievances about your soldiers, and in order to please them you have not pleased me when it is I who has given you everything and wished you nothing but good. You repay my good will and my efforts badly. Your soldiers have offended me and tired me when I have not deserved this abuse: keeping me locked in chains as if I were your llama— *which means calf*—in greedy torment, no feat of prowess. For it is clear that you have imprisoned me out of your insatiable greed, out of your need to overpower me, and as you have seen and witnessed, you did not defeat me by force of arms but by beautiful words. For had you not told me you were the sons of Wiraquchan and that you were sent by him, and because of the carefully planned signs you used with me, I do not know how else you could have entered my land. And you repay my hospitality in this manner. How generously you repay me for the good will I have shown you. Here, I have given you I don't know how much gold and silver in response to your requests, leaving you alone to distribute it all as you wished. You are a good Apu, ordering them to anger me no longer as I do not wish to anger them, and I will have you know that if they anger me any further, I will make my retribution a heavy burden for them to carry.

The governor was pleased by my father's reply and ordered the Spaniards to receive the treasure, saying:

Receive what Lord Manku Inqa Yupanki has given us, showing us such good will, and he will continue to do so in the future. All of you present, look well upon your gifts, for we have received much from Lord Manku Inqa after having stayed in his land and we repay his good will badly. From now on, upon penalty of death, you must respect and esteem him as he deserves.

All of the soldiers, happy to receive the treasure that my father had given them, joyously replied to the governor with these words.

Response to the Governor by Hernando Pizarro, Gonzalo Pizarro and Juan Pizarro and the other Soldiers

Certainly, your Lordship is right to reproach and reprimand us for such things for if we had a conscience we would not have done such a thing. Instead we would have thanked him for doing us good and so shall we do from now on.

Having finished these speeches, the Spaniards rationed the treasure one by one, according to their rank. Hernando Pizarro gave out the treasure because he was the principal author of the deal, having imprisoned my father in the first place. The treasure was handed out in bits because it had to be weighed by peso.[46] *When they had distributed the treasure among themselves, my father gave the governor thanks, saying these words:*

Apu, it seems that you have played a part in my release from prison, which I innocently suffered by your soldiers. Do not leave so soon I beg you, but as a sign of friendship let us break bread together for I do not wish to break a promise.

And the governor, in order to please my father, and because his request was fair and considerate, thought well of it and they all sat in the hall where my father was and ate with much merriment and chacota.[47] *They received their food and were united with my father. The Spaniards went home that night, each satisfied with the ration they had received during the last treasure campaign. You would have thought that they would have been happy to heed their governor and to be merry among themselves with their bounty, but their joy, as we will see later, did not last them long, because the devil, being as evil as he is, is the friend of differences and dissidence and never sleeps.*

The Revolt by Gonzalo Pizarro against the Inqa

Three months, my father told me, did not pass before envy—which is the enemy of all kindness—took hold of Gonzalo Pizarro: firstly, because he saw that his brother had received so much more gold and silver even though he had imprisoned my father (out of greed) when he was corregidor,[48] *and secondly, because now that he had a* vara *and commanded in the absence of the Marquis Don Francisco Pizarro, who at the time had left for Lima, taking his leave from my father with much love and affection, he wished to be commanding and authoritative with his* vara[49] *at my father's expense, accusing him of wanting to revolt, saying that one of these nights he would attack while they were sleeping. And with this false accusation, Gonzalo Pizarro was able to arm himself and convince his brother Juan Pizarro and others to imprison my father and they all went to the feast where my father was rejoicing with his people, and upon their arrival, my father unaware of their brewing betrayal, received them with great benevolence and generosity, and they, as they were full of rotten betrayal, waited for him to leave his house and pursued him and took hold of him; Gonzalo Pizarro said these words:*

The Second Imprisonment of Manku Inqa by Gonzalo Pizarro

Lord Manku Inqa, the other day you agreed with my brother Hernando Pizarro not to plot or scheme, and it seems to me that you have not kept your promises. And as we are informed of the way in which you have conspired to attack us tonight, we have, for this reason, gathered so many people. You are now imprisoned by order of the king and do not think it will be like the other day when you said you thought little of our shackles, for now can you can see whether they will break or not.

And later, hands to mouth, he ordered Gonzalo Pizarro to bring shackles and a chain to lock my father in, and with these shackles and chains he had him bound, and my father, seeing the eagerness with which they forced him to this lot, tried to defend himself, saying:

Manku Inqa's Response

Why do you offend me at every opportunity? Are you not aware that I am the son of the Sun and the son of Wiraquchan, as you would like to boast? Am I nobody or an Indian with a sorry lot? Would you raise the entire land and have them tear you all apart? Do not mistreat me for I have done you no harm. Why do you think that I receive nothing for your shackles? Can they not be found about my ankles?

Gonzalo Pizarro and his captains, as they saw my father so infuriated, grabbed him and placed a chain at his gullet, saying:

Do not defend yourself, Manku Inqa. Look well, for we will bind your hands and feet in such a way that the entire world could not undo your bonds. Since we seize you, not by our authority, but in the name and voice of the Emperor himself, you must now give us much more gold and silver than what you gave us the other day and the Lady Quya Kura Uqllu, your sister, as my wife.

And together they bound his gullet with a chain and bound shackles at his feet.

Manku Inqa's Speech, when He was Imprisoned for the Second Time

My father, when he found himself bound and imprisoned in such an igno-minious and dishonorable fashion, said with these pitying words:

Am I, by any chance, your dog or calf or uywa[50] that you should bind me in this fashion? Am I a thief, or have I betrayed Wiraquchan, or your king? Since I am and have done none of these things, why do you treat me in this way? I verily say and confirm this: you are sons of the Supay before you are servants of Wiraquchan, for if you were true sons and not mere servants of Wiraquchan you would never treat me in the way you do, for you would first look well on whose son I am, and to my past and present might, which out of respect for you I have set aside, and look well that there has been nothing in all the land, high and low, small and large, that has been denied you since your arrival. Instead, my riches you now possess, your servants, men and women, young and old, the best lands in all the land are at your command. So, what have I not provided that you ingrates now desire? You are unworthy of all forgiveness.

Gonzalo Pizarro and Juan Pizarro and the rest who came with them, did not listen to what my father told them, and with a kind of loathing, said:

Calm down, calm down Lord Sapay Inqa and rest a bit for you are enraged. Tomorrow we will talk awhile. Above all else you must command for a collection of gold and silver and remember to give us the Quya because I desire her.

Said, Gonzalo Pizarro. After saying these good reasons to my father, the Spaniards went to their houses to eat because his arrest had taken place in the morning. And the Spaniards, leaving for their homes, left good wardens to guard my father. Afterwards, all the people who had been in the plaza called Pomacorco[51]—where my father had risen that morning to eat with all of them, only leaving for a moment to do something at his house when he was seized by the Spaniards—came fearful to the house where my father was to see why he had not gone to the pampa[52] which was so far away, time wise, and when they arrived at the door they found all of my father's servants panic-stricken and crying at the sight of their master's lot, caged as he was. The captains and people who arrived asked,

What is wrong?

And they all were silenced, exclaiming among themselves, and asking one another, incredulously:

What could this be? What could this be?

And thus panic-stricken, the foremost captains in the land entered to ver-ify the situation and to see what my father was doing. And further inside, after having received permission to enter, they arrived where my father was being kept, in the manner described above, and seeing him in this way they wailed at the sight, which was a sight in and of itself, until Wila Uma—who governed the land as my father did[53]—called out to them, questioning and interrogating my father in this way:

Sapay Inqa, what are these Wiraquchas up to? Today they seize you, tomorrow they release you; it looks like they are playing children's games with you. But I am not surprised that they are treating you in this way for you have wished it so: you brought such evil people into your land by your own will, without our consent. I tell you that had you left me to decide on my own when they arrived in Cajamarca they never would have arrived here because Challku Chima and I, though they wished to stop us, would have blocked their entrance with our people. I do not think that we would have done as badly as we are doing now because of your undue kindness. Had you not told us that they were Wiraquchas and sent by Hatun[54] Wiraqucha—*which means great god*—and did not order us to obey and respect them as you did, we would not be in this present predicament: vexed and disturbed by our lot—dispossessed of our lands, of our women, of our sons and daughters and of our chakras,[55] seeing ourselves vassals of those whom we do not know, so oppressed and fatigued for they even have us wipe the excrement of their horses with our own cloaks. Look, Lord, how low we have stooped because of your whims. And as you have desired it so, do not now be perplexed if they treat you in this way. You know full well that even when you left to receive them in Vilcacunga, I blocked them from you and many times advised you not to invite them into your land.[56] And if you remember, I told you when we heard the news that they had landed, that I would go with ten or twelve thousand Indians and would make piecemeal out of them and you never let me, instead, "calm down, calm down, these are Wiraquchas or their sons," as if we would not be bothered with this type of people who come to command and not to obey from such a faraway place. I, and all of your people, are pained by this past and by the sight of you and are moved with compassion, and because you know who I am, please give me permission to free you and quickly finish off these bearded men, for you are well aware that in all the higher and lower lands,[57] after you there is none other that the people respect more than myself, as I am their general.

Having finished his pronouncement to my father, the aforesaid captain Wila Uma with another called Tikuq, his cohort, turned to the Spaniards, who were there, and with dire and bitter faces, said these words:

Interrogation of the Spaniards by the Inqa's Captains as to their Ill Treatment of their King and Lord

What are you doing with our Inqa? Back and forth every day, binding him today, harassing him tomorrow, and offending him another day. What has this man done to you? This is how you repay his good will that brought you into this land against our own will? What do you want from him? What more can he do? Did he not let you enter his land in peace and security and with much honor called you from Cajamarca? Did he not honor the messengers you sent with much silver and gold and with many people to escort you and carry in great litters? Did you not receive two large houses filled with gold and silver that belonged to him, in addition to what Ataw Wallpa gave you, which belonged to my Inqa and what he sent to Cajamarca from here, yet another large amount of gold and silver as well? Along the one hundred twenty leagues from here to Cajamarca, did he not have you treated well, giving you refreshment and people to lead you? Did he not receive you himself along the road six leagues from here? In Jaquijahuana did he not, out of respect for you, burn one of the foremost persons in all the land, Challku Chima? Upon your arrival here, did he not give you houses, lands, servants, women and fields? Did he not command all of his people to give you tribute? Have they not paid you their tribute? Have they not paid you, yes or no? The other day, when you imprisoned him, to redeem your vexation, did he not give you a house filled with gold and silver? Have not the foremost people of the land been robbed of their women and sons and daughters? And we are silent because we would not cause him grief when his intentions are good. Our people, do they not serve you and even wipe the excrement of your horses and houses with their own cloaks? What more do you want? The other times you have said, "gold here, silver there, gold here, silver there, gather this, gather that," has he not given you his very servants to serve you? What more can you ask from this man? Did you not deceive him, saying that you came by the wind by Wiraquchan's mandate, that you were his own sons? And you said that you came to serve the Inqa, to love him, to treat him and his people as your very selves. You know full well and can see if you wish to look attentively, that in all things you have disappointed us and, instead of treating him as you promised in the beginning, you have upset him and upset every credo without their deserving this treatment or having given you occasion. Where do you think he will find the gold and silver you ask when he has given you everything by taking all of our jewels, all of the riches of the land? What should he give you now that you have imprisoned him? Where is he supposed to find what you ask for when he has nothing to give? All the people of this land are so distressed and disconcerted by your actions that they know not what to say nor where to go, because they see themselves dispossessed of their king, their women, their children, their homes, their lands, their fields and all they possess, and their tribulation leaves them no choice but to hang themselves or risk everything and they have told me this many times. Thus, lords, I believe it would be best if you let my Sapay Inqa rest, for your faults he suffers now. Release him from this prison to lessen the grief of these Indians.

Response of the Spaniards to Wila Uma

Who has given you the authority to dare speak to the *corregidor* of the king? Do you know who we are? Be silent, if not for your life than for the life of his Majesty, for I will seize you and play a game with you and your cohorts that you won't forget for the rest of your lives. I swear that if you don't be quiet I will slice you open and quarter you alive. Who dares you to speak with such authority before me?

Gonzalo Pizarro said this to scare Wila Uma and all of the rest with him. He then added to what he had said, saying:

Hurry up and gather the silver and gold that I have ordered otherwise I swear to you that your king will not leave this prison until it has been collected even if this be in a year's time. Do not reply, nor act out feats— whence he left, whence he came.

Having finished all of these things between the Spaniards and this captain Wila Uma, the Spaniards told them to go home and he came to my father to tell him everything that had been said and the reply that they had given them; and my father, as he saw them in this way with such pity for his travails, said the following:

My sons and daughters, I know that I have deserved this treatment for having invited these people into my land and I understand your reasons for hating me. Yet there is no other solution: for your own lives, gather all that you can as soon as possible to redeem my vexation; be pained by the sight of your king, bound like a dog, with a chain at his throat, and like a fugitive slave with shackles at his feet.

The captains and people with great compassion at the sight of my father's ill treatment could only reply with silence and their dying eyes. One after another, they left to find what my father requested so that they could soon release him; but they weren't quick enough and more than two months passed before they could gather what they collected. And the people began to strip themselves of their clothing, and there were so many of them that they were able to fill a large bohío,[58] *along with the vessels that had remained in my father's house that had been used to serve him. And with everything amassed the men, who always besieged them, continued saying:*

There is not enough. Where is the silver? You haven't finished. How long will we have to wait? Finish now.

With these and other words, which tired my father endlessly, he called for them saying that in order to stop this ordeal they should be called for, so that he could give them what had been gathered. And so they called for them, and they came and upon their arrival where my father was imprisoned, they greeted him, saying:

Sapay Inqa, what do you command and why have you called for us?

My father, seeing them come this way, because he knew they would soon free him from his chains, said these words:

The Inqa's Speech to the Spaniards

Apu-kuna[59]—which means Lords—these days past, when you seized me for the first time, I told you that you could not possibly be the sons of Wiraquchan, for you treated me so badly after I had wished and done you so much good. And I gave you good reasons. And now, this second time, you have been so onerous and pitiless, galling my misery, doubling my chains and jail time, for it has been two months now that I am imprisoned and manacled like a dog. I won't stop from saying to you that you are not Christians and not the sons, as you say, of Wiraquchan but servants of the Supay, whose steps you follow, doing evil to those who do you good. And you are even worse than he, who does not want gold or silver when there is no need, and you search for it and seize it by force when there is none. You are worse than the Yungas, who for a bit of silver would kill their own mother and father and deny the world. And you are alike, forgetting the welcome you received from me, loving you with such good will and wanting your friendship. You have betrayed me for a bit of silver and treated me worse than your dogs, for it seems that you esteem a little silver more than the friendship of all the men in the world. For your love of silver you have lost my friendship and that of my people; because of your greed and demands we have been dispossessed of our jewels and wealth, which you have taken by pure force and abuse and bitter demands. I tell you now that you do not shine brightly in all of this, when you treat my people and me without justice or reason and have gathered these poor Indians to do this hard work—for what? Receive your treasure and release me from this prison.

My father said this with much pity and with tears in his eyes, at his own lot.

The Way the Spaniards wanted to Release Manku Inqa from his Second Imprisonment and how He gave them the Quya

When the Spaniards heard what my father said to them, with some happiness and pleasure because of the silver that had been collected, they said that they were pleased and pretended to release him. It was all a feint until Gonzalo Pizarro appeared and said:

What is going on? Do not release him. First he must give us the Lady Quya, his sister, whom we saw the other day. Why do you hurry to release him without my command? Hey, Lord Manku Inqa, bring me the Lady Quya, but the silver is good and all the rest; that's what we really wanted.

How the Quya was Given

My father, seeing how they demanded the Quya, and that he could not elude them any longer, ordered them to bring a beautiful Indian woman, bedecked and adorned to hand her over instead of the Quya whom they desired and when they saw her, they did not recognize the Quya and said that she was not the Quya but some Indian woman from around here, that they should give them the Quya and stop with the funny business. And my father, in order to tempt them, brought more than twenty Indian women before them; in beauty and grace alike, and none of them pleased the Spaniards. And when my father thought it was time, he had the foremost woman of his house enter, a friend of his sister the Quya, and she was like the Quya in everything, especially when she dressed like her. Her name was Inkill—which means flower[60]—and she appeared dressed and perfumed like a Quya—which means queen—and she entered to be given in the Quya's stead, and as the Spaniards saw her enter in this way, beautiful and elegant, they joyously and merrily exclaimed:

She is the one, she is the one! She is the Lady Quya, not the others!

Gonzalo Pizarro, who desired her more than the rest, as he had pursued her, said these words to my father:

Lord Manku Inqa, if she is for me give her to me now because I just can't stand it any more!

And my father, who had instructed her well, said:

You can enjoy her in good time.

And so, in front of everyone, not thinking much of anything, he kissed and embraced her as if she were his legitimate wife, which made my father laugh and everyone else gape.[61] Inkill, out of fear and horror, as she saw herself being embraced by people whom she did not know, started screaming like a crazy woman, saying she did not wish to submit to these men, that she would rather flee than see them in her thoughts. And my father, seeing her so defiantly resist leaving with the Spaniards, and knowing that his release depended on her compliance, ordered her, infuriated, to go with them. And she, seeing my father so angry, out of fear, did what he commanded and left with them.

How Gonzalo Pizarro received the Treasure and Quya in Hand and how Manku Inqa, in a Sign of Friendship, shared a Meal with Him

Gonzalo Pizarro received her and ordered my father to be released from his shackles, and once he was released he received the treasure, which was then distributed among them. Once distributed, Gonzalo Pizarro begged my father, saying that as he had given them so many things in gold and silver, and, above all else, the Lady Quya whom he so desired, begged him that, as a sign of friendship, which was to last a long time because they were now related, to honor him, along with those knights and to be served in his house, which he offered him from now on as his own. And my father, wanting to see the countryside and to please him, thinking that in this way the friendship with the Spaniards would last a long time, did what Gonzalo Pizarro begged and went with him and his cohorts to eat that day in his house, where there was a grand feast and much merriment. And when all had eaten, my father said that he wanted to return to his house because it was late and the Spaniards accompanied him there, and leaving him there, happy, they returned to their homes. Let the reader understand that when this business with the Quya and the prison with its chains and shackles was over with, the Marquis Don Francisco Pizarro had already left for Lima and was not in Cuzco at the time (and let nobody think that he was involved).

After the second imprisonment and the gift of Inkill in the house of Gonzalo Pizarro, many days did not pass before my father Manku Inqa made a large feast in which we pierce our ears and amongst we Inqas this is our foremost feast of the year, for this is when we are given our names and change old names for new ones, similar to the ceremony of the Christians whence they are confirmed.[62] In this feast my father entered with all of his royal authority as our customs demand, taking his royal scepters and the foremost scepter was made of pure gold and the tassels were of pure gold, and all who followed him bore one made of silver and copper, more than a thousand of them, to be re-baptized, what we call wakaruq.[63] And when all the Indians and Spaniards were gathered in a plain before a hill called Anahuarqui,[64] where the ceremony was held, when it was done—how it is held will be said further on—when those who had been re-baptized in the baptism—which is shearing and piercing the ears[65]—had left to wash themselves, the Spaniards, maybe out of greed for the silver in the scepter or some jealousy that must have befallen

*them, armed themselves and started tormenting all the gathered people with
their hands at their hilts, saying:*

Villains, you wish to revolt but it will not be so! Wait! Wait!

*And in this way they snatched the scepters from their bearers with the
desire to grab my father's and, as they saw so many guards about his sleeves,
they dared not approach him so they took what they could from the others,
which was a lot. My father heard the noise and murmurs of the crowd and
once he knew that the Spaniards had shamed themselves in that manner, he
raised his voice, saying:*

What is this?

And the Indians, wailing and mourning their lot, said:

Sapay Inqa, what kind of people do you welcome into your land? They
are not content with all the gold and silver that we have given them that by
force they take our yawris[66] of silver—*which means scepters*—which they
have stolen with threats, and this gives us great grief. Tell them to return
these to us and to be satiated by the gold and silver that we have given
them.

*And my father, seeing how anxiously these Indians protested, was dis-
tressed and speaking to the Spaniards he said this:*

Reasoning of the Inqa to the Spaniards
when they tried to Seize him for the Third Time

Lords, it seems that you still mean to give me and my people grief when I
do not wish to nor do I keep such thoughts. The other day, did you not
promise me and my people that you would give us grief no longer? You are
not right for I have given you no reason to cause me such anguish. Are you
not brimming with silver that you must come to rob me of the crumbs I
serve at my feasts? If you do this to incite me or the people of my land to
revolt against you, be frank so that my people and I may be wary. I will not
be as careless as I was just now, simply because we exchanged words the
other day in the Apu's house and mine promising that all of us would keep
the peace and love so that neither you would be wary nor we would be
fearful.

And the Spaniards listening, to what my father said to them, said:

Lord Manku Inqa, we do not wish to give your Majesty grief. Some soldiers must have caused a ruckus for fun. Do not be distressed your
Majesty, it's nothing.

*And my father, seeing that the people were still and at peace, was silent and
finished the festivities, and the Spaniards went to their homes because it was
late and time to go to sleep.*

Death of Paskaq, Brother of Manku Inqa

Having finished the festivities and what has been said above, when my father was still and at peace in his home, a terrible thing happened to him. His brother, named Paskaq, was overcome by vanity because of someone's suggestions and thought to kill my father, saying that when he was dead he would be king; and I don't know who insisted or who gave him the dagger, with which he went to see my father, whom he was going to muchay,[67] *as to a lord, and then stab with his dagger and be hailed as king and so give a lot of silver to the Spaniards who must have given him the dagger for that purpose. And as there is nothing so secret that sooner or later will not reveal itself, a certain Spaniard whose name is unknown, who was my father's servant and was always in his house, said:*

Know this, Lord Manku Inqa: your brother Paskaq wants to kill you and carries a hidden dagger, and he means to kill you when he gives you mucha. When you see him you must be ready, and, if you order me to do so, I will kill him myself.

And my father, warned by his Spanish servant, thanked him very much and was ready for his brother when he came, as he was wont, to revere him. And, when he saw Paskaq give him mucha, he raised his head and with a dagger he had at hand he stabbed him, and the Spaniard who had given the warning finished him off. Seen by all who were present, they were all shocked to see such an extraordinary and violent event and nobody dared say a word.

After all of these things had passed and many more, whose telling would only lengthen the telling, which I avoid for the sake of brevity, I will continue with my intent to make my father's story known and what the Spaniards did after all of this. Know that Gonzalo Pizarro, the corregidor *of Cuzco (named as such by the Governor Don Francisco Pizarro), Hernando Pizarro and Juan Pizarro and many others were with him. It so happened that when Juan Pizarro, the brother of Hernando Pizarro and Gonzalo Pizarro, saw that my father had given his two brothers a large amount of bullion, he became envious, saying:*

Since they will only give my brothers silver and won't give me any, I swear this must end! They must give me as much gold and silver; otherwise I will give them a game that they will never forget.

And with these rogues he started firing people up, saying:

Let us seize Manku Inqa! Let us seize Manku Inqa!

And when my father heard of the treason that was being plotted against him in the town, he ordered all of the leaders in the land to gather—many of them were in Cuzco as his bodyguards—and, once he had them all gathered before him, he spoke, advised by the aforesaid Wila Uma:

Speech of the Inqa to his Captains about the Siege of Cuzco

My beloved sons and brothers, I never thought that it would be necessary to do what I am thinking, because I thought and believed that these bearded people, whom you call Wiraquchas, as I told you once because I thought they came from Wiraquchan, would not be rude nor give me grief in all things. But now I realize, from what I have seen and from experience—and you have seen how badly they have treated me and how badly they have thanked me by insulting me a thousand times and seizing me and binding my feet and neck like a dog—and after having given me their word that I with them, and they with me, would live in love and friendship, saying that we could perpetually forget the past—once again they are riling themselves up to seize and kill me. I will not forget to remind you, as my sons, the many times you begged me to do what I now wish to be done, saying that I should revolt against them and why did I welcome them to this land in the first place? And I did not want to because I thought that what I am now witnessing would not come to pass. And since all they want to do is anger me and torment me, I will be forced to do the same to them and not make any further pacts out of respect for your own lives, for you always have shown me so much love and wished me so much happiness. You would please me, gathered as you are before me, to unite as one, and send your messengers to all the land so that twenty days from now you will return to this town without these bearded ones knowing a thing. And I will send Qisu Yupanki, my captain, to Lima, to govern that land, and let him know that the day we attack the Spaniards, he is to attack their people there.[68] United as one, he there and we here, we will finish them off, so that not one will remain and we will be rid of this nightmare and will rejoice.

Having finished his speech before his captains, as to what they were to pre-pare for their battle with the Spaniards, they all replied with one voice that they rejoiced at the news and were ready and prepared to do what my father commanded. And without delay they started to work, sending their own to each quarter of the earth: to Chinchaysuyu Wila Uma sent Quyllas and Uskay and and Quri Ataw and Taypi to bring the people from that quarter; and to Qullasuyu, Liqlis[69] went with many other captains to bring people from that quarter; to Kuntisuyu, Suranwaman, Kikana and Suri[70] Wallpa and many other captains went; and to Antisuyu, Rampa Yupanki and many other captains, so that each and every suyu would unite the necessary people. Note that these four suyus that are named here, it is good to know, as I have said above, are the four quarters in which the earth is divided and spread, as I have declared more extensively above. After having sent them off to the aforesaid four quarters, with Juan Pizarro up to his evil plotting, an Indian tongue who worked for the Spaniards, named Antonio, warned my father that Juan Pizarro and the rest would be seizing him one of these days and that they would kill him if he did not give them a lot of gold and silver. And my father, hearing what the Indian said, believed him and pretended that he was going to Calca to hunt and the Spaniards believed him, thinking to go ahead with their plans upon his return.

When my father had been in Calca for several days, while the people he had called for gathered, he sent for Qisu Yupanki, who was in Lima, so that he would be advised of the day and hour that he would attack the Spaniards so that he could attack at the same day and hour and all would be as one: Qisu Yupanki in Lima and my aforesaid father in Cuzco. At the time that my father did this, the Spaniards sent him many letters, telling him to hurry and return home because they could not do a thing without him. My aforesaid father responded saying that he had not finished hunting and that he would return as soon as he could. And the Spaniards, seeing that on all of the occasions whence they had called for him, on all he had refused to come, and that he moved further and further away and sent worsening replies, decided to find him to bring him by force or kill him. So they gathered their captains in Cuzco and sent one of their captains and people to Calca to do the aforementioned, and the rest stayed in Cuzco on the threshold of war to follow them if necessary. When they arrived at the bridge of the river in Calca, they fought with its guards, who defended the bridge and there the Spaniards challenged my father's people, and having defied them, returned to Cuzco with my father's people in pursuit, shouting and yelling. Upon their arrival in Cuzco, the Spaniards, somewhat shaken by the past guazábara[71] and the people that came in their pursuit from Carmenca,[72] which is a part of Cuzco, they shouted to their cohorts asking for aid, and their cohorts who were on alert ran to their aid, and in Carmenca there was a great battle with the people that followed and others who heeded their call. And when the battle ended, they had them all surrounded in Cuzco, without having killed any of them, and that same night they rattled their nerves with their screaming, surrounding them on all sides, and they waited to attack because they were waiting for the people who would arrive the next day and because my father had told them not to attack them until the people arrived, and because he said he wanted to see them.

The Siege of Cuzco

After they were brought back to Cuzco, having placed many guards that very night to keep watch over all of the entrances, the next afternoon a throng of *people arrived and did not enter because they thought it was too dark and that they could not use the night against their enemies because of the great darkness. And so they watched from the hills and knolls which lord over the town, placing guards and sentinels in the fields.*

The morning, at nine, when all of the Spaniards were ready in a squadron in the plaza of Cuzco, whose numbers are unknown although it is said that they had many black men with them, on all of the hills of Cuzco, in a circle, with many whistles and horns and trumpets, shouts and voices that surprised the entire world, and they must have been more than four hundred thousand Indians who entered in this way:

Entrance of the People into the Enclosure

By Carmenca, going towards Chinchaysuyu, Quri Ataw and Quyllas and Taypi and many others closed that entrance with the people they brought. By Coacachi, going towards Kuntisuyu, Wamani, Kikana and Quri Wallpa and many others closed off a large mile, more than half a voice league, all well-equipped for war; going towards Qullasuyu, Liqlis and many other captains with many people, the largest number found in this siege, entered; and going towards Antisuyu, Anta Allka and Rampa Yupanki and many others finished off the enclosure that had been placed on the Spaniards that day.

And after they had made the barricades, which was something to be seen, they wanted to attack the Spaniards but dared not do so without my father's orders, whom, as we have said above, had commanded that, upon penalty of death, nobody was to move from their places. And Wila Uma, Captain General of these people, seeing them ready and set, had my father, who was in Calca, informed, saying that he had them encircled and terrified and if he was to kill them or not. And my father sent back word that they should leave them in this same anxious torment that they had left him in and that they should suffer as he had suffered and that he would arrive another day and finish them off. When Wila Uma received this response, the aforesaid Wila Uma, seeing what my father had ordered, was aggrieved because he wanted to finish them off as they were so ready for it, but he did not dare to because of what my father had ordered. So he commanded the entire army that, upon penalty of death, nobody was to move from their places until he ordered and he ordered all of the water reservoirs of the town to be released to flood the fields and roads about and within the city—in case the Spaniards wished to flee, they would find the earth flooded and, by goring their horses, they would be lords of their enemies on foot and in the mire, because clothed men survive badly in the mud. And all was done as the general Wila Uma commanded. The Spaniards, when they saw themselves besieged and with so many people attacking them, began to suspect among themselves that these were the last days of their lives, not seeing any remedy, not knowing what to do because on the one hand they saw themselves besieged in that way and on the other hand they saw the wounds and insults that the Indians gave and made, throwing rocks on their tents and pulled the wool over their eyes because nobody paid them any attention, so they started burning the houses, and would have burned the church but for the blacks who were above them, and stopped them. Although many arrows from the Sati and Antis Indians[73] stopped them, they did not do them any harm because God watched over them as they shielded themselves and, since they doubted any other remedy, they commended themselves to God for aid, and all that night they were in the church calling to God to help them, on their knees and with their hands to their mouths. And many Indians saw them and even those who were in the plaza, in the fires, did the same and many were Indians on their side who had come with them from Cajamarca.

Battle of the Spaniards against the Indians at the Fortress

Another day, in the early morning, they all left the church and rode their horses as if to fight, and started looking one way and another and spurred their horses at a gallop and broke the barricade that was barred like a wall, and, in spite of their enemies, fled over the hills above in a mad dash. The Indians who were above the siege of Cuzco, seeing them flee, cried out, saying:

They are leaving for Castilla! They are leaving for Castilla! Stop them!

And so the blockade that had been done came undone, some in their pursuit, others to seize them, some to inform the bridge guards so that none could escape anywhere. And the Spaniards, seeing themselves chased by so many people, reined in their horses and rounded the hill called Quencalla and were at the backs of Wila Uma and his people, who had climbed up to the fortress[74] of Cuzco to be strong. And there they fought hard and took the four gates of the fortress, and from these walls which are very strong, they threw many stones, they threw many arrows, many darts, many spears which direly tired the Spaniards and with one of these stones they killed Juan Pizarro and two blacks and many Indians that helped them. When Wila Uma ran out of munitions the Spaniards through divine favor were able to enter and take the fortress by force, killing and destroying many Indians who were inside. Some threw themselves from the walls above and, as these are high, the first to fall died and some of those that fell thereafter, because of the large pile of corpses, fell upon them and were saved. This battle, for both sides, was very bloody because of the many Indians who favored the Spaniards, among whom were two brothers of my father, one named Inkill and the other Waypar, with many people of their faction with many Chachapoyas and Cañaris joining their side.

This battle lasted three days after this fortress was taken, for the next day they returned and regrouped the Indians to see whether they could regain the fortress they had lost and with much vigor they attacked the Spaniards who were in the fortress but they could not touch them because of all the guards they had placed—Cañaris who helped them and the Spaniards themselves. The Indians also say that a white horse that was there, the first to enter the fortress when it was taken, had injured many. And this encounter lasted for a day and in the black night the very darkness impeded them from startling their enemies and so they pulled back to their encampments, and the Spaniards, so as not to leave the fortress and abandon it, allowed them to leave. And the next day, in the morning, they returned and the battle began once again, and they fought fiercely on both sides, and in the end, seeing the great vigor with which the Indians fought against the Spaniards, who defended themselves with great effort, the Indians pulled back to where my father was, which was in Calca, many followed behind them, killing and destroying a large number of people as far as the river of Yucay, where the Indians gave way before the Spaniards who headed straight for Calca—where my father was—and there they did not find him because he was feasting in a town called Sacsasiray. And as they could not find him there they made a half turn and returned to Cuzco by a different road with many losses in the rear where the Indians surprised them from the rearguard, and with these spoils they headed straight for the place where my father was feasting.

Having feasted, my father left this town of Sacsasiray for Tambo, passing Yucay—there he slept for one night. And upon his arrival in Tambo, he ordered all the land to gather because he wanted to build a strong fortress to defend themselves from any Spaniards, who wished to attack them, and this gathering was brief and, once they were gathered, he made the following speech:

Speech made by the Inqa to all of his Captains and People that were in the Town of Tambo. How they turned to him after the Destruction of Cuzco

My beloved sons and brothers, in our past conversations, you must have understood how I always blocked you from doing ill to those evil people, who through deceit and because they said they were sons of Wiraquchan and sent by his mandate to enter my land, to whom I gave my consent, and because of this and many good acts whereby I gave them what I had—silver and gold, clothes and corn, livestock, subjects, women, servants and many other innumerable things—they seized me, insulted and tormented me without my deserving such treatment, and then they tried to kill me, which I knew because of the warning given by Antonico, their tongue, and he is present because he has escaped from them as he could suffer them no longer. And as you understood, by the instructions on the blockade of Cuzco that I gave you, I returned to Calca to await the siege so that from there, without their knowledge, we would strike at their head. It seems to me that this has been done as I ordered, though I was not present as I thought I would be, and for this reason you were defeated in Sacsahuaman. Because of your carelessness they took Sacsahuaman and then pursued you as far as Yucay and you could do nothing. I pity you, being so many, and they being so few that they should escape through your hands. Maybe the Wiraquchan helped them because, you have told me, they were on their knees all night begging him, because if he had not, how else could they have escaped from your hands when you were innumerable? It is done, and for your entire lives, from now on, look well on how you act with them for they are our foremost enemies and we will be theirs forever and they have wished it so. I wish to gather strength in this town and construct a fortress that none can enter. Upon your lives, fulfill this wish with the hope that one day it will be of use.

Response that the Captains gave the Inqa

Sapay Inqa, we, your humble servants, kiss your hands and with much confusion and shame we come before you for having allowed such an important objective, as were these evil and ungrateful people, having treated you so badly after all that you did for them, escape through our hands. We are so confused that we do not dare look you in the face, but at the same time are somewhat relieved that you as well are to blame. When we asked you what we were to do with them, when they were surrounded and without hope or remedy, and you sent for us saying that we should let them suffer as they had made you suffer and that you would come and finish them off. And we, not willing to disobey your command, waited one day and one night for you and, when we thought we had secured them and had them in the palms of our hands, they escaped us and we could do nothing. We know not the cause other than it was our regret not to attack them at once and your sorrow not to let us do so. And what you ask, that we should build you a fort in this town in order to defend you, we will do so willingly, for we owe you more than this.

And so they built one of the strongest forts that exist in Peru, during the year and a half that they stayed in Tambo.

During this interlude, when he had spoken to the Indians and made them understand the misfortune that had befallen them, messengers of the destruction that had befallen Lima and Cullcomayo—which is in Jauja—arrived in the aforesaid town of Tambo, wherein the Spaniards and the Indians had fought in a battle in which the Indians had been victorious and they brought my father many Spaniards' heads and two living Spaniards and a black man and four horses. They arrived, rejoicing at the victory, and my father received them honorably and encouraged the rest to fight in the same way. And at the same time, Diego Ordoñez and a squadron of soldiers approached the aforesaid town of Tambo to fight against my father and knowing this he left to encounter the Spaniards with many Indians on a plain called Pascapampa and Pachar, past the river, before they arrived at the Tambo fort, and there, they both fought hard and none could claim a victory because the very Spaniards, due to the thorns of that plain, were cut and one of them and three black men even died in the mayhem. And the Indians captured another in their fort when he had tried to escape. And when the night scattered them all, they gathered, each to his fort and the Spaniards put up a fort at night and shot their lightning at dawn under the guise that they wanted to continue fighting but before sunrise they had left for Cuzco. When the Indians thought they were there, the next morning they found nobody which made them laugh, saying that they had run in fear. After all of this had passed and the Spaniards had returned to their homes, my father remained in Tambo hurrying the construction of the fortress. And when they were in Tambo, two imprisoned Spaniards that he had with him, whom he treated very well, even dining with them, escaped when signaled from Cuzco and, not knowing how to avoid capture, they were stopped in a town called Maras, two leagues from the aforesaid town of Tambo. When my father asked them why they had escaped they could give him no reason. And my father, seeing that they still repaid him the good that he did them so badly—one of them was even the aforesaid Antonico who had warned my father in Cuzco of what the Spaniards were plotting against him—ignoring the treatment my father had given him and did him, bringing him in a litter and treating him as his own son, he fared the same fate as the rest: my father handed them over to some Moyo Moyo Indians to be quartered and eaten.

Having finished this and the fortress, my father decided to leave for the Andes and to leave that land because of the grief the Spaniards gave him and because the Antis often begged him to leave for their land, that they would guard him well and serve him as their lord and king. And when he decided on his exit, he had his people gather to instruct them as to how they were to live with the Spaniards. And he spoke thus:

Document that Manku Inqa gave to the Indians when he wished to Retreat to the Andes on how they were to Live with the Spaniards

My beloved sons and brothers here before me who have followed me in all of my trials and tribulations. I believe you ignore the reason why I have commanded you to gather before me, and I will be brief. For your own sake, do not be distressed by what I tell you for you well know that necessity often times compels men to do what they would not and for this reason, seeing myself forced to please these Antis who have so implored me to visit them, I will go please them for a few days. I beg you: do not feel despondent for I wish to give you no grief because I love you as my own children, and I beg you to please me by your strength.

You already know that many times, besides the present, I have told you how these bearded people entered my land under the pretense that they were Wiraquchas. Because of their clothes and faces, so different from our own, you and even I believed, because of the assurances and certification of the Tallanes Yungas of the things they saw them do in their homeland, I had them brought to my land and town and gave them the treatment now notorious in all the earth and gave them things that you already know and I was repaid in the way you have seen. And not only they, but my brothers Paskaq, Inkill and Waypar dispossessed me of my land and even tried to kill me and I was saved, as I have told you, by Antonico's warning. He was eaten by the Antis the other day for his betrayal. And seeing all of these things and many others that I leave aside for the sake of brevity, I gathered you all to Cuzco to give them a taste of the bitterness that they had given us, and it seems that because their God helped them or because I was not present, you were not successful in your attempt, which I have lamented. But men will not always succeed in what they desire most and we should not be overly anguished and distraught, because, in the end, we have not done so badly: for in Lima, Chulcomayo and Jauja, we did take some of their things and that gives us some respite, though in no way do they equal the grief they have given us.

It is time for me to leave for the land of the Antis, as I said before, and I will be forced to stay there for a few days. Look well on what I command; do not forget what I have told you. I mean to tell you now to remember all the time that my forefathers and their forefathers and I have nourished and kept you, favored and governed your homes, providing for them in the way you needed, so that all of you are obliged not to forget us, my forefathers and myself, during your lives nor the lives of your descendants, and to respect and obey my son and brother Titu Kusi Yupanki and the rest of my sons who may follow him. For in this, you will greatly please me and they will thank you as I command. Enough has been said.

Response of the Indians given to the Inqa

Sapay Inqa, with what heart do you wish to leave your sons alone who with such faith have only desired to serve you and desire always to serve you and if necessary would give their lives a thousand times for you when the time comes. To which king, to what lord, to whom do you leave us? What betrayal, which treason, what evil have we committed that you should now abandon us and leave us with no lord or king to respect, for we have never known another lord or father besides you and Wayna Qhapaq, your father and his forefathers. Instead, please take us with you, wherever you go, for the young and mature, old men and old women are ready to follow you though you may not permit us.[75]

And my aforesaid father, seeing how anxiously his people wanted to serve him, said the following:

Children, I thank your good will and your desire to follow me wherever I go. I will not forget to repay you and I will be grateful and thank you before you know it. And now, for your own sake, behave and do not grieve so, for we will soon meet again. And until I return, or until I send my messengers with orders, you will live in this way:

The first thing you will do is not believe a word of what those bearded men say for all of the injury I have suffered has been due to my trust in them. They lie a lot, as they lied to me in all the promises they made, and so they will to you. What you can do is give outward signs of obedience to their orders, giving them some *camarico*[76] or what your lands can offer, because these people are so brutish and so different from us that, if you refuse outright, they will take it by force and hurt you. To avoid this, you would do well to heed my advice. The other thing: always be alert for my call or command, on what is to be done with these people, and should they attack you or take your lands, defend yourselves and even risk your lives if necessary; and if you should be in extreme need and desire of my person, call for me by post wherever I may be, and look well for these people deceive with good words and later ignore their promises. For you have seen how they told me that they were the sons of Wiraquchan and showed me, in the beginning, much kindness and love and later did with me what you have seen. If they were truly sons of Wiraquchan as they boasted they would not have done what they have done because the Wiracha[77] can level the hills, flood the waters and raise mountains where there are none; he does evil to none and we have seen how they have done none of these things. Instead of doing us good deeds they have done us evil deeds, seizing our lands, our women, our sons, our daughters, our chakras, our sustenance, and many other things we had in our land which they took by force and deceit, against our will, and people who do such things cannot be called sons of Wiraquchan but, as I have said on many occasions, Supay and worse for their actions mirror his and are so shameful that I would not speak of them.

You must do this: if there should come a time when they tell you to adore what they adore—what they say is Wiraquchan are but painted clothes, and when they say to adore them as a waka,[78] which is but cloth, do not obey. Instead, adore what we hold dear, for, as you can see, the Willkas[79] speak to us; and the Sun and the Moon, see them through our own eyes and what they speak of we do not see well. I believe that at some point, by force or deceit, they will have you adore what they adore. When you cannot resist any longer, make the motions before them but never forget our own ceremonies. And if they tell you to shatter your wakas, and do so by force, show them what you must and hide the rest. In this, you will greatly please me.

Having finished all of the things said above and many others, my father took leave of the Indians, bringing me there before them to say that I was his son and how when his days had ended, they were to have me in his stead and then he stood to take leave of his people. When they saw him stand, their wailing seemed to bore through the mountain peaks, and the people were anxious to follow but my father did not allow them and he said, to those who would follow, how could they leave their fields, their homes, their women and their children, their uywas[80] or animals only to follow him? He told them to behave for he would soon return to see them once again or would send for them instead. And so he left them all for the town of Vitcos.

Arrival of the Inqa in Vitcos

Upon their arrival in Vitcos, a town thirty leagues from Cuzco, with the people following my father, we founded our town and center with the intention of resting there for a few days. My father had a house built to sleep in because the other houses there were of ancient times, belonging to my grandfather Pachakutiq Inqa, Thupaq Inqa Yupanki and Wayna Qhapaq and the others whose bodies we had taken there because we did not dare leave them in Cuzco or in Tambo. And after this, when my father was calm and at peace, believing that none could enter that land, he wanted the Antis and the people of that land to host a very solemn feast. And while they were feasting, unaware of their setting, they found themselves surrounded by the Spaniards. And as the Indians were heavy with drink and their weapons were at home, they could not defend themselves from this surprise attack. Don Diego de Almagro and Diego Ordoñez and Gonzalo Pizarro and many others, whose names would make this long, brought before them all of the Indian men and women they could find and the bodies of my ancestors, whose names were Wayna Kawri,[81] Wiraquchan Inqa, Pachakutiq Inqa, Thupaq Inqa Yupanki and Wayna Qhapaq and many other bodies of women with many jewels and riches of the feast, more than fifty thousand head of livestock, chosen among my father's and my forefathers' finest, and they took me and many other Quyas, and my father escaped as best he could.[82] The Spaniards happily returned to Cuzco with their plunder and with me. And upon our arrival in Cuzco, a man called Oñate took me into his home and gave me many gifts and treated me well. And when my father knew of this he called for him and thanked him and gave me and his sisters to him to look after, promising to repay him. After all of these things had passed, when I was staying in Cuzco with the aforesaid Oñate, my father left Vitcos because some Chachapoya Captains took him to Rabantu where there was a good fort whence he could defend himself from his enemies, and so he followed them. And on the road to Rabantu, he stopped in a town called Oronocoy because the townspeople held a feast there in his honor. And having finished these feasts, resting a bit, he sent his runners on the roads to ascertain whether there were any Spaniards or people. That very night, in the early morning, they came with the news that more than two hundred Spaniards, armed to the teeth, were riding their horses in search of my father. They had told them that my father was in the town of Oronocoy, so that they, leaving their guards behind, one after the other, ran to the top of the hill, thinking that they would find my father there, sleeping. And it so happens that when my aunt Kura Uqllu, my father's sister stepped outside, she saw the people coming from afar and heard the clattering of the hooves and ran to my father, in his bed, to warn him in a clamor that his enemies were coming, to please wake up and arm himself. My father, seeing her so terrified, was calm, and dressed quickly to see for himself whether what his sister told him was true. And he quickly returned home and had his horse readied to speedily warn his people to make haste so that his enemies would not take them by surprise. And when he was armed he ordered his horse to be saddled for the enemy was near, and when they were sighted he had the women line the hillside, spears in hand, so that the Spaniards would think they were men. And having done this, with great ease upon his horse, spear in hand, he alone surrounded his people so that they would not flee before the enemy until the runners had crossed through the fields. When they arrived, in the nick of time, and saw my father, their master, in dire straits, though tired from running up above, they were eager to fight their enemies down below. Their spirits renewed, they trampled the Spanish soldiers over with their spears and daggers and forced their retreat and were able to rest and catch their breath after the skirmish. And when the Spanish saw them sitting and drinking, they thought they were exhausted and were eager to fight these warriors up above who had not been careless, rather they were now stronger and with more people gathered to their aid. And whence they saw their enemies return, they were so determined to defeat them that with one push, one above, and one below, they destroyed them and threw them into the gorge and chasm below. And they could not control themselves and destroyed one another for they had lost control in such a rough fall with the weight of their weapons, and the heat that drowned them, that killed them. And not one man or horse survived but two, one of whom by swimming was able to ford the river and the other hid beneath the bridge.

And so my father's people rejoiced and gathered the Spanish spoils and stripped them of all they had, rid them of their clothes and weapons and took everything up above to the town of Oronocoy; they and my father, because of their victory, rejoiced and feasted and danced for five days to honor the victory and pillage.

When these aforesaid feasts were finished, my father and his people left for the town of Rabantu, going towards Quito, and on the way, in the valley of Jauja, in a town named Llactapallanga, he learned that the Wankas, natives of that land, had joined the Spaniards and he was angered and decided to give them a punishment that would ring throughout the earth, saying that he would burn them and their houses and leave none alive for they had sworn allegiance to the Spaniards and submitted to them, and had placed their women and children at their service, along with their foremost waka of the valley called Wari Willka, which is fifty leagues from Llactapallanga.

Knowing my father's anger, and that he said he would burn them and Wari Willka, their idol, because of the allegiance they had made with the Spaniards when he was their native lord, the Wankas decided to close off the entrance and to aid the Spaniards, under whose protection they had placed themselves, so that they would come and relieve them of their danger. And knowing of my father's retribution against the Wankas, the Spaniards came at once to their aid, one hundred strong, and when they arrived my father was warned and headed in that direction, and he had many skirmishes and battles with the Wankas along the way, killing and destroying them all, telling them to go help their masters. And in this way, he arrived many days later in Jauja the Great, as it is called, where he had a grand battle with the aforesaid Spaniards and with the Wankas and this battle lasted two days, and my father in the end defeated them because of all the people he was of greater skill. And they killed fifty Spaniards and the rest escaped by the skin of their teeth. And some of our own followed them awhile and when they saw them hurry so, they joined my father who was riding his horse, blandishing his sword, on which he had bravely fought the Spaniards. And when this battle was over, my father, somewhat tired from the fighting, dismounted from his horse and rested among his own, many of whom were tired and injured from the prior battle.

The next day, when the people were somewhat renewed, he left for the journeys he had left aside, for a town named Vayocoche, which is where the idol named Wari Wilka was, and in one day he rested there and ordered it to be removed from where it had been buried up to its shoulders and when they had dug it out, he ordered all of the treasure that had been offered to it removed; and he had all of the yana-kuna[83] *and servants who served the waka killed, in whom the people of that land confided, so that it would be understood that he was their lord. And he had a rope tied about the neck of the idol, and they dragged him back along the twenty leagues of road, along hills and stones, and swamps, saying:*

Herein lies the confidence of those Wankas who worshiped this idol instead of Wiraquchan. Look what has happened to them and to their masters, the Spaniards.

And along the way they came upon a town named Acostambo and there they rested for a year. There they built their houses and tilled the fields that the Spaniards now own and call Vinaca because Castilian vines grow there. The waka and idol called Wari Willka was thrown into a large river.

After this, because of the pleas of the Anti Captains, he went to the land and town called Pilcosuni, where he had another battle with the Spaniards that came to find him and he defeated them; how would take too long but know this, he took much artillery, muskets, crossbows and other weapons. After they battled in Icñupay, he rested there for a year and returned on his journeys and towns, which for the sake of brevity I will not narrate, and to the town of Vitcos and thence to Vilcabamba, where he rested and relaxed, building his houses and lodgings to make it his headquarters, for it is of good climate, and is the main center to his person.

After he had rested some days and thinking that the Spaniards would now leave him be, he heard from spies that he had posted along the roads, that Gonzalo Pizarro and Captain Diego Maldonado and Ordoñez and many others that came with them, including his own three brothers, it is worth knowing, Don Pablo and Inkill and Waypar, who led the way, saying that they wanted to join my father in his fight against the Spaniards. And my father received them in a fortress he had for his defense, three leagues from here. Upon his arrival, he found I don't know how many Spaniards, and because the forests of these hills are thick, they could not be counted, and he fought with them on the river banks. On one side and on the other they fought for ten days, the Spaniards against my father's people and my father, and they always were the worse off because of the fort we had. And it came to this that a blood brother of my aunt Kura Uqllu, named Waypar, came and my father was angry because this brother had come to find him and his brother's business would cost him his own life. And my father wanted to kill him, he was so angry, but Kura Uqllu, out of the love she had for her brother, tried to stop him, and my father, not wanting to heed her pleas, beheaded him and his other brother named Inkill, saying these words:

It is fairer for me to cut off their heads than for them to take mine.

And my aunt, angered by the death of her brothers, never more wished to be moved from the scene of their deaths.

And certain Spaniards came and when my father saw them come, seeing that he could not escape, jumped into the water to ford the river crossing. And when he reached the other side, he cried:

I am Manku Inqa! I am Manku Inqa!

The Spaniards, when they saw they could not seize him, decided to return to Cuzco, taking my aunt Kura Uqllu and Kusi Rimachi, my father's brother, before them, and other things, and when they arrived with my aunt in the town of Pampa Cunac, they tried to rape my aunt and she, refusing to give in, defended herself and filled her body with vile and gruesome things to cause revulsion in those who would approach her. And in this way she defended herself many times until they arrived in the town of Tambo where the Spaniards were so enraged with her because she would not submit to what they wanted and because she was my father's sister. They buried her alive, which she suffered for her chastity. And she said these words when they whipped her:

You lash out all your anger on a woman. Any other woman would do the same. Hurry up and finish me off so that you can satiate your appetite in everything.

And so they finished her off, and she bound her own eyes.

Wila Uma, my father's General Captain, Tisuq and Taypi and Llamki Wallpa and Urqu Waranka and Atuq Suyru and many other of my father's captains, when they saw that the Spaniards had taken the Quya and had treated her in that fashion, bemoaned her fate, and when the Spaniards heard them, they captured them, saying:

You must return. You must love your Inqa and serve him well. You cannot end your lives alongside your mistress.

And they protested and said they wanted to be with the Spaniards forever to serve them, but the Spaniards did not believe them, thinking them deceitful, and ordered them all to the stake to be burned. And having burned them, and killed the Quya, they left for Yucay where they burned Usqullu[84] and Quri Ataw[85] and many others so that they would not return to my father and to keep their own backs safe. After all of these things had passed and many others, which I have set aside for brevity's sake, my aforesaid father returned to Vilcabamba, the center of this province, where he rested a few days. And from this town, because he missed me, my father had me sent for from Cuzco, where I had been living (in the aforesaid house of Oñate) ever since they had taken me from Vitcos. These messengers kidnapped me from Cuzco and hid me along the way to the town of Vitcos. There, my father had gone out to take fresh air, because this is a cold land. And there, my father and I were for many days, when seven Spaniards arrived at different times, saying that they were fugitives for crimes they had committed and that they promised to serve my father with all their lives' strength; they pleaded with him, if he would let them enter his land and there finish their days. My father, seeing their good will, even if they were Spaniards, ordered his captains not to hurt them for he would receive them in his land as servants and that they should build them houses where they could live. And so my father's captains, even though they wanted to kill them, did what my father ordered. And my father kept them for many days and years, treating them well and giving them what they needed, even ordering his own women to make them food and serve them drink, and he kept them at his side and fed them as his own person and entertained them as though they were his very brothers.

After days and years, these aforesaid Spaniards were in my father's company in the aforesaid town of Vitcos, in my father's very home. One day they, my father, and I—only a boy at the time—were happily playing herrón alone, and my father, without a thought to the word of warning given to him by one of their Indian women, a woman called Wuwa, who had told him, many days beforehand, that the Spaniards wanted to kill him. Unsuspecting, he played with them as before and in this game, when my father lifted the herrón to play, they beset him with daggers, knives and some swords, and my father, when he felt himself stabbed, with the fury of death, tried to defend himself from one side and the next, but as he was alone, and they were seven and my father was unarmed, they brought him to the ground with many wounds, and they left him for dead. And as I was small and I saw my father treated in this fashion, I tried to cure him and they turned against me, angered, and flung me aside with the tip of my father's spear that was in the room, and they must have erred because they did not kill me as well. And I, *fearful, fled to the forests below so that they could not find me even if they searched. And as they left my father behind to perish, heading out the door, they joyously cried out:*

We have killed the Inqa, do not be scared!

And some Antis who arrived and the Captain Rimachi Yupanki stopped them before they could flee, knocking them off their horses, and captured them for sacrifice. And they all received cruel deaths and some of them were burned. And after all of this my aforesaid father lived for three days, and, before he died, he called me and all of his captains to him to speak to us. And he had these words for his captains:

Speech that Manku Inqa made to the Indians when he was Dying and he said:

Sons, if you see me in this way it is because I trusted these Spaniards too much, especially these seven that you have seen here, who have plotted against me for so long and whom I have treated as my own sons, and to repay my hospitality they have given me this lot. I do not think I will escape this time. For your sake, remember what I have said and reprimanded in Cuzco and Tambo and in all of the other places where you have gathered at my call and all the time you have followed me, and because I know you keep this all in your memory, I will be brief. The pain is excessive and why, ay, should I trouble you any longer? I give you my son, Titu Kusi Yupanki, so that you may look after him, for you know that he is the light of my eyes and I esteem this young man not only as a son but as a brother because of his intelligence, and so I leave him and all of my sons in your care—do unto him as you would do unto me, for I greatly respect him and I will thank you and repay you well. Call him to me so that I may give him my blessing and tell him what he is to do.

Speech of Manku Inqa to his Son on his Deathbed

My beloved, darling son. You can see how I am and so I need not make you understand in words the pain I feel. Do not weep, for I should be the one weeping at my lot, for having trusted such people and presenting them with gifts as I did, when they did not deserve such treatment, and you know full well how they arrived, fleeing from their cohorts from the crimes they had committed amongst them. And I took them in, and favored them with a father's tolerance. I order you never to live with these people in peace so that what has befallen me may never befall you. Do not allow them to enter your land, no matter how inviting their words may be, for their honeyed words deceived me as they will deceive you if you believe them.

Take care of your brother and sisters and your mother. Look out for them, heal them and favor them as I would favor you and do not give my bones grief by treating your brothers and mother badly.

Take care of these poor Indians and look after them as you should and look well on how they have followed me, and guarded me and aided me in all of their needs, leaving their lands and customs out of their love for me. Do not overwork them, do not attack them, do not fight with them, nor punish them without reason because doing so you will anger Wiraquchan. I have ordered them to respect and esteem you as lord in my place, for you are my firstborn and the heir to my kingdom and this is my dying wish. I trust in the goodness of them all, that they will accept you and respect you as such and will do no more than what I have ordered and what you order them.

And then he came to an end, and left me in the town of Vitcos whence I came to Vilcabamba, where I have been for more than twenty years until some Indians from Huamachuco came to find me with orders from Gonzalo Pizarro, who was at the time, up in arms against the king.[86]

Here begins the Manner, Method and Way that I, Don Diego de Castro Titu Kusi Yupanki came to Live in Peace with the Spaniards and in this Peace, by the Grace of God— whom We called Wiraquchan of Old—came to be a Christian. The Story is the Following:

In my aforesaid declarations, I explained, simply and concisely, how my father Manku Inqa Yupanki was the native lord of these Peruvian kingdoms and the method and the manner in which these Spaniards entered his land and how and why he revolted against them, which was due to their foul treatment of him and how he was forced to live his last years and then was killed. Here I wish to declare the manner and method in which I came to be a Christian and be at peace with the Spaniards after his days, which was through God, because his Lordship, through the Lord Governor Licentiate Lope Garcia de Castro, reigned and governed these Peruvian kingdoms.

During the period that the Marquis of Cañete was viceroy of these Peruvian kingdoms,[87] *he sent a Dominican Father to speak with me about leaving this place for Cuzco, saying that the Lord Viceroy has an order from the Emperor Don Carlos that upon my exit from Vilcabamba, and showing my will to be a Christian, they would feed me according to my rank.*[88] *And I, remembering the way the Spaniards had treated my father in Cuzco, in his company, and what he had told me during his last days, thinking that what had happened to my father might happen to me, did not then wish to give my consent to that Father, Friar Melchor de los Reyes,*[89] *who accompanied the* embassy, and one Juan Sierra, his companion, who had told me they came by the Lord Viceroy's command. In order to verify what the Father and his companion were saying, I sent with the aforesaid Father a certain number of my captains[90] to the Marquis so that they could assure me of the business at hand, and if it was as they had said I would send a brother of mine in my stead so that he could experiment a life with the Spanish and tell me how they treated him, and if they did him well, I would leave for Cuzco.

After a year had passed, the aforesaid Father returned with my aforesaid captains who gave me their assurance in everything and I—seeing that such a person entreated me so and gave me such a verifiable certification of what I was to be fed—sent my aforesaid brother named Sayri Thupaq, to whom I gave orders on how he was to behave. And he left with the aforesaid father to see the Viceroy who received him well and fed him in the valley of Yucay and other repartimientos,[91] where he died a Christian.[92] And I, when I learned of the death, was greatly aggrieved, thinking that the Spaniards had killed him as they had killed my father, and so I grieved for days until the Licentiate Polo[93] and Martín de Pando,[94] the notary who still serves me to the present day, along with Juan de Betanzos,[95] were sent from Cuzco to certify that my brother, Don Diego Sayri Thupaq, had died a natural death. And I detained the aforesaid Martín de Pando in my land to certify things that were convenient to me, and I allowed Juan de Betanzos to leave with my answer.[96] And so I was for a few days until by order of the Count of Nieva,[97] the successor to the Marquis of Cañete, other messengers came with things concerning the peace I was negotiating with the Spaniards, and he said the same things as the Marquis. I responded that I was very pleased that the king possessed my father's lands and was ready to live at peace. And his messengers left with this reply.[98]

And I knew that the Spanish were trying to procure this peace for three reasons: thinking that I was leaping about their lands attracting many of the natives to me; or because the king's orders to negotiate were dictated by his conscience that his possessions had been my father's; or perhaps because he would rather keep me there, in his land, to assure himself that I could do no harm amongst them. I believed these things because I had not been instructed in the Faith and could not see that it would be the main cause for peace as I now know my conversion was, for the Fathers tell me so, that this is the main reason for the peace negotiations.

After these aforesaid messengers, who had come at the behest of the Count of Nieva, the treasurer, García de Melo,[99] returned with the same message: begging me to live in peace with the Spaniards, to be still, not to move about so much, because the king gave me his word that he would repay me as soon as I allowed priests to preach the word of God in my land. And I said I would *be still and would do no ill to the Indians nor worry the Spaniards, and that I gave my word that if they did not give me occasion to do otherwise, I would happily be at peace and at work, as they could well see. And to their request that I should allow priests into my land, I replied that I knew nothing of their work, that first peace should be had, and later what was fair would be done. And with this response the treasurer Melo returned, for the first time.*

And at the time of these comings and goings from Cuzco to my lands and from my lands to Cuzco, the corregidor *was Doctor Cuenca,* oidor *of his Majesty,*[100] *and it came to pass that some Indians that belonged to Nuño de Mendoza, who resided along the limits of my land, along the river called Acobamba, escaped because of the bad treatment they received from a Spaniard who was in charge of them and entered my land to acknowledge me as their lord. When Doctor Cuenca was informed of these events, believing that I had brought them by force, he wrote me an offensive letter in which he ordered me to return these Indians to their rightful owner because otherwise he would wage the cruelest war known to man against me. When I received this letter I was quite saddened and I responded that it was not for war that they had not been begging me and if that was what they wanted I was ready for them. Angered, I prepared my men for war, and had spies placed, oh I can't remember where, so that those who would do me ill would not catch me by surprise. This Doctor Cuenca nevermore gave a reply and I inspected the road he would have to cross in order to see if they still wanted to go to war and I returned with more than five hundred Indians, from many places. And I returned to be still in my home where I received a letter, written in Lima, from the aforesaid Doctor Cuenca, I don't know how I overlooked it, in which he offered me much and begged me to let dead dogs lie.*[101]

After this, the treasurer García de Melo returned with the orders of Your Lordship, in which you advised me, because of what I had told you, to marry my son Don Felipe Kispi Titu with his cousin Doña Beatriz[102] *and then we agreed to be at peace, which we later signed in Acobamba*[103] *by orders of Your Lordship and myself. The witnesses, at Your Lordship's request, were Diego Rodríguez, as* corregidor,[104] *and Martín de Pando, as my secretary. The hows and whys of this treaty and capitulation are in Your Lordship's possession and you can show these to His Majesty. I will not go into the treaty's details because Your Lordship is their author, but I will explain the importance of Chuquichaca and the arrival of Hernando Matienzo*[105] *and my conversion and baptism and I would like His Majesty to know that all of this was your doing.*

As Your Lordship is well aware, when you sent Diego Rodríguez to be the corregidor *of my land, I received him as Your Lordship commanded, and to see whether the peace ratification was convenient—as I had given my word to* live in peace with the king, our lord, and his subjects—which I did ratify, by receiving the oidor Licentiate Matienzo on the Chuquichaca bridge,[106] informing him of recent events in my land and by receiving priests into my land to instruct me and my people in the matters of God. Father Vera,[107] whom Your Lordship sent me, baptized my son Don Felipe Kispi Titu and was in my land for almost a year and a half and then left because the Augustine friars had come to baptize me.

My renunciation that I made to Your Lordship, in the name of His Majesty, of all my kingdoms and fiefdoms that had been the possessions of none other than my father, is a testimony to this peace that was signed with the treasurer Melo in Acobamba. Leaving these things aside, as Your Lordship is a witness to these events, being their protagonist, this is how I became and have been a Christian until the present day:

Because Your Lordship wrote many letters begging me to become a Christian, saying it was necessary to secure the peace, I inquired of Diego Rodríguez and Martín de Pando who in Cuzco was the foremost person among the clergy and which religion was the most appropriate and most widely followed. And they told me that the most approved and widely followed religion with the most authority and which flourished most, in all the land, though with fewer friars, was that of the Lord Saint Augustine and his prior (I mean the monks who reside in Cuzco) was the foremost cleric in all of Cuzco.[108] And having heard and understood all of this, I studied this order and religion, more than any other, and decided to write to this prior many letters begging him to baptize me in person, because I would be pleased to be baptized by his hand, he being such an important cleric, more than any other. And so this honorable cleric, graced me with the trouble of coming to my land to baptize me, taking with him another cleric and Gonzalo Pérez of Vivero and Tilano of Anaya, who arrived in Rayangalla on August 12, 1568, where I arrived from Vilcabamba to receive baptism, as I understood they were to give me.[109] And there, in this town of Rayangalla, the aforesaid prior named friar Juan de Vivero and his companions spent fourteen days instructing me in matters of the faith, at the end of which, on the day of the glorious Doctor Saint Augustine, I was baptized by the aforesaid prior. My godfather was Gonzalo Pérez of Vivero and my godmother was Doña Angelina Sisa Uqllu. And after they baptized me, I spent another eight days with the prior educating myself in all of the matters and mysteries of our Holy Catholic faith. When we were done, this aforesaid prior left with Gonzalo Pérez of Vivero, leaving behind one of his companions, Friar Marcos García[110] so that he would remind me, little by little, of the matters in which the aforesaid prior had instructed me so that I would not forget and so that he would teach and *preach to the people of my land the word of God. And I, before he left, told my Indians the reasons for my baptism and why I had brought these people to my lands and what effects baptism had on men and why this aforesaid Father would stay in the land. They all replied that they rejoiced at my baptism and the Father's decision to stay in our land, and that they too would soon try baptism (for this purpose our Father was staying in the aforesaid land).*

Two months after the aforesaid Father had been in Rayangalla and the prior had left, teaching and instructing in matters of the faith, and baptizing children with the consent of their parents, I decided to go with Martín de Pando to visit the land on the other side of the ports, towards Huamanga, where I stayed for four months doing the same job, erecting crosses and building churches in the towns where I arrived, and in these churches and beneath these crosses more than ninety infants were baptized. When all this was done, and having left young men to preach the Doctrine, he returned to the aforesaid town of Rayangalla, where he was baptizing and teaching the Indians in the entire province. And around the month of September, another Father[111] came and we worked together in that land until I brought them to Vilcabamba where we are now. They have not baptized anyone yet because the people are still new to these matters of God's laws and commandments, which they should first know and understand. Thus, so that Your Lordship comprehends me and graces me before His Majesty, I have tried to be brief in my above declarations without going into more detail on how my father lived or the success and the aim of my business up until now. If you need to know anything more extensively, on how things have been up until now, when Your Lordship so desires you should not hesitate to ask me as Your Lordship commands. Until then, it seems to me that this is enough, though there was more to say and inform, especially as to our origin and beginning and the ways of our people and their customs which I leave aside for the sake of brevity alone and because they do not directly fulfill our purpose. I will only beseech Your Lordship, for you have graced me in everything, to warmly and truthfully convey everything written to His Majesty in order to receive his favor, for I know he will favor me as it becomes my lordship; and because it seems to me that I have lengthened this too much, I finish here.

All of this written above was made and ordered with the declarations of the Illustrious Lord Don Diego de Castro Titu Kusi Yupanki, son of Manku Inqa Yupanki, who was the Native Lord of these Peruvian Kingdoms, by the Reverend Father Friar Marcos García, Presbyterian Friar of the Order of Lord Saint Augustine, who resides in this province of Vilcabamba, in charge of the administration of the souls that reside within it, in the honor and glory of all mighty God, Father, Son and Holy Spirit, three persons and only one true God and of the Glorious Kingdoms of the Angels, the Mother of God, Saint Mary, our Lady, now and forevermore, Amen.

I, Martín de Pando, scribe by commission of the Illustrious Lord Licentiate Lope García de Castro, who was the governor of these kingdoms, give faith that everything that the aforesaid Father dictated and ordered was at the insistence of the aforesaid don Diego de Castro, which I wrote with my own hands. Witnesses who saw the dictation and writing were the Reverend Father Friar Diego Ortiz, professed Presbyterian of the aforesaid order who resides in the company of the author, and three of Don Diego de Castro's captains named Suta Yupanki, Rimachi Yupanki and Sullka Waraq. And as I give faith of all that is said above, I sign it with my own name. Done in the town of San Salvador de Vilcabamba on February 6, 1570. To give further faith, the aforesaid Father Friar Marcos García, and Friar Diego Ortiz and I, the aforesaid Martín de Pando, sign our names. Fray Marcos García. I say I have witnessed all of this being written, Friar Diego Ortiz. In true testimony, Martín de Pando, scribe.

I, Don Diego de Castro Titu Kusi Yupanki, son as I am of Manku Inqa Yupanki, native lord of these Peruvian kingdoms, seeing as it was necessary to give a relation to the King Don Felipe, our lord, of things concerning me and my descendants (and I know not all the phrases and gestures that the Spanish use on these occasions), begged the Reverend Father Friar Marcos García and Martín de Pando to, according to their native custom, order and compose this aforesaid relation to send it to the kingdoms of Spain to the very Illustrious Lord Licentiate Lope García de Castro so that he, in my name, in my representation, might favor me by showing it and telling his Majesty the King Don Felipe our lord, so that, seeing the reasons why I should be repaid, favor me and my children and their descendants, according to his Majesty's station; and as all of the aforesaid is true, and is signed with my name, done on the aforesaid day, month and year. Don Diego de Castro Titu Kusi Yupanki.

Power of Attorney for the Lord Governor the Licentiate Lope Garcia de Castro

Let all who see this power of attorney know that I, the Sapay Inqa Don Diego de Castro Titu Kusi Yupanki, firstborn son of Manku Inqa Yupanki and grandson of Wayna Qhapaq, who were the native lords of these Peruvian kingdoms and provinces, say that inasmuch as I need to discuss many things and business with the King Don Felipe our lord and other authorities, of whatsoever rank and condition they may be, secular or ecclesiastic, and together with some other people who have left for the

Spanish kingdoms, who may reside there or now reside there, and, not finding among them another besides the Lord Governor Licentiate Castro who, on his way to Spain, could more warmly or solicitously represent me, who could more lovingly favor me, and who has been accustomed to gracing me with his favor, and in whose person I confide, I give him free and ample power to represent me, as the law commands, as I have and hold, and as the law in this case requires, that for me and in my name and as my very person he may appear before his Majesty and present to his royal name whatsoever petition or appeal, and say and declare everything that may be asked of him respecting my business, as though I were saying and declaring and appearing before whatsoever councils, audiences, mayor and regiment or any other of his Majesty's justices, ecclesiastic or secular, and ask and demand, defend and secure, all and whatsoever things he sees that can and should belong to me, which he may possess, rule and adjudicate as if I myself possessed, ruled and adjudicated with my own person, and if I were to receive *pesos* in gold and silver, lands, rents, livestock and whatsoever things possible, he may send them to these kingdoms at my cost and liability, and in my name. Should he be given any *pesos* in gold that may belong to me, he may buy whatsoever lands, rents, or merchandise he deems fit, like furniture or properties. Likewise, so that he can make whatsoever requests, appeals, calumny and slander oaths, tell the truth, respond to the contrary, conclude, present witnesses, evidence, documents, provisions, royal decrees, and any other kind of proof and bring it forth, contradict those in opposition, place any suspicions, reservations, objections, oaths and remove these as well. Take and assume in my name whatsoever possession of whatsoever goods and lands convenient to me, and upon this assumption, do what is just and convenient for these aforesaid goods; hear sentences in my favor, or agree to the contrary; appeal and plead wherefore the laws back me, and follow cases until their final conclusion; ask for costs and swear upon them, do everything that I could, even if it may not be expressly declared here and may require my presence, for as much power I have to give and bestow, I give and bequeath to this purpose, with all of the incidences and dependencies, annexes and corollaries and for a free and general administration, and with this aforesaid power may substitute with one or more persons or revoke them as he deems fit, and to them and to him I trust. With all formality to confirm the above, I require that the goods, tributes, rents, and lands that may benefit me, properties had and to be had; in testimony of the aforesaid, I sign this by my name on February 6, 1570. Witnesses who saw this through were the Reverend Father Friar Marcos García and Friar Diego Ortiz and Don

Pablo Wallpa Yupanki[112] and Don Martín Kusi Waman and Don Gaspar Sulka Yanaq. I, Martín de Pando, scribe by commission of the most Illustrious Lord Governor and Licentiate Castro—who governed these kingdoms, in the form and manner required by law—in whose testimony I have placed his name, Don Diego de Castro Titu Kusi Yupanki, witnessed by Friar Marcos García, witnessed by Friar Diego Ortiz. And in truthful testimony, I signed. Martín de Pando, scribe by commission.

Endnotes

1. Cf. Cerrón Palomino 1998: 435.

2. <Cusi> according to González Holguín, means "dicha, o ventura, o contento" 'joy, fortune or happiness' although he has no suggestion for <Titu>
other than "nombre de un Inga" 'name of an Inga' (56;344). Cf. Cerrón
Palomino 1998: 435 for his Aymara etymology for /Yupanki/; Cerrón
Palomino 1997b for his analysis of the copulative verb in Quechua and
Cerrón Palomino 1994 for his discussion of parallel grammatical structures
in Quechua and Aymara.

3. "The Inca account recorded who was descended from Manco Capac and his
sister [the pair of dynastic progenitors] in the male line. A knowledge of
genealogy was important because it was used in the calculation of a status
which flowed through this patrilineage. A claim that its members were *Capac*
was asserted [. . .] Capac status flowed through both males and females
descended from the pair of dynastic progenitors" (Julien: 296). "Huayna
Capac was the first ruler born to the union of a brother and a sister from the
preceding dynastic generation [. . .] a concentration of capac status resulted
from the pairing of individuals who were closest in descent terms, to the
dynastic line" (30). The claim to *Qhapaq* status became increasingly important following Pachakutiq's reign because it became associated with the
expansion of the Inqas out of the Cuzco valley, and the restructuring of
Cuzco into Hanan and Lurin sectors (243). Hanan Inqas were those who
lived physically above the old Cuzco, or Lurin Cuzco, and were descended
from generations who were associated with the empire and in whom a status linked to the solar supernatural was concentrated (i.e. Qhapaq status)
(261).

4. "Montes" in 16th-century Peruvian Spanish meant forest, wild or fallow land
and not elevated land as it can be sometimes understood in modern usage.
Although Sebastián de Covarrubias Orozco glosses this term in 1611 as
"montaña" 'highland' (812), the *Diccionario etimológico de la lengua caste-*
llana notes that although "montes" had taken on the meaning of "highlands"
in Peninsular Spanish by the late 16th century, the Old Castilian usage of
"forests" was retained and transmitted in Peru (Sandoval de la Maza; Vol. 4,
131). Vilcabamba is a region of cloud forest, or in a literal translation of the
Spanish *ceja de selva* it lies on the brow of the Amazon, a mountainous
region at 2,000 meters above sea level.

5. See Franklin Pease, *Las Crónicas y los Andes*: 15–34 for an overview of the
chronicles and relations written about Peru before 1570.

6. City in the northern Peruvian highlands. See Chapter 1 of Antonio Cornejo
Polar, *Escribir en el aire* for his discussion of the confrontation between orality and the written word in Cajamarca and the significance of the massacre
in Andean collective memories. For historical information, see Lockhart's

Men of Cajamarca, probably the best account of the Cajamarca encounter between Pizarro and Ataw Wallpa.

7. According to John Hemming, the Castilian league was equivalent to 3.5 miles or 5.57 kilometers (321).

8. Gonzalez Holguín notes the following: "Era epicteto, del sol honrroso nombre del Dios que adorauan los indios y de ay ygualandolos con su Dios llamauan a los españoles viracocha" 'Was an epithet for the only honorable name for God whom the Indians worshiped and then they equated the Spanish with their God by calling them viracocha" (353). Tzevetan Todorov follows this same thesis in *The Conquest of America: the question of the other* notwithstanding texts such as the *Instrucción* which place in question the image of Indians who allowed for the 'rapid' conquest of these vast territories of the Andean region because they thought the Spanish conquistadors were "gods." Cf. Guillén Guillén 1994 and Pease for alternate visions, which conclude that the Spaniards projected the conflation of the conquistadors with Wiraqucha after the conquest. Furthermore, attempts to equate Wiraqucha with the Christian God were declared counterproductive by the 3rd Council in Lima in 1583 and priests were prohibited from making such cultural translations (Cf. Harrison 1994). Significantly, it is precisely at this Council that the preaching in the official native languages (Quechua, Aymara, and Puquina) becomes compulsory and the Christian doctrine is translated into these three "general" languages of Peru. Nonetheless, this cultural translation will continue to be used by other authors including, most notably, el Inca Garcilaso in an attempt to reconcile his own mestizo heritage (although he prefers the name of Pachakamaq over Wiraqucha). Wiraqucha is often cited as the creator of nature in an empty universe. However, in *The Huarochirí Manuscript*, he can also appear as "Cuny Raya," a trickster, and reappears in flood and solar eclipse stories (cf. Salomon and Urioste). Cf. Jan Szeminski, *Wira Qucha* for his comparison and analysis of the webs of meaning surrounding this pan-Andean deity in prayers, chronicles, plays and other colonial documents. Julien emphasizes the creation stories involving <Viracocha> with the Lake Titicaca region as a backdrop. These stories, however, are problematic because their "universality" is difficult to separate from Christian belief (289). Nonetheless, <Atun Viracochan> appears to have had a physical presence as a <huaca>, to the South of Cuzco in Urcos, and was fed on a daily basis by attendants (289). In the accounts of Sarmiento and Betanzos, <Ticci Viracocha> in the former and <Contiti Viracocha> in the latter, the scenes of these creation stories move from the Lake Titicaca area to Tiahuanaco to Cacha in Canas territory and then to Urcos in Cuzco where he later traverses the Andes and disappears into the sea off the Ecuadorian Coast (287). The course of <Viracocha> in these stories is thus closely associated with that of the sun from sunrise to sunset. Furthermore, in Betanzos, "there are parallels between Viracocha's sweep through the Andes and the march of the Inca armes [. . .] an Andean motif

that assimilates the Inca conquest to the actions of the supernatural [i.e. the Sun] most closely associated with the dynastic descent group" (291). See note 3.

9. One of the Andean deities who had announced his return (Millones 1985: 9). See note 8. Also, Domingo de Santo Tomás glosses <Ticssin> as "principio, o fundamento de edificio; elemento o principio; o fin de qualquier cosa" 'the beginning or foundation of; element; the end of something' (363).

10. It is significant that González Holguín not only glosses the term as "rayo" 'lighting' but also "arcabuz" 'musket' and "artilleria" 'artillery' (367). Like the rainbow, Illapa was an important deity for the Inqas.

11. Millones suggests in his edition that "Yuyan" is an error for "yungas," or Yunka, meaning inhabitants of the lower lands (1985 Edition: 3). Regalado de Hurtado transcribes "yugan" but likewise suggests "yungas" as a possibility (1992 Edition: 5). Urteaga directly transcribes "yunga" (1916 Edition: 9).

12. González Holguín translates <quellcca> [qillqa] as "Papel carta, o escriptura" 'letter paper or writing' (301). Though Domingo de Santo Tomás likewise translates <quillca> as "letra, o carta mensagera; libro, o papel generalmente" 'letter or messenger letter; a book or generally, paper' he translates <Quillcanigui> [qillqay] as "pintar, o escrevir generalmente; labrar alguna cosa con colores generalmente" "generally, to paint or write; generally, to work with colors" (357). Cf. Mignolo 1995: Chapter 2 for his discussion on the "book" in the European tradition and Spanish perceptions of Mesoamerican and Andean writings.

13. Chicha is a Tahina word, which the Spanish later applied to the fermented corn beer they encountered in the Andean region. Martha Hildebrandt proposes a probable Cuna origin, from the Indians of Panama. See *Peruanismos*. The Quechua word for fermented corn beer is *aqha* in Southern Quechua dialects (Cerrón Palomino 1994a: 34). Among Quechua and Aymara speakers, the offer to drink chicha is a sign of welcome and an invitation to initiate a relationship of reciprocity and a rejection to this invitation to drink is still seen as a great offense today. It is a sacred drink used to propitiate to the Pachamama and the Apus as well as to one's ancestors. During festivities, large quantities of chicha are drunk to encourage social as well as cosmological integration. Cf. Thierry Saignes, ed. for discussions of colonial perceptions of ritual drunkenness of Andean peoples, the creation of identities surrounding the drinking of chicha and the relationship between cosmos, memory and drinking in Andean rituals and code-switching (between Spanish and Quechua) in ritual drinking contexts. Titu Kusi Yupanki, in his letter to Lope García de Castro of 24 November 1568, describes the importance of chicha drinking among the Anti (or peoples of the Amazon) for ritual cannibalism (1916 Edition Apéndice B: 122). Cf. *Mummies and Mortuary Monuments* for Isbell's discussion of pre-Inqa and Inqa ancestor worship in general.

14. Seed 1991 reads the preceding passage in the following manner: "According to Titu Cusi's account, Atahualpa's gesture of throwing the book on the ground mirrors the gesture that preceded it—the Spaniard's pouring the chicha on the ground—and thus establishes a symmetry between Inca and Hispanic behavious, each one causing an object sacred to the other to end up on the ground" (21). Salomon 1982 similarly finds that the text establishes a parallel between both parties' forms of conquest, thus equating the Spanish and Inqa acts of aggression.

15. See note 3.

16. The *Relación de los Agustinos* gives an insight into the native Huamachuco perception of the war of succession waged between Waskar and Ataw Wallpa as well as a description of these festivities celebrating the local *wakas*. In this *Relación* however, Ataw Wallpa is remembered as the Inqa who ordered the desecration of the *Waka* <Cataquil> because his prophecy favored his brother Waskar (Castro de Trelles: 20). The Huamachuco region is not a native Quechua or Aymara speaking region and was fiercely resistant to these two languages before the Spanish conquest, its native inhabitants preferring their native Culli, which may explain the rapid hispanization of the region (including the provinces of Cajabamba, Otuzco, Pallasca, Santiago de Chuco and Sánchez Carrión). Cf. Torero 1989; Andrade Ciudad 1995. This toponym should not be interpreted as a Quechua word.

17. Tumis are knives used for ritual sacrifice. Like chicha drinking, the use of these knives was not limited to Quechua or Aymara speaking cultures, rather the finest extant specimens of this metalwork are Moche, in gold-plated copper, and later Lambayeque and Chimu, in arsenical bronzes using depletion gilding *tumbaga* technology (Cf. Lechtman 1974). One of the measures the Inqas took to establish their hegemony in this northern coastal region of the Tawantinsuyu, i.e. Chinchaysuyu, was to prohibit native production of tumis in native bronzes (i.e. arsenical bronze) and to replace them with the import and production of tin bronzes native to the Southern altiplano (Cf. Lechtman 1987).

18. Urteaga asserts that there is no place called Conoc in the area surrounding Cajamarca (1916 Edition: 11). Conoc is a believable toponym for the hot springs mentioned, however, because it is a colonial spelling of the Quechua word for 'warm.'

19. Santo Tomás translates <Osno> as an "altar donde sacrifican" 'altar where sacrifices are made' (332). González Holguín adds that the <usnu> is a "tribunal de juez de una piedra hincada" 'judge's bench made with steps' (358). Cf. Harrison 1989: 97.

20. Note that distance among Andean peoples can be conceived of in terms of space and time and not necessarily in linear units of measurement (such as the Castilian league) (Harrison 1994: 40).

21. Significantly, Juan de Betanzos writes that the Inqa Pachakutiq "named the whole of [Cuzco] Lion's Body, saying that its neighbors and inhabitants were like the members of the body and that he was its head" (Betanzos: Parte I Capítulo XVII).

22. González Holguín writes that <Çapay Inca çapay apu> means "el rey desta tierra' 'the king of this land' (78). Because *sapay* means "the one and only" Sapay Inqa is a form of address which literally means 'Only Lord.'

23. See Note 6 and Chapter 1 of Rama as well as Chapter 2 of Mignolo 1995; also Cummins for his discussion of Andean referents. Though many of the conquistadors were themselves illiterate, the written word provided a source of political and divine legitimacy for their actions. The introduction of the written word to indigenous societies of the Americas was often a violent punishment for resisting (uncomprehending) submission to the Pope and Holy Roman Emperor outlined in the *Requerimiento*. Thus the written word introduces a system of signs and signifiers based on the violent exclusion of the native population. At the same time, if we remember the iconography surrounding Saint Augustine holding a Church founded on the Gospel, the written word offered the church and the conquistadors an image to create, or map out in "empty spaces," these 'new' territories as ordered Christian communities or Cities of God (in contrast to the chaotic and violent early years of the colonies and the reality of churches being founded over the sites of 'pagan' or 'idolatrous' native temples). Ironically, a silver model of the Church founded on the Gospel is stored in the Quri Kancha of Cuzco, also a Dominican monastery, and exemplifies the contradiction between the theoretical and concrete activity in the projection of the written word over "new" cultural spaces. Cf. Rama: Chapter 1.

24. In his introduction, Millones finds a parallel in this passage to the enigmatic deity that led the messianic movement Taki Unquy (Millones 1985: 10). The 10 year long Taki Unquy movement, c. 1560–70, called for a return to Waka worship and for the casting out of Spanish ideology from the highlands (Cf. Millones 1990: 14). See Lienhard, for his analysis of epic tropes and oral structure in Titu Kusi Yupanki's *Instrucción* (Chapter VII).

25. Francisco Pizarro was conferred the title of Marquis of Atavillos by the Crown in 1541, but the actual location was left pending and Pizarro was murdered before he was able to establish an actual location for his marquisate. Thus, there exists no Peruvian parallel to the Oaxaca marquisate that was granted to Hernando Cortés in Mexico (Varón Gabai 1997: 217–218).

26. Note that among the chroniclers of the conquest there is no unanimous opinion as to the identity or number of the Spaniards who were first sent to Cuzco (cf. Lockhart 1972).

27. Huánuco Pampa, an administrative center of the Inqa empire, lies 150 km outside of the Huánuco, capital of the modern Peruvian department in between Cajamarca and Cuzco. The Inqa resistance in this region, from 1537

to 1545, was the strongest and also the bloodiest of the "War of Reconquest" (Guillén Guillén 1994: 117). For an archaeological study of the site, see Craig Morris and Donald E. Thompson, *Huánuco Pampa*.

28. Machu means old in Quechua and "Kapitu" is the Quechua pronunciation of the Spanish "capitán."

29. González Holguín writes, " Señor grande o juez superior o curaca principal" 'Principal Lord, Judge or Curaca' (Holguín: 31). Ludovico Bertonio in his *Vocabulario de la lengua aymara* glosses Apu in Aymara as "Señor corregidor or príncipe" 'Lord *corregidor* or Prince" (Bertonio: 24). The term also refers to the mountain and glacier deities venerated by Andean peoples.

30. González Holguín glosses <hu hu> as "sea a si que me plaze, o norabuena" 'I agree or in good time' (163).

31. "Significantly, although Atahualpa was garroted, he is remembered in Andean tradition as having had his head cut off by the Spanish [. . .] This imagined dismemberment of the Inca's body mirrored the dismemberment of the imperial body that occurred with the execution of the Inca, for the strictly vertical nature of the Inca hierarchy, with all the power flowing from the Inca downward, made the loss of the Inca symbolically analogous to a decapitation" (Classen: 114). See Waman Puma, f. 390 for a visual image of Ataw Wallpa's decapitation (Murra y R. Adorno 1980 Edition: 362–63). In the myths surrounding the return of Inkarri, * *inqa* and *rey* (Spanish for King), once the Inqa has found his head and his body complete once again, he will do battle to the Spanish and oust them from his lands and restore the Inqa social order to the Andean peoples (Chang-Rodríguez 1994: 22).

32. González Holguín glosses <Quisquis> as "parasite" (310). Many names in Quechua and Aymara are also names of animals such as Atuq 'fox' or Amaru 'serpent.'

33. <Guazábara> was originally an Antillean word for skirmish or guerrilla warfare. (Sandoval de la Maza: Vol. 3 p. 251)

34. Jaquijahuana, modern-day Anta, is a village that lies on a plain twenty miles northwest of Cuzco. Here, Gonzalo Pizarro discovered and burned the mummy of Inqa Wiraqucha and was himself later hanged when he lost the battle of Jaquijahuana to La Gasca on April 9, 1548, for his treason against the Spanish Crown. Polo de Ondegardo later visited this small village and wrote in his *Tratado y averiguación sobre los errores y supersticiones de los indios (1559)* that Wiraqucha's ashes were still being venerated. Jaquijahuana was one of three major estates that were later given to Sayri Thupaq, Titu Kusi Yupanki's brother, when he left Vilcabamba in January 1558; these had been confiscated from the rebel Francisco Hernández Girón. Jaquijahuana is also important in prehispanic Inqa history as the battlefield where the Inqas defeated the <Chancas>; there the cowardly Inqa Wiraqucha abandoned his son Kusi Yupanki to his fate, who proves to be a worthy leader in battle, indicative of his later successes in expanding the territories of the empire. He

later names himself Pachakutiq (or Maker or Renewer of the Land). See Rostworowski, for her discussion of the myths surrounding Yupanki's initiation as Inqa leader (55–68).

35. Hernando de Soto. Titu Kusi Yupanki mistakenly calls him Antonio de Soto.

36. Carrillo notes in his edition that this should read Cupi. The pre-Hispanic settlement of Cupi is now a town in the district of Colcabamba in the Aimaraes province, in the department of Apurimac (1973 Edition: 31).

37. El Inca Garcilaso de la Vega writes that Kiskis had offered the Inqanate to Pawllu but that he respected the election of his brother Manku Inqa (*Comentarios Reales* Lib. I, Cap. XXXIX). He proves to be an important general, along with Wila Uma, in the war against the Spanish, but later betrays Manku Inqa and fights alongside the Spanish. Pawllu was later named Inqa by Diego de Almagro, with whom he had fought side by side in Chile, following Manku Inqa's retreat into Vilcabamba (Nowack and Julien: 37). As a part of Viceroy Toledo's campaign to incorporate all Inqa-owned *encomiendas* into Spanish domains, he accused the sons of Pawllu Inqa of sending letters to their relatives in Vilcabamba in order to impede the Viceroy's negotiations for peace with the rebellious Inqanate (16). Through these accusations, Toledo was able to divest the Inqas with a high position in colonial Cuzco society as well as dispossess all of the Inqas of Vilcabamba of their property once the rebellious province was conquered by Toledo in 1572. Inqa women were not stripped of their land holdings; rather they were incorporated into Spanish colonial society through marriage with Spaniards or forced into a religious life, thus integrating their *encomiendas* with Church property (37).

38. Contrast with the description of the dead Thupaq Amaru in Capitán Baltasar de Ocampo's "Account of the Province of Vilcapampa and a Narrative of the Execution of the Inca Tupac Amaru [1610]": referring to Thupaq Amaru's execution in 1572, Ocampo writes that "when the head was cut off, it was put on a spike, and set up on the same scaffold in the great square, where the execution had taken place. There it became each day more beautiful, the Inca having had a plain face in life" (Markham 1907: 229). In Ocampo's account, Thupaq Amaru is of a "lordly mind" with "self-possession," a defeated enemy who should be respected (227). Kiskis, on the other hand, in the *Instrucción* is a traitor, blood thirsty and tyrannical so that even in death, he is offensive to the living with his ugliness and is not worthy of veneration.

39. Manku Inqa is referring to the *peso* system. Hemming writes, "a 'peso de oro' was not a coin but a weight of gold roughly a sixth of an ounce or 4.18 grams. A thousand pesos de oro was thus about ten pounds or 4.2 kilos. At the time of the Conquest, 450 maravedís made one peso de oro, and 100 pesos de oro made one libra de oro. Later, a 'peso de oro' became known as a 'castellano,' worth 490 maravedís. [. . .] Prices in the early days of the

Conquest of Peru were naturally very erratic because of the scarcity of European goods and the relative abundance of precious metals" (Note to p. 63 Hemming: 554). The coins produced for the American Kingdoms were often devalued (despite their status as prime producers of the metal) because of the Crown's expenditures in the European wars and on luxury imports, which often emptied the Spanish treasury (Cf. Galeano).

40. "The *qoya* brought a great deal into the marriage [with the Inqa], including counsel, status, legitimacy for offspring, and wealth. Once in the alliance, she wielded some independent power and was also a persuasive political adviser for her husband and son who succeeded him. Even though she may well have been voicing the interests of her kin group, a *qoya* mother could also impede the marriage of her daughter to the king. Similarly, a prospective *qoya* could reject the proposal [. . .] The lineage of the candidates' mother [to male royal succession] was crucial, because sitting rulers did not belong to their father's kin group. Instead, they founded their own *panaqa* and identified closely with their mother's" (D'Altroy: 103–104). *Pana*, the root of *panaqa*, means "man's sister" in Quechua (Cerrón Palomino 1994b: 58). See note 3 for Julien's views on the role of a Quya's genealogy in the determination of her son's Qhapaq status.

41. "Supay" was originally a Quechua word for 'ghost' or 'spirit' (Cerrón Palomino 1994a: 73) or a mischievous creature living in the lower earth but was given the negative meaning of "demon" or "devil" by Catholic missionaries (Harrison 1989: 48).

42. The civilized world inhabited by "runa" or people: "The most populous of the four parts, called *Chinchaysuyu* took its name from the respected Chincha *etnía* of Peru's south-central coast: it encompassed the lands and peoples of the Peruvian coast, the adjacent highlands, and the north Andes. *Antisuyu* lay to the north and northeast of Cuzco: it was named after the warm forests of the montaña, known in Hispanic form as the *Andes*. *Kollasuyu* formed the largest part of the empire: it ran from Peru's southern highlands through the altiplano all the way to Central Chile and adjacent Argentina. This division took its name from the Qolla (Kolla, Colla) peoples who lived on the north side of the Lake Titicaca. *Cuntisuyu*, the smallest part, took in the stretch of lamd that ran southwest from Cuzco to the Pacific.[Like Cuzco, the Tawantinsuyo] also contained ranked parts. The Upper part [Hanan] included Chinchaysuyu and Antisuyu, while the Lower [Lurin] included Kollasuyu and Cuntisuyu" (D'Altroy: 87–89). Cuzco represented the geographical and spiritual center of the Empire, leading el Inca Garcilaso to propose an apocryphal etymology for the city's name (Cf. Cerrón Palomino 1997a). "The Andean landscape is imbued with sacredness, human destinies are in part determined by chthonian powers, in the spirits of mountains, rocks, springs, rivers, and other topographic features, and generalized in the earth matrix, Pachamama" (Sallnow: 141). See also Bauer, for an archaeological study of the "ceque" system, or the distribution

of Inqa shrines and lands in radial lines beginning in Cuzco, according to parallel royal kin groups (*panaqas*).

43. See note 39.

44. The notorious "Quinto Real." The Kings in Spain received one fifth of all of the treasure pillaged and mined in the Americas (Hemming: 89).

45. Hernando Pizarro handed over the first shipment of treasure corresponding to the Emperor Charles the V to royal officials in Seville, Spain in January 1534 (Varón Gabai 1997:44).

46. See note 39.

47. According to Ludovico Bertonio <chacutha> in Aymara means "hazer rodeo" 'to round up' and <chaccuthapitha> means "juntar la gente o ganado esparzido" 'to gather the scattered people or livestock' (68). Sebastián de Covarrubias gives a Latin etymology for *chacota* from *cachinnus*. "Hazer *chacota* de un negocio, echarlo en burlas." "to make *chacota* of a particular activity." In his entry for *burla*, Covarrubias specifies that *echarlo en burlas* is "disimular lo que en un colérico sería occasion bastante para reñir" 'to 'save face on an occasion in which an irate man would find a substantial reason to fight.' The RAE 2001 lists *chacota* as an onomatopoeic word meaning "bulla y alegría mezclada de chanzas y carcajadas, con que se celebra algo. 2. Broma, burla" 'a ruckus and festivities mixed with fun and laughter, with which something is celebrated. 2, a trick, a joke.'

48. "Royal rule extended into the provinces by means of the 'corregidor,' an official who lived in each Spanish municipality and presided over its council. The *corregidor* was originally an unpaid, honorary official, generally a leading encomendero" (Hemming: 381). Gonzalo Pizarro was never 'corregidor' of Cuzco, but Juan Pizarro replaced Hernando de Soto as lieutenant governor of Cuzco on August 28, 1534 (Varón Gabai 1997: 77).

49. Literally "staff" in Spanish. To be a staff holder meant that you had a position of authority. In pre-Hispanic iconographies as well, most notoriously in Wari ceramics and in the Portal del Sol at Tiahuanaco in Bolivia, staff ornamentation and quality is a form of establishing hierarchies among several staff-holding deities.

50. Domingo de Santo Tomás writes that <oyuanigui> or [uyway] means to "criar niño o otro qualquier cosa" 'raise a child or anything' and that <oyuac> or [uywaq] means "criador o criadora" 'a breeder' (330). We can thus infer the meaning of "uywa" is a domesticated or docile animal or a small child. Cf. Cerrón Palomino 1994b: 80.

51. Pomacorco Street, parallel to Tullumayu, presently runs from Cuzco proper to the base of Sacsahuaman and was one of the Chinchaysuyu <ceques>; Wayna Qhapaq had a house there (Bauer: 55).

52. Domingo de Santo Tomas translates "pampa" as "campo raso, como vega" 'a level plain or meadow' (335).

53. Bertonio writes that <Vila> in Aymara means "la sangre" 'blood' and that <Vilamasi> means "consanguineo, pariente de una misma sangre" 'consanguinity, a relative of the same blood' (Bertonio 1984: 385); Uma in Quechua means "head." As we saw in note 31, the Inqa was considered the "head" of the Inqa Empire which was imagined as a body. Wila Uma's very title reflects his importance as a "co-ruling" warrior-priest related to the Inqa. (He belonged to the *panaqa*, or parallel royal lineage, of Wayna Qhapaq i.e. he was in equal standing for the Inqanate to Manku Inqa). Spanish chroniclers, understandably, compared the relationship between Manku Inqa and Wila Uma to that between their own Holy Roman Emperor Charles V and the Pope (Hemming: 177).

54. According to González Holguín *hatun* means "lo mayor, o major, o superior mas principal y mas conocido" 'the greatest, best, superior, or most principal, and most known' (154).

55. Domingo de Santo Tomás translates <chacara> as "heredad, lugar de labor" 'property, workplace' (255). González Holguín writes <chaccra> and glosses "heredad de lauor tierras o huertas" 'property for tilling land or gardens' (91). In Peruvian Spanish "chacra" means a small farm or a plot of farming land. In modern Southern Quechua, *chakra* (Cerrón Palomino 1994b: 36).

56. Kiskis and his men killed five or six Spaniards and wounded eleven men and fourteen horses and had Almagro not arrived with reinforcements, the small group led by Francisco Pizarro may have been decimated (Hemming: 108–110). What Titu Kusi suggests through this speech is that Wila Uma had supported the "rebels," Kiskis and Challku Chima.

57. See note 42.

58. Antillean word meaning "a windowless house."

59. "Kuna" is a plural marker, although it is not always needed. Increasingly, due to the external pressure of Spanish norms on Quechua, the use of "kuna" is required to mark the plural number of a noun although in 16th-century Quechua it was purely optional (cf. Cerrón Palomino 1987: 202).

60. According to Holguín, <Ynquillcuna> are "flores de oler" 'perfumed flowers' (526), specifically orchids (Cerrón Palomino 1994b: 45). The <Ynguill> in this passage could be referring to Francisca Ynguill who was affiliated to the *panaqa* of Inqa Ruqa, sixth Inqa of the dynastic line and first Inqa of Hanan Cuzco. According to Inqa witnesses in a lawsuit over the claims of Juan Pizarro's children whose mother was Francisca Ynguill, Francisco Ynguill was "very young" and had been kept in seclusion by Manku Inqa because "she was of his descent and lineage, to create in her his caste and children" (AGI, Patronato 90b, no.1, ramo 55, fol. 109 u in Julien: 40–42). Ynguill was too young to be married at the time of Manku Inqa's accession and he was waiting for her to mature before taking her as principal wife (or Quya). She could have been his *yanasa*, or promised woman (Cf. Cerrón Palomino 1994b: 84). Julien remarks, "the story [in the *Instrucción*] illustrates the

importance of these women [who could claim descendence from the dynastic line from mother and father] to the Incas and the knowledge on the part of the Pizarros of what it meant to espouse a woman with this status" (note 13 p. 305). Díaz-Rivera stresses the significance of the young girl's name, Inkill 'flower', in European ideas of virginity and comments that the conquistador's lust was as large as his desire to humiliate the 'colonized other' when he takes possession of the woman he believed to be the wife and sister of the Inqa (246).

61. The various layers of deceit in "How the Quya was Given" is an example of the "economy of lies" which Díaz-Rivera has proposed as the governing form of exchange 'between the Spaniards and the Indians' in the *Instrucción*: "Denomino economía de la mentira a, por un lado, la presencia en el texto de una minuciosa enumeración de las repetidas ocasiones en que los españoles le mienten a Manco Inca y a sus súbditos como forma de contabilidad mediante la cual se cuantifican los engaños y traiciones de los enemigos, y por el otro, a la presentación de la mentira como método básico de intercambio entre el indio y el español a través de la cual el embuste se convierte en la moneda que permite el trueque o la interacción entre ambos" 'I call 'economy of lies' the presence in the text of a minucious enumeration of the repeated ocassions in which the Spaniards lie to Manco Inca and to his subjects as a form of accounting [or accountability] through which these deceits and betrayals by the enemy are quantified and, similarly, the presentation of lying as the basic method for exchange whereby the Indian and the Spaniard convert deceit as the money that permits bartering or interaction between the two parties' (197). In light of Inkill's possible historical identiy, as we have seen in note 60, the layers of deception and shame within the text become more complex. According to the Spanish codes of social conduct of the era, the forced possession, especially in public, of Manku Inqa's principal wife and sister would have been an affront to his honor and a stain on his *honra* (Díaz-Rivera: 246). The laughter of the Inqas, in the text, however, is meant to signify the vengeance of the Inqas on the Spaniards because they deceived Pizarro by handing him a Quya who was not in fact the Quya and thus ridiculed the Spanish conquistador in the same manner, through artifice and malice (251–252). Yet the *Instrucción* seems to have masked the historical players in this passage, Juan Pizarro and Francisca Ynguill, with laughter and deceit in order to veil the Inqas' shame from its readers at the ravishing of the *yanasa* truly intended to be Quya by the Spanish Conquistador Juan Pizarro. The "errors" in the text, which repeatedly mistake Gonzalo for the other Pizarro brothers, betray an intention to construct a Pizarro character whose actions embody the collective misdeeds of the Pizarros and the conquistadors in general. Gonzalo Pizarro makes for an excellent scapegoat as the historical personage was repudiated both by the Inqas of Vilcabamba and the Spanish Crown.; he led a failed Spanish invasion of Vilcabamba following Manku Inqa's uprising and was also one of the *encomenderos* who led the rebellion against the Viceroy's rule in Peru.

62. Cf. Millones 1985: 13; Classen: 42, 102. This celebration occurred in January, around the summer solstice or December 23, during Qhapaq Raymi which was when noble Inqa boys went through rites of passage that marked the transition from child to adult (D'Altroy: Table 7.2). Inqa boys who had reached the age of fourteen received their breechcloth, woven by their mothers and also received their names during these rites (190). "The piercing of the ears to receive golden spools was only part of the rite of male initiation. Initiation marked the first wearing of the breechcloth, a rite called *huarachico* in the historical narratices whose name incorporates the term for breechcloth (*huara*)" (Julien: 278).

63. The directional suffix *rqu can sometimes lose its second consonant in Quechua Cusqueño and has a "dynamic totalizing" function with verbs (Cerrón Palomino 1987: 194; 283). The agentive suffix *-q* means "he or she who" (272). Thus, "wakaruq" can be understood as "he who keeps or honors the wakas." For a discussion of "waka" see note 78.

64. The mummy of <Mama Anaguarque>, Pachakutiq Inqa Yupanki's wife, was kept in Pomamarca, in the Antisuyu quadrant of Cuzco, the northeast quarter and one <ceque> may have been named after her in Kuntisuyu, the southwest quarter (Bauer: 25). Bauer notes that in Cobo's descriptions, this <ceque> runs over the ridge of Anaguarque, which is a major shrine of the village of Chocco, whose inhabitants were traditionally thought to be descendants of Mama Anawarki (Bauer: 48). The male initiation rite "also involved three pilgrimages by the intitiates to different mountains around the Cuzco valley, each followed by an assembly in the main plaza of Cuzco at which the ruling Inca, the images of the major supernaturals and the residents of the city, and the intitiates were present. The mountains visited were Huanacauri, Anahuarqui and Apo Yavira" (Julien: 278). Anahuarqui was the site of the foot race. At Huanacauri the initiates were given slings and bags similar to those used by the ancestral Inqas, the Ayar brothers. There they also received their short haircuts. At Apu Yawira they were given their breech clothes, their golden ear spools, feather crowns and other ornaments. Huanacauri is a *waka* directly linked to the origin story of the Inqa dynastic line. When one of the Ayar brothers realized he had been turned to stone upon reaching the Cuzco valley (the site was recognized as the *waka* of Oma on the mountain Huanacauri), he asked his remaining brothers that he should be the first *waka* to receive the offerings of the Inqas when they performed their male initiation rites (276).

65. "The piercing of ears that took place during the male puberty rite was [. . .] associated with sound and fluidity. This rite was the male counterpart to first menstruation and thus an inauguration of fertility. However, the fact that the organ made to bleed was not the penis but the ear suggests that men were supposed to control their sexuality by listening to and obeying oral tradition [. . .] Significantly, while the ears might ordinarily attract less attention than the other organs of the face, the Incas highlighted them by keeping their hair

short and wearing distinctive large gold ear ornaments. This drew attention to the Incas' privileged access to sacred orality" (Classen: 70). See also note 62.

66. Bertonio translates <yauri> as "cobre" 'copper' in Aymara (305). Neither González Holguín nor Santo Tomás offer a gloss of yawri from Quechua, which means 'plough blade' in modern Southern Quechua (Cf. Cerrón Palomino 1994b: 84).

67. Transistive verb in Quechua meaning 'to kiss' or 'to adore, venerate' (Cerrón Palomino 1994b: 55).

68. Qisu Yupanki attacked Lima in late 1536 (Guillén Guillén 1994: 77).

69. Name for a webfooted animal that lives in altiplano lakes (Cf. Cerrón Palomino 1994b: 49). See note 32.

70. A type of bird (González Holguín: 352). See note 32.

71. See note 33.

72. In the Chinchaysuyu quadrant of Cuzco, Carmenca is a prominent hill lying at the foot of the larger hill bearing Sacsahuaman and is where the shrine of Marcatampu once stood and where the Church of Santa Ana stands today (Bauer: 66). InqaThupaq Amaru was brought through the gate of Carmenca before his execution in the Plaza Mayor of Cuzco (Baltasar de Ocampo in Markham 1907: 223).

73. Jungle peoples from Antisuyu, the eastern sector of the Tawantinsuyu.

74. Sacsahuaman. John Rowe has argued that this temple overlooking the Cuzco valley was built in the shape of a puma's head and that the city itself had the shape of a puma's body. His hypothesis has been questioned, however, by Tom Zuidema who has demonstrated that the archaeological remains of Cuzco do not suggest such a design was intended. Though Cuzco may not have been constructed in the shape of a puma by the Inqas, the city's sacrality was conceived of in these terms. Cf. Rowe and Zuidema.

75. Martin Lienhard writes, with respect to this passage, that to his subjects the Inqa's gesture effectively converts them into waqchas—orphans, the ostracized, those poor in social wealth—the most feared status in Andean communities (191).

76. Offering or gift in Peruvian Spanish < * Qu. *Kamarikuq*. According to González Holguín, <camaricuk> in Quechua means "el que apareja algo, o asi mesmo se dispone o apareja" 'he who gives something or offers himself' (48). I have retained the Spanish orthography because "camarico" was assimilated early on in Peruvian Spanish with the meaning of "gift" and not "giver" and appears, in this context, with the latter meaning. As early as 1552, "camarico" can be found in Spanish legal documents signifying "gift" (*Testimonio dado por Benito de la Peña*: f. 21 v.)

77. Millones suggests there may be an error and advocates "Viracocha" in its stead (1985 Edition: 26); Regalado likewise finds an error but proposes no substitution (1992 Edition: 52). Urteaga replaces <viracha> with "Viracochan" without noting that a substitution had been made (1916 Edition: 80). However, Bertonio significantly glosses <Virachatha> [Wirachatha] in Aymara as "hazer que el suelo tenga corriente o esté mas alto de una parte que de otra" 'to give a current to the ground, or to raise one area higher than the other,' where <vira> means "el suelo, o qualquiera cosa que va cuesta abaxo" 'ground or anything downhill' (388), which seems especially appropriate given that the passage speaks of the raising and leveling of hills; "cha" could be the factual suffix –*cha* which creates verb phrases expressing the idea to make someone or something do what is being referred to in the nominal root in Aymara (Cerrón Palomino 2000: 260) so that "Wiracha" would literally be a verb meaning "to move or become earth" in Aymara. The "tha" in Bertonio's cited <Virachatha> is most probably the ablative suffix which gives a spatial or temporal origin to a material, a conversation etc. (cf. Cerrón Palomino 2000: 209). Missing, however, is the agentive suffix i.e. which adds the meaning "he who"—in Aymara this is –*ri* and in Quechua –*q*.

78. González Holguín glosses <huacca> in Quechua as "Ydolos, figurillas de hombres y animals que trayan consigo" 'idol, human and animal figurines they bring with them'; "hombre de nariz partida o labio hendido" 'man with a split nose or a hare lip'; "quando tiene seis dedos en manos y pies como león" 'when a man has six fingers on their hands and feet like a lion' (165). These homophones or homonyms are distinguished in Cuzqueño Quechua with a glottal: *waka* means deity or sacred place; *wak'a* is a crevice, crack, cleft or flaw as in a hare lip (Cerrón Palomino 1994b: 80). Santo Tomás only glosses <guaca> as "templo de ydolos o el mismo ydolo" 'a temple of idols or the idol itself' (279). Cf. Classen: 67.

79. Bertonio gives <Villca> several entries in Aymara: "El Sol como antiguamente dezían, y agora dizen inti; adoratorio dedicado al solo o otros idolos; es tambien una cosa medicinal, o cosa que se dava a bever como purga, para dormir, y en durmiendo dize que acudia el ladron que avia llevado la haziendo del que tomo la purga y cobrava su hazienda; era embuste de hechizeros" 'it meant sun in ancient times although now inti is used; a shrine dedicated to the sun or other idols; it is also a medicine, or a drink given to purge, or to sleep, and when sleeping it is said that the robber came to rob the sleeper of his lands; they were the lies of sorcerers' (386). Willka in modern Southern Quechua also means grandson/ granddaughter or great grandson/granddaughter (Cerrón Palomino 1994b: 83).

80. See note 50.

81. See note 64 for the importance of Wayna Kawri in Qhapaq Raymi or the initiation rite for Inqa males. "Huanacauri is clearly a major supernatural and

was presented to the people dominated by the Incas as such. He was fed in the same manner as the Creator [Wiraqucha], the Sun [Inti or Willka], and the Thunder [Illapa]. They were fed three times a day, each time by the burning of a camelid" (Julien: 280).

82. The Spaniards, however, did not manage to pillage Punchaw. Until the Inqas of Vilcabamba's defeat in 1572, the Spaniards had never manged to see Sun idol (or Punchaw) because it was not in Cuzco when the Quri Kancha, its original house, was sacked (Duvoils 1976: 165). Manku Inqa had taken Punchaw as an emblem of "national resistance" to the European invasion (166). Betanzos had described Punchaw as a child hammered and cast in gold (166). Pachakutiq Inqa had ordered Punchaw to be made as a symbol of Imperial Cuzco's refoundation under his rule. "Punchao is related to the transformation of Cuzco from an agricultural community to its 'consecration' both as a place and as a people" (Julien: 256). According to Antonio de Vega's descriptions, the innards or intestines of the idol was made up of a "pineapple" filled with the ashes of the burnt hearts and livers of prior Inqas (*Crónica Antonio de Vega* in Duvoils 1976: 170). For Toledo, the retrieval of Punchaw from Vilcabamba was another important trophy symbolizing his military victory over the neo-Inqanate. Duviouls has reconstructed the figure of Punchaw as one made of two serpents coiling outwards from its sides, two pumas, and an interior boz with the ashes of the Inqas's hearts (171).

83. González Holguín translates <yanocona> in Quechua as "los criados o un criado" 'servants or a servant' (364). Recall that <cona> /kuna/ is the plural marker in Quechua (cf. note 59.) Bertonio writes that <yana> in Aymara means "sirviente, hombre que sirve" 'servant, man who serves' in contrast to <supari> "muxer que sirve" 'woman who serves' (391).

84. González Holguín glosses <Ozcollo> as "Mountain Cat" in Quechua (265).

85. Name meaning "Golden Fortune." Quri means "gold" in Quechua and <Atau> is translated by González Holguín as "fortunate in wars or honors [. . .] in games [. . .] in very dire or good things, as in salvation or twists of fate" "la ventura en guerras, o honores [. . .] in games [. . .] in cosas muy graves, o excelentes, como es la salvación o los dones de gracia" (36).

86. See note 61. The figure of Gonzalo Pizarro is highlighted as an example of treachery both against the Inqa's welcome, goodwill and customs, and against the Spanish Crown, and Spanish mores of *honor* and *honra*.

87. Don Andrés Hurtado de Mendoza, Marquis of Cañete, was the third Viceroy of Peru. His term began on June 29, 1556 and lasted until March 30, 1561. He completed the diplomatic negotiations, started by President La Gasca, for the submission and incorporation of Sayri Thupaq and his sister-wife, Quya Kusi Warqay, into Cuzco's colonial society. The Marquis of Cañete was also responsible for the creation of the Audiencia de Charcas, or La Plata, in 1559; presidents of the subsidiary audiences (to Lima) acted as local governors or

captain-generals and each *audiencia* had four or five *oidores* and a *fiscal* (Hemming: 381).

88. Titu Kusi Yupanki only began to be courted for peace negotiations in 1565 under the administration of Licentiate Lope García de Castro. Until then, all diplomatic efforts had been focused on Sayri Thupaq's capitulation and exit from Vilcabamba. The Spanish had assumed that by luring the Inqa out of Vilcabamba they would immediately be in possession of it. The viceroy, however, soon realized his diplomatic fiasco when he received a letter from Titu Kusi Yupanki, dated June 20, 1569 which clarified the 'legitimate' line of succession: that his younger brother, Thupaq Amaru, was the true heir of his father Manku Inqa and that Sayri Thupaq had been chosen among them as a kind of regent (Guillén Guillén 1994: 134). Titu Kusi Yupanki clarified Inqanate succession to Diego Rodríguez de Figueroa in the following manner: "I then observed that the report was that he was an illegitimate son. He then told me that among them, when there was no legitimate son, the custom was that a bastard succeeded. He was, therefore, high priest in what we call spiritual things. This was in default of another brother, at least one who was older than himself. He thus inherited the temporal lordship. He was in possession and was recognized by the other Incas. They all obeyed him, and if he had not the right they would not obey him. For the rest the question had better be settled by arms and not by talking" (Markham Translation 1913: 189).

89. Urteaga and Regalado de Hurtado in their editions read, "Melchor de los Reies" (1916 Edition: 99; 1992: 62); Millones suggests "Marcos" as a possibility (1985 Edition 31). Guillén Guillén notes that the Dominican Friar Melchor de los Reyes was accompanied on this mission not only by Juan Sierra Leguísamo, a mestizo son of a Spaniard of the same name and Beatriz Yupanki (daughter of Wayna Qhapaq), but by Juan de Betanzos (see note 93) as well (Guillén Guillén: 132).

90. Quri Pawkar, Sutiq and Yawri (Guillén Guillén 1994: 132).

91. Sayri Thupaq left Vilcabamba on October 7, 1557 and arrived in Lima on January 5, 1558. He was the first and only Inqa ruler to visit the Spanish City of Kings (Lima). He was made the Mariscal of the Yucay Valley although his chief repartimiento was made up of Oropesa, Jaquijahuana (see note 34), and Pucará (Hemming: 294). This gave the rebels in Vilcabamba a strategic control over two of the major gateways into Cuzco: through the valley of Yucay (known as the "Sacred" or "Urubamba" Valley) as well as the higher valley entrance through the Chinchero area. The testimonies given in favor of Doña María Kusi Warkay (Cf. *Información dada a pedimento de la Doña María Cusiguarcay*) suggest that the Inqa rebels received supplies and shelter in these areas (funded from the pension in silver *pesos* that Sayri Thupaq, and later his widowed wife, received from the Spanish Crown).

92. He died in 1561, in his early twenties, less than three years after leaving Vilcabamba and he was buried in the monastery of Santo Domingo in Cuzco (also the Quri Kancha). His early death, which soon followed that of the Viceroy Marquis de Cañete, who was apparently poisoned in early 1561, left room for speculation as to the cause of death: some held that the Cañari kuraka of Yucay, Francisco Chilichi, an unconditional servant to the Spaniards, poisoned Sayri Thupaq (Guillén Guillén 1994: 134) and he was indeed imprisoned on these charges and later released when they could not be proved; another theory held Titu Kusi Yupanki responsible for his death, supposedly to make way for his own succession; still another theory held that Pawllu's son Don Carlos Inqa had been involved in Sayri Thupaq's death because of the continued rivalry between the *panaqas* of Pawllu and Manku Inqa (Hemming: 301). (After Pawllu had switched loyalties to the Spanish and had been crowned Inqa under Almagro in Cuzco, he later switched loyalties again to the Pizarros and was able to lead a comfortable life in Cuzco.)

93. Hemming notes that the corregidor of Cuzco at the time, Juan Polo de Ondegardo, sent Juan de Betanzos and Martín de Pando (301).

94. The mestizo scribe of this narrative. He was the confidant of Titu Kusi Yupanki and taught the Inqa European fencing. According to Diego Rodríguez, Pando carried a sword and shield and wore "Spanish dress and a very old cloak" (Markham 1913: 179). Martín de Pando betrayed his master to the corregidor in Cuzco in his own letter written from Talawara on November 9, 1567, accusing Diego de Plaza, Francisco de Chávez, Pedro Bustinza and Doña María Kusi Warkay and the Inqa captains being sent from Cuzco to Vilcabamba as conspirators against the Spanish Crown (Pando: 255–258).

95. Juan de Betanzos, famous for his intimate knowledge of the Quechua language and husband to Angelina Añas Yupanki, herself the niece of Wayna Qhapaq and wife to Ataw Wallpa, wrote the *Suma y narración de los incas(1551)* at the behest of the Viceroy Antonio de Mendoza and had been instrumental in the negotiation which led to Sayri-Thupaq's exit from Vilcabamba. The *Suma y narración de los incas* seems to follow the historical *relación*, as other Spanish chroniclers, but Betanzos, as a faithful "translator," decides to "keep the manner and order of Cuzqueño speech" in his narrative which displays many oral tropes of song for the ritual homage to the Inqa (Cf. Lienhard: 182–186). The text presents Cusqueño cosmogeny (Cap. I-V), and dedicates one chapter to all of the Inqas until Wiraqucha Inqa (VI) and later dedicates twenty-seven chapters just to Pachakutiq Inqa (his Inqa sources belonged to this Inqa's *panaqa*). After 1987, when the eighteen missing chapters dating to 1556 were found and published, a song transcribed in an indigenous language, though not in Quechua, whose composition had apparently been ordered by Pachakutiq Inqa Yupanki to celebrate his victory over the Soras, caught the attention of researchers in the field of Andean linguistics. Cerrón-Palomino has been able to recognize a Puquina subtext

within an overall Aymara grammatical and syntactical structure, leading him to propose Puquina as the legendary "secret language" of the Inqas (Cerrón Palomino 1998). Cf. Torero 1994 for his arguments in favor of Aymara.

96. Their embassy failed and Juan de Betanzos returned empty-handed to Cuzco (Hemming: 302). After Sayri Thupaq's death, Thupaq Amaru and Titu Kusi Yupanki reignited their guerrilla campaign against the neighboring Spanish encomiendas, near the Apurimac and Vilcanota (Willkamayu or Urubamba) rivers especially the Amaybamba and Pichu localities (Guillén Guillén 1994: 135; Nowack).

97. Don Diego López de Zúñiga, Count of Nieva, arrived in Lima in April 1561 and tried to negotiate a peace treaty with Inqa Titu Kusi Yupanki.

98. The Count of Nieva offered terms similar to those proposed by Cañete. Titu Kusi replied that if he were rewarded with "some of the large amounts of my father's lands now in the possession of the King," he would be prepared to enter into peace negotiations (Hemming: 302). At the same time, he and Thupaq Amaru intensified their guerrilla campaign, directing a general insurrection—with military and religious overtones—of the Tawantinsuyu (Guillén Guillén 1994: 136)

99. The royal Treasurer García de Melo offered Titu Kusi Yupanki a political marriage between his niece, Beatriz Clara Quya—the only daughter of Sayri Thupaq and Kusi Waykay—and his own son, Kispi Titu. In this way, the lands of Yucay and Oropesa would remain in Inqa hands, and the Spanish Crown would not have to go through the trouble of finding another sizeable estate to offer the Inqa of Vilcabamba (Hemming: 302). This marital alliance was also a source of political legitimation for Titu Kusi Yupanki because it could strengthen his son's bid for the Inqanate upon his death. Thupaq Amaru had a stronger claim as he was the son of Manku Inqa and the Quya, whereas Titu Kusi Yupanki was not. A marriage with the rich heiress Beatriz, who also claimed direct descent from Manku Inqa and his Quya, could favor Kispi Titu in his aspirations for the *maska paycha* (Hemming: 313).

100. Urteaga writes that this "Doctor Cuenca" was Don Juan Cuenca, Oidor of the Audiencia in Lima and was visitador of the corregimientos in Peru and that between 1564 and 1566 he was in Cuzco trying to procure the submission of Titu Kusi Yupanki as well as visiting and distributing lands in the Cuzco area (1916 Edition: 101 note 92). Hemming also mentions that the name of the corregidor of Cuzco was "Dr. Juan Cuenca" (Hemming: 310). Guillén Guillén, on the other hand, notes that the corregidor of Cuzco, was a "Gregorio González de Cuenca," who had been sent on a diplomatic mission to Vilcabamba by the Count of Nieva in 1561 (Guillén Guillén: 135–136).

101. In his *Gobierno del Perú*, Oidor Matienzo mentions that he spoke of Doctor Cuenca's notorious letter to Titu Kusi Yupanki and understood that the Inqa has taken many "Indians and livestock" from neighboring towns and from Cuzco because of his insult and that he wished to know the truth so that

Cuenca would not go unpunished; an investigation was indeed opened (296); Lohmann adds that, among the many epithets Doctor Cuenca had directed against the Inqa, "jumpy drunken dog" was perhaps the most insulting (note 2). Cf. Nowack.

102. Lope García de Castro succeeded the Count of Nieva in September 1564 after the latter's scandalous death in Lima. The marriage proposal had first been offered by Melo to Titu Kusi Yupanki during the administration of the Count of Nieva (see note 99) but García de Castro sent Treasurer Melo back to Vilcabamba in early 1565 and added to the previous offer: any heirs of the marriage between Kispi Tutu and Beatriz would receive their estates in perpetuity in addition to two towns of Indians which would not pay any tribute as well as the Indians belonging to the Cathedral and to La Merced monastery in Cuzco (Hemming: 303). Cf. Nowack and Julien; Nowack.

103. The treaty of Acobamba was signed on August 24, 1566. Titu Kusi Yupanki received full recognition as Inqa and the definitive possession and jurisdiction over the territory belonging to Vilcabamba which included the provinces of: Abancay, Sicuani, Chacumanchay, Nigrias, Opatari, Paucarmayo, Pilcosuni, Huarampay, Peati, Chirinahua and Chiponahua in addition to Vitcos, Manari and Huaranico and two towns, Cahora and Zanora, in the outskirts of Cuzco; the authorization to marry his son Kispi Titu to Beatriz daughter of Sayri Thupaq so as to control the repartimientos of Yucay, Jaquijahuana, Hualaquipa and Pucará; an annual rent of 5,000 pesos for the rest of his life to be inherited by his descendants (according to primogeniture or *mayorazgo*); he was able to keep the people of the neighboring *repartimientos* of Huamanga and Cuzco whom he had liberated during his guerrilla attacks and also the authorization to settle Amaybamba and Pichu. In exchange for these rights, Titu Kusi Yupanki was obliged to "keep perpetual peace" with the Spaniards and to be the vassal of the King of Spain, return the black slaves, Indians and Spaniards who had sought refuge in his domains to the Spanish judicial authorities and to accept a Spanish corregidor and friars to preach the Catholic faith in his lands (Guillén Guillén 1994: 144).

104. Diego Rodríguez de Figueroa was sent to Vilcabamba in April 1565 on behalf of the authorities in Cuzco when García de Melo's negotiations failed. In his *Relación* , dated November 4, 1567 and written in Talawara, we learn of the conversation Rodríguez had with Pando in which the latter accused several mestizo messengers to the Inqa of encouraging Titu Kusi to revolt. Rodríguez also notarized Martín de Pando's letter, written in Talawara on November 7, 1567 (Rodríguez de Figueroa: 254.). Rodríguez describes the entrance of the Inqa in this way: "Many lances were drawn up on a hill, and messengers arrived to say that the Inca was coming. Presently the escort of the Inca began to appear. The Inca came in front of all, with a head-dress of plumes of many colours, a silver plate on his breast, a golden shield in one

hand, and a lance all of gold. He wore garters of feathers and fastened to them were small wooden bells. On his head was a diadem and another round the neck. In one hand he had a gilded dagger, and he came in a mask of several colours" (Markham 1913: 179). He described the Inqa as a "man of forty years of age, of middle height, and with some marks of small-pox on his face. His mien rather severe and manly [. . .]" (182). Rodríguez also describes a significant encounter with chicha drinking with Inqa Titu Kusi Yupanki: "Then he gave me a cup of chicha, asking me to drink it for his service. I drank a quarter of it, and then began to make faces, and wipe my mouth with a handkerchief. He began to laugh, understanding that I did not know that liquor [. . .] Then the mestizo came with a very small cup of chicha, with a message from the Inca asking me to drink it, that he looked upon me as a friend, and that when I liked, we could treat of the matters about which I had come. I took a sip, and gave the rest to one of the Indians who had come with me" (180–181).

105. Licentiate Juan de Matienzo de Peralta, not Hernando Matienzo, was a Lecturer of the Chancellery of Valladolid, Oidor of the Charcas and Lima Audiencias, and later president of the former. He helped, along with Licentiate Polo de Ondegardo, to write several of the laws, which make up Viceroy Toledo's *Gobierno del Perú,* and later wrote his own account of his experience in Peru under the same title. He had come to Cuzco, as Oidor of Charcas, in order to conduct an investigation into the administration of the *corregidor* Doctor Cuenca (see note 101); after hearing Rodriguez's reports of his travels to Vilcabamba he decided to meet with the Inqa himself.

106. The encounter between the Oidor Matienzo and Titu Kusi Yupanki at Chuquichaca, occurred on June 18, 1565. During this interview the Inqa asked for several concessions that were given to him later in the Treaty of Acobamba (see note 103). Matienzo describes his first impressions of the Inqa and Martín Pando as follows: 'he was well armed in his own way, wearing many feathers, and wore no paint or markings on his face as the others did; he wore a golden breastplate upon his chest and upon it lay bare a drawn golden dagger; beside him, to his left, walked Martín Pando, mestizo, his secretary, with a shield and sword' (301).

107. Father Antonio de Vera, Augustine Friar of Cuzco, was the first to give Titu Kusi Yupanki catechism in Vilcabamba in 1566. Rodríguez de Figueroa brought to the Inqa's attention, however, that he had already been baptized (presumably when he was younger, in the Spaniard Oñate's care): "for I had seen in the baptismal book of the principal church (in Cuzco) that the Inca had been baptized and named Diego. He told me that it was true, and that he was a Christian, and he confessed it before the Indians" (Markham 1913: 192).

108. Juan de Vivero was the prior of the Augustine convent in Cuzco and entered Vilcabamba in August 1568 to baptize and catechize the Inqa.

109. Gonzalo Pérez de Vivero was a *vecino* (prominent citizen) of Cuzco and Atilano (or Tilano) de Anaya was also a *vecino* who kept Beatriz as his ward. Atilano de Anaya was later killed in March or April 1572 for crossing the Chuquichaca bridge without the Inqa's permission (Guillén Guillén 1994: 302).

110. Friar Marcos García began his rounds of Vilcabamba with Martín Pando in October 1568 and was later joined by Friar Diego Ortiz in mid-February 1569; that same year, Lope García de Castro finished his term as governor and he was replaced by Francisco de Toledo whose bellicose policies towards Vilcabamba represented a drastic shift from the diplomatic negotiations that were at hand. Soon after this *Instrucción* was finished, Friar Marcos García and Friar Diego Ortiz desecrated the shrines at Chuquipalpa~palta, near Vitcos, and the former was subsequently expelled from Vilcabamba in March or April 1570 (Guillén Guillén 1994: 302).

111. Friar Diego Ortiz. (See note 110.) Friar Diego Ortiz and Martín de Pando were killed to avenge the death of Titu Kusi Yupanki, believed to have been poisoned, in April or June 1571 (Guillén Guillén 1994: 146).

112. Wallpa Yupanki was later Thupaq Amaru's "captain-general" during the war against Francisco Toledo's troops in 1572 (Guillén Guillén 1994: 161).

Works Cited

ADELAAR, WILLEM F.
1997   "Spatial Reference and Speaker Orientation in Early
            Colonial Quechua." Rosaleen Howard-Malverde, ed.
            135–167.

ADORNO, ROLENA, ED.
1982   *From Oral to Written Expression: Native Andean
            Chronicles of the Early Colonial Period.* New York:
            Syracuse University.

ADORNO, ROLENA
2001   *Guaman Poma and His Illustrated Chronicle from
            Colonial Peru. From a Century of Scholarship to a New
            Era of Reading.* Copenhagen: Museum Tusculanum
            Press, University of Copenhagen, The Royal Library.

ANDRADE CIUDAD, LUIS
1995   "La lengua culle: un estado de la cuestión." *BAPL.* 26:
            37–130.

ASCHER, MARIA
2002   "Reading Khipu: Labels, Structure and Format." Jeffrey
            Quilter and Gary Urton, eds. 87–102.

ASCHER, ROBERT
2002   "Inka Writing." Jeffrey Quilter and Gary Urton, eds.
            103–118.

BAKHTIN, M.M.
1981   *The Dialogic Imagination.* Ed. Michael Holquist. Austin:
            University of Texas Press.

BAUER, BRIAN S.
1998   *The Sacred Landscape of the Inca: the Cusco ceque system.*
            Austin: University of Texas Press.

BEAUCLERK, JOHN
1980   "La Cordillera Vilcabamba." *Boletín de Lima.* 4. 78–79. 5.
            78–79 (cont.)

BERTONIO, LUDOVICO
1984 [1610] *Vocabulario de la lengua aymara.* Xavier Albó and Félix
            Layme, intro. Cochabamba, Bolivia: CERES.

BETANZOS, JUAN DIEZ DE
1987 [1551] *Suma y narración de los incas.* María del Carmen Martín
            Rubio, ed. Cusco: Fondo Editorial de la UNSAAC.
1996   *Narrative of the Incas.* Ronald Hamilton and Dana
            Buchanan, tr. and ed. Austin: University of Texas Press.

BINGHAM, HIRAM
1963 [1948]   *Lost City of the Incas: the story of Machu Picchu and its builders.* New York: Athenium.

BOONE, ELIZABETH HILL, AND WALTER D. MIGNOLO, EDS.
1994   *Writing without Words: alternative literacies in Mesoamerica and the Andes.* Durham: Duke University Press.

CASAS, BARTOLOMÉ DE LAS
1989   *Brevísima relación de la destrucción de las indias.* 4ta. Ed. México, D.F.: Fontamara.

CASTRO DE TRELLES, LUCILA, ED.
1992   *Relación de los agustinos de Huamachuco.* Lima: PUCP.

CERRÓN PALOMINO, RODOLFO
1987   *Lingüística quechua.* Cuzco, Peru: Centro de Estudios Rurales Andinos "Bartolomé de las Casas."
1990   "Reconsideración del llamado quechua costeño." *Revista Andina.* 8. 2: 335–409.
1994a   *Quechumara: estructuras paralelas de las lenguas quechua y aimara.* La Paz: Centro de Investigación y Promoción del Campesinado.
1994b   *Quechua sureño diccionario unificado: quechua-castellano, castellano-quechua.* Biblioteca Basica Peruana. Lima: Biblioteca Nacional del Peru.
1997a   "Cuzco y no Cusco ni menos Qosqo." *Histórica.* XXI.2: 165–170.
1997b   "Reducción y ensamblaje en la formación de sufijos del quechua." Julio Calvo Pérez and Juan Carlos Godenzzi, eds. *Multilingüismo y educación bilingüe en América y España.* Cuzco: C.E.R.A. "Bartolomé de Las Casas." 283–308.
1998   "El cantar del Inca Yupanqui y la lengua secreta de los incas." *Revista Andina.* 16. 2: 417–452.
2000   *Lingüística aimara.* Lima: Centro de Estudios Regionales Andinos "Bartolomé de las Casas."
2003   *Castellano andino: aspectos sociolingüísticos, pedagógicos, y gramaticales.* Lima: PUCP, Fondo Editorial.

CEVALLOS-CANDAU, FRANCISCO JAVIER, ET AL., EDS.
1994   *Coded Encounters: Writing, Gender, and Ethnicity in Colonial Latin America.* Amherst: University of Massachussetts Press.

CHANG-RODRÍGUEZ, RAQUEL
1988   *La apropiación del signo: tres cronistas indígenas del Perú.* Temple, Arizona: Center for Latin American Studies.

1994   "Cultural Resistance in the Andes and Its Depiction in
               Atau Wallpaj P'uchukakuyninpa Wankan or *Tragedy of
               Atahualpa's Death.*" Francisco Javier Cevallos-Candeau
               et al., eds. 115–134.

CLASSEN, CONSTANCE
1993   *Inca Cosmology and the Human Body.* Salt Lake City:
               University of Utah Press.

CORNEJO POLAR, ANTONIO
1983   "La literatura peruana: totalidad contradictoria." *Revista
               de Crítica Literaria latinoamericana.* 18. 37–50.
1994   *Escribir en el aire: ensayo sobre la heterogeneidad socio-
               cultural en las literaturas andinas.* Lima: Editorial
               Horizonte.
1997   "Mestizaje e Hibridez: Los riesgos de las metáforas."
               Cuadernos de Literatura. 6. La Paz, Bolivia.

COVARRUBIAS OROZCO, SEBASTIÁN DE
1994 [1611]   *Tesoro de la lengua castellana o española.* Felipe C.R.
               Maldonado, ed. Madrid: Nueva biblioteca de Erudición y
               Crítica, Editorial Castalia.

CUMMINS, TOM
1994   "Representation in the Sixteenth Century and the
               Colonial Image of the Inca." Elizabeth Hill Boone and
               Walter D. Mignolo, eds. 188–219.
               Declaración de los quipocamayos a Vaca de Castro. c.1541–43 (pp.
               4–26). 1608 (pp. 26–53) additions attributed to Fray
               Antonio Calancha. In Urteaga, ed. 3–53.

DEDENBACH-SALAZAR SÁENZ, SABINE
1997   "Point of View and Evidentiality in the Huarochirí Texts
               (Peru, 17th Century)." Rosaleen Howard Valverde, ed.
               149–167.

DE GRANDA, GERMÁN
2001   *Estudios de lingüística andina.* Lima: PUCP, Fondo
               Editorial.

DÍAZ-RIVERA, ADABEL
2001   *Del discurso colonial en la 'Relación' de Titu Cusi
               Yupanqui (1570): La ambivalencia del mimetismo
               colonial.* Dissertation. Georgetown University.

DOUGALL DE ZILERI, DAPHNE, TR.
2002   "Cusco: Nueva Ciudad Perdida." *Caretas: ilustración
               peruana.* 2 de agosto.

Dunbar Temple, Ella
1949   "Notas sobre el Virrey Toledo y los Incas de vilcabamba:
            una carta de Titu Cusi Yupanqui y el testamento inédito
            de su hijo Don Felipe Quispe Titu." *Documenta.* 2.1:
            614–629

Duviols, Pierre
1978   "Camaquen, upani. Un concept animiste des anciens
            Peruviens." *Amerikanistiche Studien. Festschrift für
            Hermann Trimborn.* Roswith Hartmann and Udo
            Oberem, eds. Vol. 1. 132–144.

Escobar, Anna María
2000   *Contacto Social y lingüístico: El español en contacto con el
            quechua en el Perú.* Lima: PUCP, Fondo Editorial.

Esteve Barba, Francisco
1968   *Crónicas peruanas de interés indígena.* Biblioteca de
            Autores Españoles. 209. Madrid: Ediciones Atlas.

Fejos, Paul.
1944   *Archaeological Explorations in the Cordillera Vilcabamba,
            Southeastern Peru.* New York: Viking Fund, Publications
            in Anthropology, no. 3.

Ferrell R., Marcos A.
1996   "Textos aimaras en Guaman Poma." *Revista Andina.*
            14.2: 413–455.

Freud, Sigmund
1997   "The Uncanny." *Writing on Art and Literatura.* Stanford:
            University of Stanford Press. 193–233.

Galeano, Eduardo H.
1997   *The Open Veins of Latin America: Five Centuries of the
            Pillage of a Continent.* Cedric Belfrage, tr. New York:
            Monthly Review Press.

García-Bedoya M., Carlos
2000   *La literatura peruana en el periodo de estabilización
            colonial (1580–1780).* Lima: Universidad Nacional Mayor
            de San Marcos (UNMSM).

Garcilaso de la Vega, El Inca
1991 [1609] *Comentarios reales de los incas. Parte 1.* Lima: Fondo de
            la Cultura Económica.

González Holguín, Diego
1989   *Vocabulario de la lengua general de todo el Peru llamada
            Lengua Quechua o del Inca.* 2nd ed. Lima: UNMSM.

GUILLÉN GUILLÉN, EDMUNDO

1974   *La versión inca de la conquista.* Lima: Editorial Milla
           Bartres.
1984   "Tres documentos inéditos para la historia de la recon-
           quista inka." *BIFEA.* XIII. 1.2: 73–96.
1994   *La guerra de reconquista inka.* Lima: R.A. Ediciones e.i.r.l.

HARRISON, REGINA

1989   *Signs, Songs, and Memory in the Andes: Translating
           Quechua Language and Culture.* Austin: University of
           Austin Press.
1994   "The Theology of Concupiscence: Spanish-Quechua
           Confessional Manuals in the Andes." Francisco Javier
           Cevallos-Candeau et al., eds. 135–151.

HEMMING, JOHN

1987   *The Conquest of the Incas.* New York: Harvest/HBJ.

HILDEBRANDT, MARTHA

1994 [1969] *Peruanismos.* Lima: Campodónico.

HOWARD-MALVERDE, ROSALEEN, ED.

1997   *Creating Context in Andean Cultures.* New York: Oxford
           University Press.

HOWARD, ROSALEEN

2002   "Spinning a Yarn: Landscape, Memory and Discourse
           Structure in Quechua Narratives." Jeffrey Quilter and
           Gary Urton, eds. 26–49.

HUERTAS VALLEJOS, LORENZO

1972 [1973] "Memorial acerca de las cuatro ciudades inkas situadas
             entre los ríos Urubamba y Apurimac." *Historia y Cultura.*
             Lima. 6: 203–205
Información dada a pedimento de Doña María Coya Cusiguarcay. 1567.
           Ms. 9. Libro 1. Libros de la Dirección del Archivo
           Regional Del Cuzco. 27. ff. 136–185.
*Informaciones del Virrey Toledo. Verificadas en Jauja, Cuzco, Guamanga,
           y Yucay.* Urteaga, ed. 102–164.

ISBELL, WILLIAM

1997   *Mummies and Mortuary Monuments: a Post-Processual
           Prehistory of Central Andean Social Organization.* Austin:
           University of Texas Press.

JAKFALVI-LEIVA, SUSANA

1993   "De la voz a la escritura: La *relación* de Titu Cusi
           (1570)." *Revista de crítica literaria latinoamericana.* XIX.
           37: 259–277.

JULIEN, CATHERINE
2000   *Reading Inca History.* Iowa City: University of Iowa
            Press.

LECHTMAN, HEATHER
1974   "El dorado de metales en el Perú precolombino." *Revista
            del Museo Nacional.* 40: 86–110.
1987   *La tecnología en el mundo andino.* México, D.F.: Fondo de
            la Cultura Económica.

LEE, VINCENT R.
c. 1989   *Chanasuyu: the ruins of Inca Vilcabamba.* Wilson, Wyo.:
            Sixpac Manco Publications.

LEMLIJ, M., ET AL.
1990   "El Taki Onqoy: reflexiones psicoanalíticas." Millones,
            comp. 425–434.

LIENHARD, MARTÍN
1991   *La voz y su huella: escritura y conflicto étnico-social en
            América Latina 1492–1988.* Hanover, New Hampshire:
            Ediciones del Norte.

LOCKHART, JAMES
1968   *Spanish Peru: 1532–1560, A Social History.* Madison,
            Wisconsin: The University of Wisconsin Press.
1972   *The Men of Cajamarca: a social and biographical study of
            the first conquerors of Peru.* Austin: University of Texas
            Press.

LOHMANN VILLENA, GUILLERMO
1939   "El teatro en Lima en el Siglo XVI." *Cuadernos de
            Estudio.* 1.1.45–74
            Mandamientos de Prelados. Notebook, Ms. XCII, 1, 5, Fol. 44. Archivo
            del Arzobispado de Cuzco, Peru, c. 1583.

MANNHEIM, BRUCE
1990   "La cronología relativa de la lengua y literatura quechua
            cusqueña." *Revista Andina.* 8.1. 139–178.

MARKHAM, CLEMENTS R., ED. AND TRANS.
1907   *The History of the Incas by Pedro Sarmiento de Gamboa
            and the Execution of Tupac Amaru by Captain Baltasar de
            Ocampo.* 1967 Reprint. Nendeln/Liechtenstein: Kraus
            Reprint Limited.
1913   *The War of Quito by Pedro de Cieza de Leon and Inca
            Documents.* 1967 Reprint. Nendeln/Liechtenstein: Kraus
            Reprint Limited.

MATIENZO, JUAN DE
1967 [1567] *Gobierno del Perú.* Guillermo Lohmann Villena, ed. and
            intro. Paris-Lima: Institut Français d'Etudes Andines.

Mauss, Marcel
2000 [1950] *The Gift: The Form and Reason for Exchange in Archaic Societies.* Halls, W.D., tr. New York: Norton & Company.

Mazzotti, José Antonio
1996 *Coros mestizos en el Inca Garcilaso: resonancias andinas.* Lima: Bolsa de Valores de Lima y FCE.

Meneses, Teodoro, tr. and comp.
1983 *Teatro quechua colonial: antalogía.* Lima: Edubanco.

Mignolo, Walter
1994 "The Movable Center: geographical discourses and territoriality during the expansion of the Spanish Empire." Francisco Javier Cevallos-Candeau et al., eds. 14–45.
1995 *The Darker Side of the Renaissance: Literacy, Territoriality and Colonization.* Ann Arbor: University of Michigan Press.

Millones, Luis
1985 "Introducción." Titu Kusi Yupanki 1985, 7–23.
1990 "Introducción." *El retorno de las huacas: estudios y documentos del Siglo XVI.* Luis Millones, comp. Lima: IEP. 11–22.
1995 *Perú Colonial: De Pizarro a Tupac Amaru II.* Lima: COFIDE, Fondo Editorial.

Morris, Craig, and Donald E. Thompson
1985 *Huánuco Pampa: an Inca city and its hinterland.* London: Thames and Hudson.

Murúa, Martin de
1987 (1613) *Historia general del Perú.* Manuel Ballesteros, ed. Madrid: Historia 16.

Nowack, Kerstin
2004 "Las provisiones de Titu Cusi Yupangui." *Revista Andina.* 38. 139–179

Nowack, Kerstin, and Catherine Julien
1999 "La Campaña de Toledo contra los señores naturales andinos: el destierro de los Incas de Vilcabamba y Cuzco." *Historia y Cultura.* 23.15–81.

Pando, Martín de
1994 Carta del escribano Martín de Pando suscrita en Talavera el 7 de noviembre de 1567. Edmundo Guillén Guillén, ed. Documento C. 255–56.

Parry, Milman
1987 "Cor Huso: A Study of Southslavic Song." *The Making of Homeric Verse: The Collected Papers of Milman Parry.* Adam Parry, ed. Oxford: Oxford University Press. 437–464.

PEASE G.Y., FRANKLIN
1995   *Las crónicas y los Andes.* Lima: PUCP, Instituto Riva-
            Agüero, Fondo de Cultura Económica.

POLO DE ONDEGARDO, JUAN
1917 (1559) Tratado y averiguación sobre los errors y supersticiones
            de los indios. *Colección de libros y documentos referentes a
            la Historia del Perú.* Horacio H. Urteaga and Carlos A.
            Romero, eds. Serie 1. Tomo III. 3–43.

PORRAS, FRAY DIEGO DE PORRAS
1952   Instrucción para los sacerdotes que se ocuparen de la
            conversion de los indios del Peru, hecha por Fray Diego
            de Porras. Transcription of the manuscript in the A.G.I.
            Legajo No3, Letra F. *Revista del Archivo Histórico del
            Cuzco.* 3. 26–37.

QUILTER, JEFFREY
2002   "Yncap Cimin Quipococ's Knots." Jeffrey Quilter and
            Gary Urton, Eds. 197–222.

QUILTER, JEFFREY, AND GARY URTON, EDS.
2002   *Narrative Threads: Accounting and Recounting in Andean
            Khipu.* Austin: University of Texas Press.

REGALADO DE HURTADO, LILIANA
1992   "Estudio Preliminar." Titu Kusi Yupanki. XI-LVII.

RAMA, ANGEL
1996   *The Lettered City.* John Charles Chasteen, tr. and ed.
            Durham: Duke University Press.
            *Relación de los señores indios que sirvieron a Tupac
            Yupanqui y Huayna Capac.* In Urteaga, ed. 55–86.

RIVAROLA, JOSÉ LUIS
2000   *Español andino: textos de bilingües de los siglos XVI y
            XVII.* Vervuert: Iberoamericana.

RODRÍGUEZ DE FIGUEROA, DIEGO
1994   *Relación escrita en el pueblo de Taraura el 4 de noviembre
            de 1567.* Edmundo Guillén Guillén, ed. Selections.
            Documento B. 248–254.

ROSTWOROWSKI DE DIEZ CANSECO, MARÍA
1999   *Historia del Tahuantinsuyu.* 2nd Ed. Lima: IEP.

ROWE, JOHN H.
1967   "What Kind of Settlement Was Inca Cuzco?" *Ñawpa
            Pacha.* 5: 59–76.

SAIGNES, THIERRY, COMP.
1993   *Borrachera y memoria: la experiencia de lo sagrado en los
            Andes.* Lima: IFEA.

SALLNOW, MICHAEL J.
1991   "Pilgrimage and cultural fracture in the Andes."
            *Contesting the Sacred: The Anthropology of Christian
            Pilgrimage.* John Eade and Michael Sallnow, eds.
            London: Routledge. 137–153.

SANDOVAL DE LA MAZA, SERGIO
1995   *Diccionario etimológico de la lengua castellana.* Madrid:
            M.E. Editores.

SANTO TOMÁS, DOMINGO DE
1951   *Lexicon o vocabulario de la lengua general del Perú.* Raúl
            Porras Barrenechea, ed. Lima: Edición del Instituto de
            Historia.

SALOMON, FRANK
1982   "Chronicles of the Impossible: Notes on Three Peruvian
            Indegenous Historians." Rolena Adorno, ed. 9–39.

SALOMON, FRANK, AND GEORGE L. URIOSTE, TR. AND ED.
1991   *The Huarochiri Manuscript: a testament of ancient and
            Colonial Andean religion.* Austin: University of Texas
            Press.

SÁNCHEZ ROMERALO, ANTONIO, ED.
1989   *Lope de Vega. El Teatro.* Vol. II. Madrid: Taurus.

SARMIENTO DE GAMBOA, PEDRO
1965 [1570] *Historia Indica.* Madrid: BAE.

SAVOY, GENE
1970   *Vilcabamba: last city of the Incas.* London, Hale, 1970.

SEED, PATRICIA
1991   " 'Failing to Marvel': Atahualpa's Encounter with the
            Word." *Latin American Research Review.* 20.1. 7–32.
1995   *Ceremonies of Possession: Europe's Conquest of the New
            World 1492–1640.* Cambridge: Cambridge University
            Press.

SEMPAT ASSADOURIAN, CARLOS
2002   "String Registries: Native Accounting and Memory
            According to the Colonial Sources." Jeffrey Quilter and
            Gary Urton, eds. 119–150.

SULLIVAN, LAWRENCE E.
1985   "Above, Below, or Far Away: Andean Cosmogony and
            Ethical Order." *Cosmogony and Ethical Order: New
            Studies in Comparative Ethics.* R. W. Lovin and F. E.
            Reynolds, eds. Chicago: University of Chicago Press.
            98–129.

SZEMINSKI, IAN
1990   "Un texto en el idioma olvidado de los inkas." *Histórica.*
            XVI. 2: 379–388
1997   *Wira Quchuan y sus obras: teología andina y lenguaje.*
            Lima: IEP.
1998   "Del idioma propio de los incas cusqueños y de su
            pertenencia lingüística." *Histórica.* XVII.1: 135–168.

TAYLOR, GERALD
1985   "Un documento quechua de Huarochirí-1607." *Revista
            Andina.* 3.1. 157–185.
Testimonio dado por Benito de la Peña en 22 de abril de 1552. Ms. Libro
            3. 29. Dirección del Archivo Regional Histórico del
            Cuzco.

TITU KUSI YUPANKI
Manuscript
(1570)   Biblioteca del Escorial. L. 116. 1–5 [ff. 132v.-196v.]
Editions
1877   *Tercero Libro de las Guerras Civiles del Perú, el cual se
            llama la Guerra de Quito, hecho por Pedro Cieza de León.*
            Marcos Jiménez de la Espada, ed., intro. and app.
            Madrid: Biblioteca Hispano-Ultramarina. Selections.
1916   *Relación de la conquista del Perú.* Horacio H. Urteaga
            and Carlos A. Romero, eds. Colección de Libros y
            Documentos referentes a la Historia del Perú.
            Serie 1. Tomo II. Lima.
1973   *Relación de la conquista del Perú.* Francisco A. Carrillo,
            ed. Lima: Ediciones de la Biblioteca Universitaria.
1984   "The Andes Edition." *New Iberian World: A Documentary
            History of the Discovery and Settlement of Latin America
            to the Early 19th Century.* John H. Parry and Robert G.
            Keith, Michael Jimenez, eds. and trans. Vol. IV. New
            York: Times Books. 135–145; 268–272.
1985   *Ynstrucion del ynga don Diego de Castro Titu Cussi
            Yupangui para el muy ilustre señor el licenciado Lope
            Garcia de Castro governador que fue destos reynos del Piru
            tocante a los negocios que con Su majestad en su nombre
            por su poder a de tratar; la qual es esta que se sigue.* Luis
            Millones, ed. Lima: El Virrey.
1985   *Titu Cussi Yupanqui. Die Eschüterunz der Welt.* Martin
            Lienhard, ed., trans. and prol.
1988   *En el encuentro de dos mundos: los Incas de Vilcabamba.
            Instrucción del inga Don Diego de Castro Titu Cussi
            Yupanqui (1570).* María del Carmen Martín Rubio, ed.
            Francisco Valcárcel, prol. Madrid: Ediciones Atlas.

1992   *Instrucción al licenciado Lope García de Castro.* Liliana
           Regalado de Hurtado, ed. Lima: PUCP.

TODOROV, TZEVETAN
1999   *The Conquest of America: the Question of the Other.*
           Richard Howard, tr. Norman: University of Oklahoma
           Press.

TOLEDO, FRANCISCO DE
1777 [1572] *A fabor de Don Francisco Chilichi.* Ms. 10. Libro 1. Libros
           de la Dirección del Archivo Regional del Cuzco. 27. f.
           187
1572   *Carta al rey.* 1 marzo 1572. Ts of original in the AGI in
           Seville, Spain. SXVI. Leg. 11. Donación de Roberto
           Samanes. Archivo Histórico Regional del Cuzco.

TORERO, ALFREDO
1987   "Lenguas y pueblos altiplánicos en torno al siglo XVI."
           Revista Andina. 5.2: 320–405.
1989   "Areas toponímicas e idiomas en la sierra norte peruana:
           un trabajo de recuperación lingüística." *Revista Andina.*
           7.1: 217–257.
1994   "El idioma particular de los incas." *Relaciones geográficas
           de Indias.* Madrid: Ediciones Atlas: 326–333.
1995   "Historias del /x/ : el proceso de velarización de /x/
           castellana según su uso en escrituras de lenguas andinas
           en los siglos XVI y XVII." Teresa Echenique et al., eds.
           Historia de la lengua española en América y España.
           Valencia: Tirant lo Blanch. 185–203.

UGARTE CHAMARRO, GUILLERMO
1968   *El teatro en el Cuzco colonial.* Lima: UNMSM. Teatro
           Universitario.

URTEAGA, HORACIO H, ED.
1920   *Informaciones sobre el antiguo Perú, Crónicas de 1533 a
           1575.* Colección de Libros y Documentos Referentes a la
           Historia del Perú. Tomo III. Segunda Serie. Lima:
           Imprenta y Librería San Martí y Ca.

URTON, GARY
2002a   "An Overview of Spanish Colonial Commentary on
           Andean Knotted-string Records." Jeffrey Quilter and
           Gary Urton, eds. 3–25
2002b   "Narrative Signs in Narrative-Accounting khipu." Jeffrey
           Quilter and Gary Urton, eds. 171–196
2002c   "Codificación binaria en los khipus incaicos." *Revista
           Andina* 35 (Cuzco): 9–68.

VARGAS UGARTE, RUBÉN S.J.
1974   *De nuestro antiguo teatro: colección de piezas dramáticas de los siglos XVI, XVII, y XVII.* Lima: Milla Batres.

VARÓN GABAI, RAFAEL
1990   "El Taki Onqoy: las raíces andinas de un fenómeno colonial." Millones, comp. 331–407.
1997   *Francisco Pizarro and His Brothers: the Illusion of Power in Sixteenth-Century Peru.* Javier Flores Espinoza, trans. London: University of Oklahoma Press.

WAMAN PUMA [GUAMÁN POMA DE AYALA]
1980   *Nueva Corónica y buen gobierno.* John V. Murra and Rolena Adorno, eds. Jorge L. Urioste, tr. 3 vols. México, D.F.: Siglo XXI.

ZUIDEMA, R. TOM
1989   "El león en la ciudad. Símbolos reales de transición en el Cuzco." *Reyes y guerreros. Ensayos de cultura andina.* Manuel Burga, comp. Lima: FOMCIENCIAS. 306–383.

ZUMTHOR, PAUL
1987   *La lettre et la voix: de la "littérature" médiévale.* Paris: Editions du Seuil.